Vimuttidhamma

From Chakra to Dhammachakra

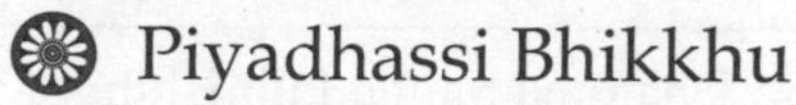

Piyadhassi Bhikkhu

Vimuttidhamma: From Chakra to Dhammachakra

Piyadhassi Bhikkhu

Published by Dhamma Publication Fund
Wat Tam Doi Tone, Chiang Mai, Thailand

First Publishing, May 2011
1,300 copies
(Free Distribution)

Cover picture: Dhamek Stupa and Image of the Buddha giving the First Sermon at Sarnath, India.

Cover design by Thaiis Co., www.thaiis.org

ISBN : 978-616-03-0372-4

Donation for Dhamma publication: please contact
Wat Tam Doi Tone, Mae Win Sub-District, Mae Wang District, Chiang Mai 50360 Thailand

Tel. 66-53-268511
E-mail: doitcmm@yahoo.com
website: www.vimuttidhamma.org

Printed at Dhamma Sapha Publishing House, 1/4-5, Baromarajachonni 119, Sala Dhammasop Sub-District, Thaweewatana District, Bangkok 10170,
Tel. 66-2-888-7940, 66-2-441-1535,
Fax: 66-2-441-1983.

Dimensions of Mind

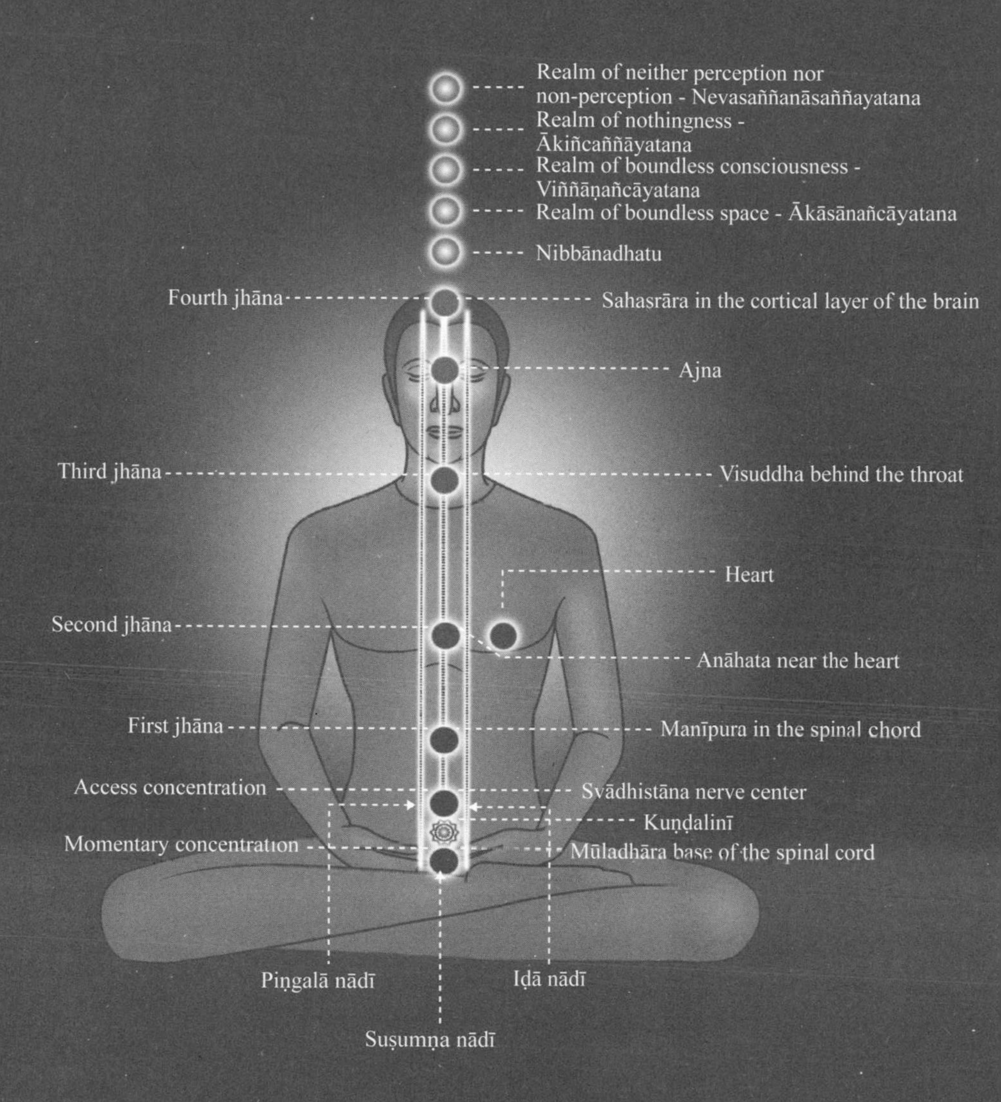

Remark : - Mind in the four arūpajhānas has the same components as mind in the fourth rūpajhāna. The only difference is that the objects of arūpa concentration are formless elements.

- **iḍā nāḍī** : Mind perceives past objects. Inner energy moves within the left channel.
- **piṇgalā nāḍī** : Mind perceives future objects. Inner energy moves within the right channel.
- **suṣumṇa nāḍī** : Mind perceives present objects. Inner energy moves within the middle channel.

CONTENTS

LIST OF FIGURES

ABBREVIATIONS

A.N. = *Anguttara Nikāya*

D.N. = *Digha Nikāya*

Kh.N. = *Khuddaka Nikāya*

M.N. = *Majjhima Nikāya*

S.N. = *Saṃyutta Nikāya*

❋❋❋❋❋❋❋❋

Like a lake unruffled by any breeze,
the concentrated mind is a faithful reflector
that mirrors what ever is placed before it
exactly as it is.

PREFACE

Vimuttidhamma is the true freedom, which does not change according to any causes or factors, transcending all kinds of conditioned phenomena. On the path to liberation (the noble eightfold path), vimuttidhamma is the final goal for all beings.

Regarding the noble eightfold path, there are three levels of learning and practice. Firstly, the *sila* level or the level of adjusting one's own physical and verbal conducts to support and be conducive to the training of one's mind. Second is the level of concentration or mind training according to the principle of the four foundation of mindfulness (*satipaṭṭhāna* practice). Practitioners will be able to experience the rising and falling states within the framework of their own body and mind. In Pali, body (*rūpa*) and mind (*nāma*) are mere aggregates of compounded things. Such rising and falling continuum appears from gross to subtler levels, namely from the worldly to the form and formless realms.

Chakra is a knowledge at the level of absorption concentration (*appanāsamādhi*) which covers both the form and formless realms. Knowledge of chakra existed prior to the emergence of Buddhism. Before enlightenment, the Buddha achieved all the eight levels of absorption concentration from two masters, the yogies Alāra Kalama and Uddaka Ramaputta. However, the knowledge of high level of concentration or chakra was not sufficient for reaching vimuttidhamma. The Buddha, therefore had to leave the two masters in order to seek, by himself, the higher and subtler kind of knowledge.

With tremendous effort and long-accumulated spiritual intuitive faculty which heightened to its peak, the Buddha was able to discover the higher kind of knowledge, or the third level of practice, namely insight or *vipassanā*. Only when absorption concentration is accompanied by insight, the ordinary kind of concentration will escalate and change itself into the noble right concentration. When both kinds of power, insight (*vipassanābala*) and concentration (*samādhibala*), develop up to the level of completion of factors of enlightenment (*bojjhaṅga*), the mind will be free from the cycle of rebirth. Before being able to reach the highest form of knowledge (*vimuttiñāṇadassana*), practitioners will experience an excellent kind of chakra, namely *dhammachakra*. Dhammachakra is a special state when ones experience only the rising and falling of aggregates without accompaniment of ignorance, craving and clinging force (which are the causes of suffering). The perception at this level is called *kiriyacitta** which functions independently of both wholesome and unwholesome factors. When dhammachakra cycles and escalates its speed, up to one point, the cycling stops, and there emerges the last and the highest kind of knowledge, vimuttiñāṇadassana which will become clear only to those who can attain it.

Vimuttidhamma was translated from Thai to English by a group of practitioners, namely, Krisda Dhiradityakul, Apinya Feungfusakul with the help of Matt Meyers, Steve Rhodes, Rudy Stoert, Arthur McKeown and Zarina Parpia. Those who financially supported the publication are Thai meditator group in Boston,Yaowalak Phenglee, Phorn Phivilay, Dalom Phivilay, Pawaranan Wisitweradilok, Nattakini Jiramanthip, Pipaspon

---

* Kiriyacitta is karmically neutral, having no karma results, both negative or positive. It is the mental state of the arahat or the fully enlightened, accompanied by two or three noble roots (greedlessness, hatelessnes and undeludedness). See detailed description on p. 256-257.

Udompolpunit, Thomas Mathsanghane, Jenjira Jenny Mathsanghane, Nupan Chalanukroa, Ubonwan Singphanomchai. The layout design was done by Thaiis Co. I would like to express my thanks and convey the blessing to all these people.

Vimuttidhamma will be a guiding friend for those who seek and practice Dhamma and will lead them to the knowledge about chakra and the higher knowledge of the excellent dhammachakra. On the noble path, may the cycling of dhammachakra reveal itself transparently to everybody who devotedly and persistently keeps on training the mind.

Piyadhassi Bhikkhu
Visaka Puja, 2011
Wat Tam Doi Tone, Chiang Mai

TRANSLATOR NOTES

In 2001, during the three month period of the rainy season known as the Vassa, Kris Dhiradityakul, who ordained and studied Dhamma at Wat Tam Doi Tone cave monastery in Thailand, got to know and befriend George, a French-born American monk. Kris was tremendously inspired by "Vimuttidhamma," the book written by his master, mentor and the Abbot of the monastery, Venerable Phra Ajahn Nawee Piyadhassi. The book was first published in October 1997 and since then has been reprinted four times. Kris felt strongly committed to making it possible for George and other westerners to read the book and taste the knowledge of his master.

Kris approached Phra Ajahn (the respectful title means "Monk Teacher" in Thai) to ask permission to translate, and then embarked upon a very difficult task. On the one hand, the book follows Theravāda tradition in its tone and style as well as its systematic analysis of the whole corpus of Dhamma. The rich quotations from the Pāli Canon help the reader to understand the interrelatedness of Buddhist core concepts. On the other hand, the book debates and challenges mainstream Theravada beliefs regarding meditation. However, the greatest challenge for the translators lay in the section of the book that deals with meditative experiences. The two last chapters of the book offer practical guidelines for beginners while allowing the reader a glimpse into the transcendental realm of higher level meditation. The book captures Phra Ajahn's more than 20 years of experience as a meditation teacher and also his own unutterable moments in the world beyond.

After years of endeavour, Kris handed his first draft to Apinya Feungfusakul, one of Phra Ajahn's close disciples, who revised the entire manuscript and spent months searching through different versions of English translations of Buddhist Scriptures and Commentaries which were quoted as references. In addition, she added more than 60 footnotes to clearly explain Pāli terms and did multiple quality and accuracy reviews of the final draft.

Many English speaking friends who practice meditation with Phra Ajahn offered invaluable help. Steve Rhodes and Arthur McKeown edited the entire book, Rudy Stoert edited chapters one to five, Matt Meyers edited chapters eight and nine, and Samaneri Pema (Karen Schaefer) edited chapter eight. Wanda Weinberger proof read a large part of the book, and Zarina Parpia edited the final version, checking the Pāli spelling, doing meticulous proof reading four times and preparing the index. Last but not least, Wanachai Wongtala, Prapasri Poung-Ngernmak and the Thaiis Co. team were in charge of the lay-out and book cover design.

Throughout the course of our journey, Phra Ajahn played a vital role in guiding us along the frequently rocky road and kept us walking on the right spiritual path. It has been an incredible experience to go through the manuscript with the author at his beautiful and peaceful monastery, Wat Tam Doi Tone. To complete the translation is a way of paying homage to our teacher and to the Triple Gem, the Buddha, the Dhamma, and the Sangha.

Though this book contains many complicated Buddhist philosophies and teachings, practitioners are always welcome to seek further discussion with the author at Wat Tam Doi Tone, where formal courses in meditation are organized to serve the needs of practitioners of all levels, from beginning meditators to those with years of experience.

The book has now been completed. We have done our job in making it available to the world. Still, the task of constant practice in order to achieve the ultimate goal continues. That is the goal our great master wants all of us to reach.

Enjoy the book, and enjoy Dhamma.

The widespread misery of the world
reveals itself to his mind
so nakedly, so powerful
that the cry for the end of it
drowns every other voice:
forth, forth, forth
to the other shore.

CHAPTER I

The Buddha's First Utterance

Namo Tassa Bhagavato Arahato Sammāsambuddhassa.

Homage to Him, the Blessed One, the Holy One, the Perfectly Self-Enlightened One.

"Monks, it is because of not understanding and not penetrating the Four Noble Truths that you and I have roamed and wandered through this long course of *saṃsāra* (the round of rebirth). What four?

"It is, monks, because of not understanding and not penetrating the noble truth of suffering… of the origin of suffering… of the cessation of suffering… of the path leading to the cessation of suffering that you and I have roamed and wandered through this long course of saṃsāra.

"That noble truth of suffering, monks, that noble truth of the origin of suffering… of the cessation of suffering… of the way leading to the cessation of suffering has been understood and penetrated. Craving for existence has been cut off; the conduit to existence has been destroyed; now there is no more renewed existence."[1]

1 S.N. (vol.2), Mahā-vagga, Sacca-saṁyutta, Koṭigāma (21), p.1852, Bhikkhu Bodhi.

The Round of Rebirth

At Savatthi, there the Blessed One said: "From an inconstruable beginning comes transmigration. A beginning point is not evident, though beings hindered by ignorance and fettered by craving are transmigrating and wandering on. Just as a stick thrown up in the air lands sometimes on its base, sometimes on its side, sometimes on its tip; in the same way, beings hindered by ignorance and fettered by craving, transmigrating and wandering on, sometimes go from this world to another world, sometimes come from another world to this.

"Why is that? From an inconstruable beginning comes transmigration ...."[2]

"An aeon is long, monks. It's not easy to count it and say it is so many years, or so many hundreds of years, or so many thousands of years, or so many hundreds of thousands of years.... Suppose, monks, there was a great stone mountain a *yojana*[3] long, a yojana wide and a yojana high, without holes or crevices, one solid mass of rock. At the end of every hundred years, a man would stroke it once with a piece of Kāsian[4] cloth. By this effort that great stone mountain might be worn away and eliminated but the aeon would still not have come to an end. So long is an aeon, monks. And of aeons of such length, we have wandered through so many aeons, so many hundreds of aeons, so many thousands of aeons, so many hundreds of thousands of aeons. For what reason? Because, monks, this saṁsāra is without discoverable beginning.... **It is enough to experience revulsion towards all formations, enough to**

2 S.N., Nidāna-vagga, Anatamagga-saṁyutta, 15.9, Bhikkhu Thanissaro, ATI.

3 An ancient Indian unit of measurement.

4 Kāsi, an ancient Indian city state, was well known for its cloth products.

become dispassionate towards them, enough to be liberated from them."[5]

"Excellent, monks. Excellent. It is excellent that you thus understand the Dhamma taught by me.

"This is the greater: the tears you have shed while transmigrating and wandering this long, long time, crying and weeping from being joined with what is displeasing, being separated from what is pleasing — not the water in the four great oceans.

"Long have you experienced the death of a mother. The tears you have shed over the death of a mother... are greater than the water in the four great oceans.

"Long have you experienced the death of a father... the death of a brother... the death of a sister... the death of a son... the death of a daughter... loss with regard to relatives... loss with regard to wealth... loss with regard to disease. The tears you have shed over loss with regard to disease while transmigrating and wandering this long, long time, crying and weeping from being joined with what is displeasing, being separated from what is pleasing — are greater than the water in the four great oceans.

"Why is that? From an inconstruable beginning comes transmigration. A beginning point is not evident, though beings hindered by ignorance and fettered by craving are transmigrating and wandering on. Long have you thus experienced stress, experienced pain, experienced loss, swelling the cemeteries — **enough to become disenchanted with all fabricated things, enough to become dispassionate, enough to be released**."[6]

5 S.N. (vol.1), Nidāna-vagga, Anamatagga-saṁyutta (5), p. 654, Bhikkhu Bodhi.
6 S.N. Nidāna-vagga, Anatamagga-saṁyutta, 15.3, Bhikkhu Thanissaro, ATI.

Rare States

"Monks, suppose that this great earth were totally covered with water, and a man were to toss a yoke with a single hole there. A wind from the east would push it west, a wind from the west would push it east. A wind from the north would push it south, a wind from the south would push it north. And suppose a blind sea-turtle were there. It would come to the surface once every one hundred years. Now what do you think: would that blind sea-turtle, coming to the surface once every one hundred years, stick his neck into the yoke with a single hole?

"It would be a sheer coincidence, Lord, that the blind sea-turtle, coming to the surface once every one hundred years, would stick his neck into the yoke with a single hole.

"It's likewise a sheer coincidence that one obtains the human state. It's likewise a sheer coincidence that a *Tathāgata,*[7], worthy and rightly self-awakened, arises in the world. It's likewise a sheer coincidence that a doctrine and discipline expounded by a Tathāgata appears in the world. Now, this human state has been obtained. A Tathāgata, worthy and rightly self-awakened, has arisen in the world. A doctrine and discipline expounded by a Tathāgata appears in the world.

"Therefore your duty is the contemplation, 'This is [suffering]... This is the origination of [suffering]... This is the cessation of [suffering].' Your duty is the contemplation, 'This is the path of practice leading to the cessation of [suffering].'"[8]

---

7 "The Perfect One," an epithet of the Lord Buddha.

8 S.N., Mahā-vagga, Sacca-saṃyutta, 56.48, Bhikkhu Thanissaro, ATI.

Existence of a Happy State

This was said by the Blessed One, said by the *arahant* (a fully enlightened person), so I have heard:

"When a *deva* (a celestial being) is about to pass away from the company of devas, five omens appear: his garlands wither, his clothes get soiled, sweat comes out of his armpits, a dullness descends on his body, he no longer delights in his own deva-seat. The devas, knowing from this that 'This deva-son is about to pass away,' encourage him with three sayings: 'Go from here, honorable sir, to a good destination. Having gone to a good destination, gain the gain that is good to gain. Having gained the gain that is good to gain, become well-established.

"When this was said, a certain monk said to the Blessed One, 'What, Lord, is the devas' reckoning of going to a good destination? What is their reckoning of the gain that is good to gain? What is their reckoning of becoming well-established?

"The human state, monks, is the devas' reckoning of going to a good destination. Having become a human being, acquiring conviction in the Dhamma-and-Vinaya[9] taught by the Tathāgata: this is the devas' reckoning of the gain that is good to gain. When that conviction is settled within one — rooted, established, and strong, not to be destroyed by any priest or contemplative deva, *Māra*[10], or *brahma*[11]; or anyone else in the world: this is the devas' reckoning of becoming well-established.

---

9 Doctrine and discipline of the Lord Buddha. The word "dhamma" has several meanings. "Dhamma" is the teaching or doctrine of the Buddha, while "dhamma" can mean the "bearer", consitution (or nature of a thing), norm, law, doctrine, justice, righteousness, quality, object of mind, or phenomenon.

10 Māra is the "tempter-figure." He appears in the texts both as a real person (i.e. as a deity, or the Lord of Evil) and as the personification of evil and passions, of the totality of worldy existence, and of death.

11 Being residing in the higher heavenly planes of the form and formless realms.

"When a deva passes away from the company of devas through his life-span's ending, three sounds sound forth the devas' encouragement. 'Go from here, honorable sir, to a good destination, to companionship with human beings. On becoming a human being, acquire a conviction unsurpassed in True Dhamma. That conviction of yours in True Dhamma, well-taught, should be settled, rooted, established — undestroyed as long as you live. Having abandoned bodily misconduct, verbal misconduct, mental misconduct, and whatever else is flawed; having done with the body what is skillful, and much that is skillful with speech, having done what is skillful with a heart without limit, with no acquisitions, then having made much of that basis of merit through giving, establish other mortals in True Dhamma and the holy life.' With this sympathy, the devas, when they know a deva is passing away, encourage him: 'Come back, deva, again and again.'"[12]

Nature of the Buddha

"On one occasion, the Blessed One was walking on the highway between Ukkatthā and Setavyā. And it happened that the Brahmin Dona was also walking along that road. Dona, the Brahmin, saw on the footprints of the Blessed One the wheel marks with their thousand spokes, with felly and hub, perfect in every respect. Seeing these marks, he thought to himself: 'It is truly wonderful, it is astonishing! These certainly cannot be the footprints of a human being!'

"Meanwhile the Blessed One had left the highway and had sat down under a tree not far off, with legs crossed, keeping his body erect, having set mindfulness before him. Then Dona the

12 K.N., Itivuttaka, 3.34, Bhikkhu Thanissaro, ATI.

Brahmin, following the Blessed One's footprints, saw him seated under a tree, of pleasing appearance, inspiring confidence, with calm features and calm mind, in perfect composure and equipoise, controlled and restrained [like] a well-trained bull elephant. Seeing the Blessed One, Dona approached him and said:

'Will Your Reverence become a deva?'

'No, Brahmin, I shall not become a deva.'

'Then Your Reverence might become a *gandhabba* (a kind of celestial being skilled in music)... a *yakkha* (an ogre)… a human being?'

'No, Brahmin, I shall not become a gandhabba… a yakkha… a human being.'

'What, then, will Your Reverence become?'

'Brahmin, those taints whereby, if they were not abandoned, I might become a deva, a gandhabba, a yakkha, or a human being - these taints are abandoned by me, cut off at the root, made barren like palm-tree stumps, obliterated so that they are no more subject to arise in the future.

'Just as, Brahmin, a blue, red or white lotus, though born and grown in the water, rises up and stands unsoiled by the water, so, Brahmin, though born and grown in the world, I have overcome the world and dwell unsoiled by the world. Consider me, O Brahmin, a **Buddha**.'''[13]

13 A.N.,The Chapter of the Fours (58), p. 87-8, Bhikkhu Nyanaponika and Bhikkhu Bodhi.

Four Kinds of Miracles

"Monks, on the manifestation of a Tathāgata, an arahant, a fully enlightened one, **four wonderful and marvellous things** are manifested. What four?

"People generally find **pleasure in attachments**, take delight in attachments and enjoy attachments. But when the Dhamma **of non-attachment** is taught by the Tathāgata, people wish to listen to it, give ear and try to understand it.

"People generally find **pleasure in conceit**, take delight in conceit and enjoy conceit. But when the Dhamma is taught by the Tathāgata **for the abolition of conceit**, people wish to listen to it, give ear and try to understand it.

"People generally find **pleasure in a life of excitement**, take delight in excitement and enjoy excitement. But when the **peaceful** Dhamma is taught by the Tathāgata, people wish to listen to it, give ear and try to understand it.

"People generally live in ignorance, are **blinded by ignorance** and fettered by ignorance. But when the Dhamma is taught by the Tathāgata for the **abolition of ignorance**, people wish to listen to it, give ear and try to understand it.

"On the manifestation of a Tathāgata, an Arahant, a Fully Enlightened One, these four wonderful and marvellous things become manifest."[14]

14 Ibid. (78), p. 109-10.

****

By what track can you trace
that trackless Buddha of limitless range,
whose victory nothing can undo,
whom none of the vanquished defilements
can ever pursue?

****

Hard is it to be born a human being
hard is the life of mortals.
Hard is it to gain the opportunity
(to hear) the Sublime Truth,
and hard to encounter
is the arising of the Buddhas.

****

The good shine even from afar,
like the Himalayan mountain.
But the wicked are unseen,
like arrows shot in the night.

Just as a solid rock
is not shaken by a storm,
even so the wise are not affected
by praise or blame.

CHAPTER II

Standard Practice for Liberation

The Path to Liberation

"There are, O monks, these five bases of liberation, and when a monk dwells diligent, ardent and resolute in any of these, his unliberated mind comes to be liberated, his undestroyed taints undergo destruction, and he attains the as-yet-unattained unsurpassed security from bondage. What five?

"1. Here, monks, the Teacher or a certain fellow monk in the position of a teacher teaches the Dhamma to a monk. Even as the Teacher **teaches the Dhamma** to him, that monk **experiences the meaning and the Dhamma**. When he gains such experience, gladness arises. When he is gladdened, rapture arises; for one uplifted by rapture, the body becomes calm; one calm in body feels happy; for one who is happy the mind becomes concentrated. This is the **first base of liberation**, and when a monk dwells diligent, ardent and resolute here, his unliberated mind comes to be liberated, his undestroyed taints undergo destruction, and he attains the as-yet-unattained unsurpassed security from bondage.

"2. Further, monks, neither the Teacher nor a fellow monk in the position of a teacher teaches the Dhamma to a monk. But the monk himself **teaches the Dhamma in detail** to others as he has learned it and mastered it. Even as he teaches the Dhamma, that monk **experiences the meaning and the Dhamma**. When he gains such experience, gladness arises… the mind becomes concentrated. This is the **second base of liberation**.

"3. Further, monks, neither the Teacher nor a fellow monk in the position of a teacher teaches the Dhamma to a monk, nor does he himself teach the Dhamma in detail to others as he has learned it and mastered it. But he **recites the Dhamma in detail** as he has learned it and mastered it. Even as he recites the Dhamma, the monk **experiences the meaning and the Dhamma**. When he gains such experience, gladness arises… the mind becomes concentrated. This is the **third base of liberation**….

"4. Further, monks, neither the Teacher nor a fellow monk in the position of a teacher teaches the Dhamma to a monk, nor does he himself teach the Dhamma in detail to others, nor does he recite the Dhamma in detail. But he **ponders, examines and mentally investigates the Dhamma** as he has learned it and mastered it. Even as he ponders the Dhamma, that monk **experiences the meaning and the Dhamma.** When he gains such experience, gladness arises… the mind becomes concentrated. This is the **fourth base of liberation….**

"5. Further, monks, neither the Teacher nor a fellow monk in the position of a teacher teaches the Dhamma to a monk… nor does he ponder the Dhamma. But he has learned well a **certain object of concentration, attends to it well, sustains it well, and penetrates it thoroughly with wisdom.** Even as he learns well an object of concentration, that monk **experiences the meaning and the Dhamma**. When he gains such experience, gladness arises. When he is gladdened, rapture arises; for one uplifted by rapture, the body becomes calm; one calm in body feels happy; for one who is happy the mind becomes concentrated. This is the **fifth base of liberation**, and when a monk dwells diligent, ardent and resolute here, his unliberated mind comes to be liberated, his undestroyed taints undergo destruction, and he attains the as-yet-unattained unsurpassed security from bondage.

"These, monks, are the five bases of liberation, and when a monk dwells diligent, ardent and resolute in any of these, his unliberated mind comes to be liberated, his undestroyed taints undergo destruction, and he attains the as-yet-unattained unsurpassed security from bondage."[15]

****

Wisdom cannot be perfectly developed

In those with unstable minds,

Who know not the noble truth,

and who live with false faith.

****

15 A.N., The Chapter of the Fives (98), p.130-31, Bhikku Nyanaponika and Bhikku Bodhi.

A Summary of the Five Pathways to Liberation

1. Listening to Dhamma
2. Teaching Dhamma
3. Reciting Dhamma
4. Contemplating Dhamma
5. *Samādhinimitta*: a method of concentration using certain mental images as concentrative objects

Standard Ways of Practice to Liberation

"Friends, whatever monks or nuns declare before me that they have attained the final knowledge of arahantship, all these do so in one of four ways. What four?

"1. Here, friends, a monk develops **insight preceded by tranquility**. While he thus develops insight preceded by tranquility, the path arises in him. He now pursues, develops, and cultivates that path, and while he is doing so, the fetters are abandoned and the underlying tendencies eliminated.

"2. Or again, friends, a monk develops **tranquility preceded by insight**. While he thus develops tranquility preceded by insight, the path arises in him. He now pursues, develops, and cultivates that path, and while he is doing so, the fetters are abandoned and the underlying tendencies eliminated.

"3. Or again, friends, a monk develops **tranquility and insight joined in pairs**. While he thus develops tranquility and insight joined in pairs, the path arises in him. He now pursues, develops, and cultivates that path, and while he is doing so, the fetters are abandoned and the underlying tendencies eliminated.

"4. Or again, friends, a monk's mind is seized by **agitation caused by higher states of mind**. But there comes a time when his mind becomes internally steadied, composed, unified and concentrated; then the path arises in him. He now pursues, develops, and cultivates that path, and while he is doing so, the fetters are abandoned and the underlying tendencies eliminated."[16]

Mind in the Path:
The Balance of Tranquility and Insight

The eightfold path[17], when fully developed to the level where their culminating power functions simultaneously, will create an overwhelming light of wisdom to realize the truth and eradicate the hindrance of defilements. **The manner in which all components of the path generate their power simultaneously is called *magga*, or path,** which signifies the very moment when all components realize themselves in full. When this process happens, the result which follows is called *phala*, or fruit, which is the penetrative understanding of the truth.

And if this enlightenment process proceeds gradually in order, magga will function more and more strongly until all four successive stages of enlightenment are completed. Therefore, these four stages of enlightenment are called four maggas and the following four states of fruition are called four phalas. These four maggas and four phalas are also called the *noble maggas* and the *noble phalas*, which can be identified as follows: *sotāpattimagga*

16 Ibid., The Chapter of the Fours (83), p.114.
17 The eightfold path consists of right view, right thought, right speech, right action, right livelihood, right effort, right mindfulness and right concentration.

(the path of the stream-enterer[18]), *sotāpattiphala* (the fruition of the stream-enterer), *sakadāgāmimagga* (the path of the once-returner), *sakadāgāmiphala* (the fruition of the once-returner), *anāgāmimagga* (the path of the non-returner), *anāgāmiphala* (the fruition of the non-returner), *arahattamagga* (the path of the fully enlightened), and *arahattaphala* (the fruition of the fully enlightened).

In terms of its components, magga can be divided into eight aspects (the eightfold path), therefore it is called *aṭṭhaṇgikamagga* (aṭṭhaṇgika means eight, magga means path). In terms of its function, there are four stages called *catumagga* or four maggas as just described.

The manner in which all factors function simultaneously within a single instant, followed by a tangible result, is also referred to as *Dhammasāmaggī* (the accordance of Dhamma) which has the same meaning as *bodhi* (enlightenment). In this very instant, not only do all components of the eightfold path culminate, but so do the components of the thirty-seven *bodhipakkhiyadhamma*[19]. However, all components of bodhipakkhiyadhamma can also be summarized and manifested in the eightfold path. Thus, when we talk about the eightfold path, it is understood to cover all other related components of Dhamma."[20]

---

18 The noble persons are those who have realized the successive stages of liberation. There are four categories of these nobles persons: the stream-enterer, the once-returner, the non-returner and the fully enlightened. See more detail in Chapter Five.

19 The requisites of enlightenment are: four foundations of mindfulness, four great strivings, four means of accomplishment, five spiritual faculties, five bases of power, seven factors of enlightenment and the eightfold path. All together, they make thirty seven factors.

20 Translated from Phra Ratchaworamuni, *Buddhadhamma*, p. 886-887.

Path Leading to the Balance of Tranquility and Insight

"These four kinds of persons, O monks, are found existing in the world. What four?

"1. Therein, monks, the **person who gains internal tranquility of mind but not the higher wisdom of insight into things** should approach one who has gains the higher wisdom and inquire of him: 'How, friend, should formation be seen? How should formations be explored? How should constructions be discerned with insight?' The other then answers him as he has seen and understood the matter thus: 'Formations should be seen in such a way; they should be explored in such a way; they should be discerned with insight in such a way.' At a later time, this one gains both internal tranquility of mind and the higher wisdom of insight into things.

"2. Therein, monks, the **person who gains the higher wisdom of insight into things but not internal tranquility of mind** should approach one who has gained internal tranquility and inquire of him: 'How, friend, should the mind be steadied? How should the mind be composed? How should the mind be unified? How should the mind be concentrated?' The other then answers him as he has seen and understood the matter thus: 'The mind should be steadied in such a way, composed in such a way, unified in such a way, concentrated in such a way.' At a later time, this one gains both internal tranquility of mind and the higher wisdom of insight into things.

3. Therein, monks, the **person who gains neither internal tranquility of mind nor the higher wisdom of insight into things** should approach one who has gained both and inquire of him; 'How, friend, should the mind be steadied?... How, friend,

should formations be seen?…' The other then answers him as he has seen and understood the matter thus: 'The mind should be steadied in such a way… Formations should be seen in such a way…' At a later time, this one gains both internal tranquility of mind and the higher wisdom of insight into things.

"4. Therein, monks, the **person who gains both internal tranquility of mind and the higher wisdom of insight into things** should establish himself in just these wholesome states and make a further effort for the destruction of the taints.

"These are the four types of individuals to be found existing in world."[21]

The Right Approach to Enlightenment

"I thought: 'Whatever recluses or brahmins in the past… in the future... (or) at present have experienced painful, racking, piercing feelings due to exertion, this is the utmost, there is none beyond this. But by this racking practice of austerities, I have not attained any superhuman states, any distinction in knowledge and vision worthy of the noble ones. Could there be another path to enlightenment?'

"I considered: 'I recall that when my father the Sakyan was occupied, I was sitting in the cool shade of a rose-apple tree, quite secluded from sensual pleasures, secluded from unwholesome states, I entered upon and abided in the first *jhāna*[22], which is

---

21 A.N., The Chapter of the Fours (72), p. 103-4, Bhikkhu Nyanaponika and Bhikkhu Bodhi.

22 Jhāna, also referred to as absorption concentration, refers to the four meditative absorptions of the form realm (sometimes called fine material realms and, in Pāli, called *rūpajhāna*) and another four higher levels of the formless realm (sometimes called immaterial realms and, in Pāli, called *arūpajhāna*). See more detail about jhāna practice in Chapter Eight.

accompanied by applied and sustained thought[23], with rapture and pleasure born of seclusion. Could that be the path to enlightenment?' Then, following on that memory, came the realization: **'That is the path to enlightenment.'**

"I thought: 'Why am I afraid of that pleasure that has nothing to do with sensual pleasures and unwholesome states?' I thought: 'I am not afraid of that pleasure since it has nothing to do with sensual pleasures and unwholesome states.'

"I considered: 'It is not easy to attain that pleasure with a body so excessively emaciated. Suppose I ate some solid food — some boiled rice and porridge.' And I ate some solid food — some boiled rice and porridge."[24]

Happiness To Be Feared / Not To Be Feared

"And, Udāyin, there are these five strings of sensuality. Which five? Forms cognizable via the eye — agreeable, pleasing, charming, endearing, fostering desire, enticing. Sounds cognizable via the ear... aromas cognizable via the nose... flavors cognizable via the tongue... tactile sensations cognizable via the body — agreeable, pleasing, charming, endearing, fostering desire, enticing. These are the five strings of sensuality. Now, any pleasure and happiness that arises dependent on these five strings of sensuality is called sensual pleasure, a filthy pleasure, a run-of-the-mill pleasure, an ignoble pleasure. And of this pleasure I say that it is not to be cultivated, not to be developed, not to be pursued, that it is to be feared.

---

23 Applied and sustained thought (*vitakka-vicāra*) are constituents of the first absorption or jhāna, but are absent in the higher levels of jhāna. Vitakka is the laying hold of a thought or the fixing of consciousness to an object and vicāra is the continued activity of the mind.

24 M.N., Mahāyamakavagga, Mahā-saccaka Sutta (36),p. 340, Bhikkhu Ñāṇamoli and Bhikkhu Bodhi.

"Now, there is the case where a monk, quite withdrawn from sensuality, withdrawn from unskillful mental qualities, enters and remains in the first jhāna: rapture and pleasure born from withdrawal, accompanied by directed thought and evaluation. With the stilling of directed thought and evaluation, he enters and remains in the second jhāna: rapture and pleasure born of concentration, unification of awareness free from directed thought and evaluation — internal assurance. With the fading of rapture, he remains equanimous, mindful and alert, and senses pleasure with the body. He enters and remains in the third jhāna, of which the Noble Ones declare, 'Equanimous and mindful, he has a pleasant abiding.' With the abandoning of pleasure and pain — as with the earlier disappearance of elation and distress — he enters and remains in the fourth jhāna: purity of equanimity and mindfulness, neither pleasure nor pain.

"This is called renunciation-pleasure, seclusion-pleasure, calm-pleasure, self-awakening-pleasure. And of this pleasure I say that it is to be cultivated, to be developed, to be pursued, that it is not to be feared."[25]

Encounter with Māra

"Monks, long ago a battle raged between the devas and the *asuras* (demons), and in that battle the asuras won and the devas were defeated. And the defeated devas simply fled, with the asuras facing north hot after them. Then thought the devas: 'The asuras give chase; let us battle with them a second time!' And a second time they fought and a second time were defeated and pursued....

25 M.N., 66, Laṭukikopama Sutta, Bhikkhu Thanissaro, ATI.

"And a third time they fought and the asuras won and the devas were defeated. Defeated and fearful, they just entered the deva city. Monks, thus gone to their city, the devas thought: 'Now that we have come to the refuge for the fearful, we will henceforth dwell by ourselves and have no dealings with the asuras.' And the asuras thought also: 'Gone, indeed, are the devas to the refuge for the fearful, henceforth they will dwell by themselves and have no dealing with us!'

"Monks, long ago another battle raged between the devas and asuras; but in that fight the devas won and the asuras were defeated. And the defeated asuras fled, pursued by the devas, facing south. Then thought the asuras: 'The devas pursue us; what if we fight a second time!' And they did so... and were a second time defeated.

"And a third time they fought and the devas won and the asuras were defeated; and defeated and fearful, they just entered the asura city; and thus gone to their city, the asuras thought: 'Now that we've come to the refuge for the fearful, we will dwell by ourselves and have nothing to do with the devas.' And the devas thought likewise....

"In just the same way, monks, what time a monk, aloof from sense desires,... enters and abides in the first [jhāna], he thinks: 'Now that I have come to the refuge for the fearful, I will henceforth dwell by myself and have no dealings with Māra.' And Māra, the Evil One, thinks: 'Now that the monk has gone to the refuge for the fearful, he will dwell by himself and have no dealing with me.' Monks, what time a monk... enters and abides in the second... third... and fourth [jhāna], he thinks likewise... and Māra too....

"Monks, when a monk... enters and abides in the realm of boundless space[26], he is said to have put a darkness about Māra, and Māra's vision, being blotted out, is without range, and he has become invisible to the Evil One.

"Monks, when a monk... enters and abides in the realm of boundless consciousness… of nothingness… of neither perception nor non-perception and by wisdom sees that the cankers are completely destroyed, he is said to have put a darkness about Māra, and Māra's vision, being blotted out, is without range; and he has become invisible to the Evil One and has passed through the world's entanglement."[27]

❁❁❁❁❁❁❁❁

Māra can destroy those

who are attached to sensual beauty,

not controlling their behavior,

lacking moderation in eating,

idle and weak,

like the strong wind

uprooting an old tree.

❁❁❁❁❁❁❁❁

26 The four higher levels of jhāna in the formless realm (arūpajhāna) are as follows: the realm of boundless space, the realm of boundless consciousness, the realm of nothingness and the realm of neither perception nor non-perception.

27 A.N. vol. 4, The Book of the Nines (9,4,39), p. 290-91, Hare.

The Yogi in States of Jhāna

Following are various arguments against the practice of jhāna from those who see no benefits or advantages of a mind in absorption concentration or *jhānacitta*.

Firstly, jhāna causes practitioners to attach themselves to its pleasure and become more likely to be misled. Most of those who hold this attitude have never had the experience of jhānacitta. Or even if experienced, they fail to develop proficiency in it. Therefore, they do not see its invaluable benefits.

Secondly, attaining the path or fruition does not necessarily require *appanāsamādhi* (absorption concentration).[28] *Khanikasamādhi* (momentary concentration) or *upacārasamādhi* (access concentration) should suffice. Truly speaking, attaining the path and fruition requires the masterful and skilled balancing of the culminating powers of tranquility and insight. The concentrative power must at least reach the level of absorption concentration in the first jhāna, which is considered the factor of right concentration in the eightfold path.

It is possible for *sekkha*[29] persons to attain jhāna in the very moment they attain the first path and fruition. After that, they might not be able to raise their mind to jhāna again. However, for once-returners wishing to attain the higher level of non-returning, they must experience and gain proficiency in jhāna before they can attain the third path.

---

28 Sometimes called attainment concentration or full concentration. It is the concentration existing during absorption in jhāna. Access concentration (sometimes called sustained attention, in Pāli upacārasamādhi) only approaches the first jhāna without attaining it, and momentary concentration (sometimes called attention stillness, in Pāli khanikasamādhi) is a state prior to access concentration.

29 Sekkha literally means 'a learner.' It signifies a person who has reached one of the earlier stages of magga, but not the last, so has still to undergo a higher learning.

The third argument against jhāna practice is that there are known cases of those who attained absorption concentration and had proficiency in supernormal powers, but still were not able to attain the noble truth. The most frequently mentioned persons are Asitta yogi (Kāladevin yogi), who enjoyed visiting heavens, Ālāra yogi, who attained the seventh jhāna, and Udaka yogi, who attained the eighth jhāna.

These commentators may have forgotten that the only types of beings who are able to develop *vipassanā* (insight)[30] without relying on other people's wisdom are the Buddha or solitary buddhas.[31] These three yogis did not possess the qualities that would enable them to be Buddha nor had the Buddha been born to the world during their time. How could they, then, attain magga by themselves?

After attaining enlightenment, the Buddha at first hesitated to teach the Dhamma as the knowledge attained by him was so profound, complicated and difficult to understand. Then, after emerging from contemplation at the end of a seven day retreat, the Lord approached the Banyan tree of the goatherds. While staying there and meditating in seclusion, a thought arose in his mind:

"This Dhamma, [known] by me, is deep, difficult to see, difficult to understand, peaceful, excellent, beyond dialectic, subtle, intelligible to the learned. But this is a creation delighting in sensual pleasure, delighted by sensual pleasure, rejoicing in sensual pleasure. So for a creation delighting in sensual pleasure, delighted by sensual pleasure, rejoicing in sensual pleasure,

30 Insight, or wisdom, attained through direct meditative observation, is the decisive liberating factor of the Lord Buddha's teaching.

31 A solitary buddha attains enlightenment by himself, but does not teach others.

this would be a matter difficult to see, that is to say causal uprising by way of cause. This too is a matter very difficult to see, that is to say the calming of all the habitual tendencies, the renunciation of all attachment, the destruction of craving, dispassion, stopping, nibbāna. And so if I were to teach Dhamma and others were not to understand me, this would be a weariness to me, this would be a vexation to me.

"And further, these verses not heard before occurred spontaneously to the Lord:

'This that through many toils I've won —
Enough! Why should I make it known?
By folk with lust and hate consumed
This Dhamma is not understood.
Leading on against the stream,
Subtle, deep, difficult to see, delicate,
Unseen 'twill be by passion's slaves
Cloaked in the murk of ignorance.'"[32]

"However, he later changed his mind. And he pondered: 'Now, to whom should I first teach Dhamma? Who will understand this Dhamma quickly?' Then he thought: 'Indeed, this Ālāra the Kālāma… and Udaka are learned, experienced, wise, and for a long time they have had only little dust in their eyes. Suppose I were to teach Dhamma first to them? They will understand this Dhamma quickly.'[33]

32 The Book of Discipline vol. 4 , Mahā-vagga I, p. 6, Horner.
33 Ibid., p.10.

"There is no concentration for one who lacks wisdom.
Nor is there wisdom for one who lacks concentration.
In whom there are found both concentration and wisdom,
Are indeed in the presence of nibbāna."[34]

Four Modes of Progress to Liberation

1. *Dukkha patipadā dandhābhiññā* – painful progress with sluggish direct knowledge.
2. *Dukkha patipadā khippābhiññā* – painful progress with swift direct knowledge.
3. *Sukha patipadā dandhābhiññā* – pleasant progress with sluggish direct knowledge.
4. *Sukha patipadā khippābhiññā* – pleasant progress with swift direct knowledge.

Painful Progress with Sluggish Direct Knowledge

"And of what sort, monks, is the painful mode of progress with sluggish [direct knowledge]?

"In this case, a monk lives contemplating the loathsomeness in the body, aware of the repulsiveness of food, aware of his distaste for all the world, aware of impermanence in all activities. Thus awareness of death is implanted in the very self. He lives dependent on these five powers of a pupil: the power of faith, the power of modesty, the power of self-restraint, the power

---

34 K.N. Dhammapada, Verses on Bhikkhu, p. 402, trans. by Sathienpong Wannapok, *The Buddha's Verses in Dhammapada*, published in commemoration of the crematory rite of Mrs. Premsri Khemasingkhi, 4 April 1999, Phra Sri Mahadhathu Royal Temple, Bangkok.

of energy, and the power of wisdom. But in him these five controlling faculties are dully manifested, to wit: the controlling faculty of faith, that of energy, that of mindfulness, that of concentration, and the controlling faculty of wisdom. Thus, owing to the dullness of these five controlling faculties, sluggish is his attainment of the concentration that follows on for the destruction of the *āsavas* (cankers or defilements). This, monks, is called 'the mode of progress that is painful with sluggish [direct knowledge].'

Painful Progress with Swift Direct Knowledge

"And of what sort, monks, is the mode of progress that is painful, but with swift [direct knowledge]?

"In this case a monk lives contemplating the unloveliness in the body same (as above). But in him these five controlling faculties are manifested in abundance, to wit: the controlling faculty of faith.... Thus, owing to the preponderance of these five controlling faculties, swift is his attainment of the concentration that follows on for the destruction of the āsavas. This, monks, is called 'the mode of progress that is painful but with swift [direct knowledge].'

Pleasant Progress with Sluggish Direct Knowledge

"And of what sort, monks, is the mode of progress that is pleasant but with sluggish [direct knowledge]?

"In this case a monk, aloof from sense-desires, aloof from evil conditions... enters upon the first [jhāna]... the second [jhāna]... the third [jhāna]...the fourth [jhāna], a state of neither ease nor discomfort, an equanimity of utter purity, and having attained it, abides therein. He lives dependent on these five powers of a pupil: the power of faith.... But in him these five controlling faculties are dully manifested, to wit... Thus, owing to the dullness of these five controlling faculties, sluggish is his attainment of the concentration that follows on for the destruction of the āsavas. This, monks, is called 'the mode of progress that is pleasant, but with sluggish [direct knowledge].'

Pleasant Progress with Swift Direct Knowledge

"And of what sort, monks, is the mode of progress that is both pleasant and accompanied by swift [direct knowledge]?

"In this case a monk, aloof from sense-desire (same as above)… But in him these five controlling faculties are manifested in abundance... Thus, owing to the preponderance of these five controlling faculties, swift is his attainment of the concentration that follows on for the destruction of the āsavas.This, monks, is called 'the mode of progress that is both pleasant and is accompanied by swift [direct knowledge].'

"So these are the four modes of progress."[35]

---

35 A.N. vol. 2, The Book of the Fours (9, 17, 163) p. 156, Woodward.

Celestial State

"Pray, Master Gotama, of what sort is that high, broad couch celestial which the worthy Gotama gets here and now as he pleases without toil and trouble?'

"In this case, Brahmin, when I am living dependent on a certain village or suburb, I get myself robed in the forenoon, and taking bowl and outer robe I enter that village or suburb to beg. When I return from my alms-round and have eaten my meal, I make for the edge of a forest. There I gather together whatever grasses or leaves there are into one place and sit down cross-legged, holding my body straight and setting mindfulness in front of me. Thus aloof from sense-desires, aloof from unprofitable states of mind, I enter on the first [jhāna]… second [jhāna]... third [jhāna]… fourth [jhāna], free of pain and free of pleasure, a state of perfect purity of balance and equanimity.

"Now, Brahmin, when I have reached such a state, if I walk up and down, at such time my walking is to me celestial. If I stand, at such time my standing is to me celestial. If I sit, my sitting is to me celestial. If I lie down, **celestial is the high, broad couch I lie on.** That, Brahmin, is what I mean when I speak of the high, broad couch celestial which I get as I please without toil and trouble."[36]

36 A.N. vol. 1, The Book of the Threes (3,7,63), p. 165-66, Woodward.

Power over the Mind

"Monks, endowed with seven things, a monk makes the mind turn according to his wish and turns not by the mind's wish. What seven?

"Herein, monks, a monk is skilled in concentration, skilled in attaining it, skilled in maintaining it, skilled in emerging from it, skilled in the well-being of it, skilled in the range of it, skilled in applying it.

"Verily, monks, endowed with these seven things a monk makes the mind turn according to his wish and turns not by the mind's wish."[37]

Wisdom Generated from Concentration

"Wise and mindful, you should develop immeasurable concentration.[38] When, wise and mindful, one has developed immeasurable concentration, five realizations arise right within one's self. Which five?

"The realization arises right within oneself that 'This concentration is blissful in the present and will result in bliss in the future.'

"The realization arises right within oneself that 'This concentration is noble and not connected with the baits of the flesh.'

"The realization arises right within oneself that 'This concentration is not obtained by base people.'

"The realization arises right within oneself that 'This concentration is peaceful, exquisite, the acquiring of serenity, the attainment of unity, not kept in place by the fabrications of forceful restraint.'

---

37 A.N. vol. 4, The Book of the Sevens (3,4,39), p. 20, Hare.

38 Concentration based on the four boundless states (also called the sublime states or attitudes) of loving kindness, compassion, sympathetic joy, and equanimity.

"The realization arises right within oneself that **'I enter into this concentration mindfully, and mindfully I emerge from it.'**

"Wise and mindful, one should develop immeasurable concentration. When, wise and mindful, one has developed immeasurable concentration, these five realizations arise right within oneself."[39]

Mind Devoid of Hindrances[40]

"Just as a man who had **taken a loan** to develop his business, and whose business had prospered, might pay off his old debts, and with what was left over could support a wife, might think: 'Before this I developed my business by borrowing but now it has prospered…' and he would rejoice and be glad about that.'

"Just as a man who was **ill,** suffering, terribly sick, with no appetite, and weak in body, might after a time recover and regain his appetite and bodily strength, and he might think: 'Before this I was ill but now I have recovered…' and he would rejoice and be glad about that.

"Just as a man might be bound **in prison**, and after a time he might be freed from his bonds without any loss, with no deduction from his possessions. He might think: 'Before this I was in prison but now I am free…' and he would rejoice and be glad about that.

"Just as a man might be a **slave**, not his own master, dependent on another, unable to go where he liked, and after some time he might be freed from slavery, able to go where he liked, might think: 'Before this I was a slave but now I am my own master…' and he would rejoice and be glad about that.

---

39 A.N., The Book of the Fives (5.27), Bhikkhu Thanissaro , ATI.

40 The five hindrances *(nīvarana)* are sensous desire, ill will, sloth and torpor, restlessness and anxiety, and doubt.

"Just as a man, laden with goods and wealth, might go on a **long journey** through the desert where food was scarce and danger abounded, and after a time he would get through the desert and arrive safe and sound at the edge of a village, might think: 'Before this I was in danger, now I am safe at the edge of a village...' and he would rejoice and be glad about that.

"As long, Sir, as a monk does not perceive the disappearance of the five hindrances in himself, he feels as if in debt, in sickness, in bonds, in slavery, on a desert journey. But when he perceives the disappearance of five hindrances in himself, it is as if he were freed from debt, from sickness, from bonds, from slavery, from the perils of the desert."[41]

The Fortress

"In the same way, monks, when a disciple of the noble ones is endowed with seven true qualities (*saddhamma*) and can obtain at will — without difficulty, without trouble — the four jhānas, heightened mental states that provide a pleasant abiding in the here-and-now, he is said to be a disciple of the noble ones who can't be undone by Māra, can't be undone by the Evil One.

"Now, with which seven true qualities is he endowed?

"Just as the royal frontier fortress has a foundation post — deeply rooted, well embedded, immovable, and unshakable — for the protection of those within and to ward off those without; in the same way a disciple of the noble ones has [faith], is convinced of the Tathāgata's awakening: 'Indeed, the Blessed One is worthy and rightly self-awakened, consummate in knowledge and conduct, well-gone, a knower of the cosmos, an unexcelled trainer of those

41 D.N., Sāmaññaphala Sutta, p. 101-102, Walshe.

persons ready to be tamed, teacher of human and divine beings, awakened, blessed.' **With [faith] as his foundation post,** the disciple of the noble ones abandons what is unskillful, develops what is skillful, abandons what is blameworthy, develops what is blameless, and looks after himself with purity. With this first true quality is he endowed.

"Just as the royal frontier fortress has a moat, both deep and wide, for the protection of those within...; in the same way, the disciple of the noble ones has a sense of shame. He feels shame at [the thought of engaging in] bodily misconduct, verbal misconduct, mental misconduct. He feels shame at falling into evil, unskillful actions. **With shame as his moat,** the disciple of the noble ones abandons what is unskillful,.... With this second true quality is he endowed.

"Just as the royal frontier fortress has an encircling road, both high and wide, for the protection of those within...; in the same way, the disciple of the noble ones has a sense of concern. He feels concern for [the suffering that results from] bodily misconduct, verbal misconduct, mental misconduct. He feels concern at falling into evil, unskillful actions. **With concern as his encircling road,** the disciple of the noble ones abandons what is unskillful.... With this third true quality is he endowed.

"Just as the royal frontier fortress has many weapons stored, both arrows and things to be hurled, for the protection of those within...; in the same way, the disciple of the noble ones has heard much, has retained what he has heard, has stored what he has heard. Whatever teachings are admirable in the beginning, admirable in the middle, admirable in the end, that, in their meaning and expression, proclaim the holy life that is entirely complete and pure: those he has listened to often, retained, discussed, accumulated, examined with his mind, and well-penetrated in terms of his views. **With learning as his weapons,** the disciple of the noble ones abandons what is unskillful.... With this fourth true quality is he endowed.

"Just as the royal frontier fortress has a large army stationed within — elephant soldiers, cavalry, charioteers, bowmen, standard-bearers, billeting officers, soldiers of the supply corps, noted princes, commando heroes, infantry, and slaves — for the protection of those within...; in the same way, a disciple of the noble ones keeps his persistence aroused for abandoning unskillful mental qualities and taking on skillful mental qualities, is steadfast, solid in his effort, not shirking his duties with regard to skillful mental qualities. **With persistence as his army,** the disciple of the noble ones abandons what is unskillful.... With this fifth true quality is he endowed.

"Just as the royal frontier fortress has a gate-keeper — wise, experienced, intelligent — to keep out those he doesn't know and to let in those he does, for the protection of those within...; in the same way, a disciple of the noble ones is mindful, highly meticulous, remembering and able to call to mind even things that were done and said long ago. **With mindfulness as his gate-keeper,** the disciple of the ones abandons what is unskillful.... With this sixth true quality is he endowed.

"Just as the royal frontier fortress has ramparts — high and thick and completely covered with plaster — for the protection of those within...; in the same way, a disciple of the noble ones is discerning, endowed with discernment leading to the arising of the goal — noble, penetrating, leading to the right ending of [suffering]. **With discernment as his covering of plaster,** the disciple of the noble ones abandons what is unskillful.... With this seventh true quality is he endowed.

"These are the **seven true qualities** with which he is endowed.

"And which are the **four jhānas** — heightened mental states that provide a pleasant abiding in the here-and-now — that he can obtain at will, without difficulty, without trouble?

"Just as a royal frontier fortress has large stores of grass, timber and water for the delight, convenience, and comfort of those within, and to ward off those without; in the same way, the disciple of the noble ones, quite withdrawn from sensual pleasures, withdrawn from unskillful qualities, enters and remains in the **first jhāna — rapture and pleasure born from withdrawal, accompanied by directed thought and evaluation** — for his own delight, convenience, and comfort, and to alight on unbinding.

"Just as a royal frontier fortress has large stores of rice and barley for the delight,... in the same way, the disciple of the noble ones, with the stilling of directed thoughts and evaluations, enters and remains in the **second jhāna — rapture and pleasure born of composure, unification of awareness free from directed thought and evaluation — internal assurance** — for his own delight....

"Just as a royal frontier fortress has large stores of sesame, green [beans], and other beans for the delight,... in the same way, the disciple of the noble ones, with the fading of rapture, he remains equanimous, mindful, and alert, and senses pleasure with the body. He enters and remains in the **third jhāna, of which the noble ones declare, 'Equanimous and mindful, he has a pleasant abiding,'** for his own delight....

"Just as a royal frontier fortress has large stores of tonics — ghee, fresh butter, oil, honey, molasses, and salt — for the delight,... in the same way the disciple of the noble ones, with the abandoning of pleasure and stress, as with the earlier disappearance of elation and distress, enters and remains in the **fourth jhāna — purity of equanimity and mindfulness, neither-pleasure-nor-pain** — for his own delight....

"These are the **four jhānas** — heightened mental states that provide a pleasant abiding in the here-and-now — that he can obtain at will, without difficulty, without trouble.

"When a disciple of the noble ones is endowed with these seven true qualities and can obtain at will — without difficulty, without trouble — these four jhānas, heightened mental states that provide a pleasant abiding in the here-and-now, he is said to be a disciple of the noble ones who cannot be undone by Māra, cannot be undone by the Evil One."[42]

Experiencing Sensual Pleasure without Attachment

"Monks, there are these five strings of sensuality. Which five? Forms cognizable via the eye — agreeable, pleasing, charming, endearing, fostering desire, enticing. Sounds cognizable via the ear — agreeable, pleasing, charming, endearing, fostering desire, enticing. Aromas cognizable via the nose — agreeable, pleasing, charming, endearing, fostering desire, enticing. Tastes cognizable via the tongue — agreeable, pleasing, charming, endearing, fostering desire, enticing. Tactile sensations cognizable via the body — agreeable, pleasing, charming, endearing, fostering desire, enticing. These are the five strings of sensuality.

"And any priests or contemplatives tied to these five strings of sensuality — infatuated with them, having totally fallen for them, consuming them without seeing their drawbacks or discerning the escape from them — should be known as having met with

42 A.N., The Book of Sevens (7.63), Bhikkhu Thanissaro, ATI.

misfortune, having met with ruin; Māra can do with them as he will. Just as if a wild deer were to lie bound on a heap of snares: it should be known as having met with misfortune, having met with ruin; the hunter can do with it as he will. When the hunter comes, it won't get away as it would like. In the same way, any priests or contemplatives tied to these five strings of sensuality....

"But any priests or contemplatives not tied to these five strings of sensuality — uninfatuated with them, having not totally fallen for them, consuming them while seeing their drawbacks and discerning the escape from them — should be known as not having met with misfortune, not having met with ruin; Māra cannot do with them as he will. Just as if a wild deer were to lie unbound on a heap of snares: it should be known as not having met with misfortune, not having met with ruin; the hunter cannot do with it as he will. When the hunter comes, it will get away as it would like. In the same way, any priests or contemplatives not tied to these five strings of sensuality....

"Suppose that a wild deer is living in a wilderness glen. Carefree it walks, carefree it stands, carefree it sits, carefree it lies down. Why is that? Because it has gone beyond the hunter's range. In the same way, a monk — quite withdrawn from sensual pleasures, withdrawn from unskillful qualities — enters and remains in the first jhāna: rapture and pleasure born from withdrawal, accompanied by directed thought and evaluation. This monk is said to have blinded Māra. Trackless, he has destroyed Māra's vision and has become invisible to the Evil One.

"Then again the monk,... enters and remains in the second jhāna,... enters and remains in the third jhāna,... enters and remains in the fourth jhāna,... enters and remains in the dimension of the boundless space,... enters and remains in the dimension of the boundless of consciousness,... enters and remains in the dimension of nothingness,... enters and remains in the dimension of neither perception nor non-perception,... enters and remains in the cessation of perception and feeling. And, having seen [that] with discernment, his mental fermentations are completely ended. This monk is said to have blinded Māra. Trackless, he has destroyed Māra's vision and has become invisible to the Evil One. **Having crossed over, he is unattached in the world.** Carefree he walks, carefree he stands, carefree he sits, carefree he lies down. Why is that? Because he has gone beyond the Evil One's range."[43]

❁❁❁❁❁❁❁❁

He must notice bliss, serenity and bright light,

and he must merely note them pass with insight.

❁❁❁❁❁❁❁❁

43 M.N., Ariyapariyesanā Sutta (26), Bhikkhu Thanissaro, ATI.

Figure 1: Forty Techniques of Concentration Exercises[44]

Concentration techniques	Dispositions fit for each technique						Levels of Achievement						
	Lustful temperament	Hateful temperament	Deluded temperament	Faithful temperament	Intelligent temperament	Distracted temperament	Conceptualized image	Access concentration	First jhāna	Second jhāna	Third jhāna	Fourth jhāna	The four arūpajhānas
Ten *Kasiṇa devices**													
- 4 color devices		x					o	o	o	o	o	o	
- Other kasiṇa devices	x	x	x	x	x	x	o	o	o	o	o	o	
10 ways of corpse contemplation	x						o	o	o				
10 Mindfulness concentrations													
- First six types of mindfulness				x				o					
- Recollection of peace					x			o					
- Mindfulness of death					x			o					
- Mindfulness of body	x						o	o	o				
- Mindfulness of breathing			x			x	o	o	o	o	o	o	
Sublime States *(Appamaññā)*													
- First three of sublime states (loving kindness, compassion and sympathetic joy)		x						o	o	o	o		
- Equanimity		x						o				o	
Concentration on loathsomeness of food					x			o					
Analysis of four elements (earth, water, fire, air)					x			o					
Arūpa													
- *Ākāsānañcāyatana*	x	x	x	x	x	x		o				o	1
- *Viññānañcāyatana*	x	x	x	x	x	x		o				o	2
- *Ākiñcaññāyatana*	x	x	x	x	x	x		o				o	3
- *Nevasaññānāsaññāyatana*	x	x	x	x	x	x		o				o	4

44 Buddhadhamma, p. 855

* *Kasiṇa* is the name for a purely external device to produce and develop concentration of mind and attain the four jhānas. The ten objects of kasiṇa concentration are earth, water, fire, air, color of blue, yellow, red, and white, space and light. See Chapter Eight for more detail.

Right Concentration

"And what is right concentration? There is the case where a monk — quite withdrawn from sensuality, withdrawn from unskillful [mental] qualities — enters and remains in the **first jhāna**: rapture and pleasure born from withdrawal, accompanied by directed thought and evaluation.

"With the stilling of directed thoughts and evaluations, he enters and remains in the **second jhāna**: rapture and pleasure born of composure, unification of awareness free from directed thought and evaluation — internal assurance.

"With the fading of rapture, he remains equanimous, mindful, and alert, and senses pleasure with the body. He enters and remains in the **third jhāna**, of which the noble ones declare, 'Equanimous and mindful, he has a pleasant abiding.'

"With the abandoning of pleasure and pain — as with the earlier disappearance of elation and distress — he enters and remains in the **fourth jhāna**: purity of equanimity and mindfulness, neither pleasure nor pain. This is called right concentration."[45]

Four Kinds of Concentration

"Monks, these are the four developments of concentration. Which four?

"There is the development of concentration that, when developed and pursued, leads to a pleasant abiding in the here and now. There is the development of concentration that, when developed and pursued, leads to the attainment of knowledge

45 D.N., (22) Mahā-Satipaṭṭhāna Sutta, Bhikkhu Thanissaro, ATI.

and vision. There is the development of concentration that, when developed and pursued, leads to mindfulness and alertness. There is the development of concentration that, when developed and pursued, leads to the ending of the [āsavas].

"And what is the development of concentration that, when developed and pursued, leads to a pleasant abiding in the here and now?

"There is the case where a monk — quite withdrawn from sensuality, withdrawn from unskillful qualities — enters and remains in the first jhāna..., enters and remains in the second jhāna..., he enters and remains in the third jhāna..., he enters and remains in the fourth jhāna.... **This is the development of concentration that, when developed and pursued, leads to a pleasant abiding in the here and now.**

"And what is the development of concentration that, when developed and pursued, leads to the attainment of knowledge and vision?

"There is the case where a monk attends to the perception of light and is resolved on the perception of daytime [at any hour of the day]. Day [for him] is the same as night, night is the same as day. By means of an awareness open and unhampered, he develops a brightened mind. **This is the development of concentration that, when developed and pursued, leads to the attainment of knowledge and vision.**

"And what is the development of concentration that, when developed and pursued, leads to mindfulness and alertness?

"There is the case where feelings are known to the monk as they arise, known as they persist, known as they subside. Perceptions are known to him as they arise, known as they persist, known as they subside. Thoughts are known to him as they arise, known as they persist, known as they subside. **This is the development of concentration that, when developed and pursued, leads to mindfulness and alertness.**

"And what is the development of concentration that, when developed and pursued, leads to the ending of the effluents?

"There is the case where a monk remains focused on arising and falling away with reference to the five clinging-aggregates[46]: 'Such is form, such its origination, such its passing away. Such is feeling, such its origination, such its passing away. Such is perception, such its origination, such its passing away. Such are fabrications, such their origination, such their passing away. Such is consciousness, such its origination, such its disappearance.' **This is the development of concentration that, when developed and pursued, leads to the ending of the āsavas.**

"These are the four developments of concentration."[47]

Mind Inclined to Nibbāna

"Monks, just as the river Ganges slants, slopes, and inclines towards the east, so too a monk **who develops and cultivates the four jhānas slants, slopes, and inclines towards nibbāna**[48].

---

46 These are the five aspects of all the physical and mental phenomena of existence which appear to the ignorant man as his ego. They are corporeality (form), feeling, perception, mental formations (also called fabrications) and consciousness.

47 A.N., The Book of the Fours (4.41), Bhikkhu Thanissaro, ATI.

48 The highest and ultimate goal of all Buddhist practices; the absolute extinction of that life-affirming will manifested as greed, hate, ignorance and clinging to existence; absolute and ultimate deliverance from suffering and rebirth.

"And how, monks, does a monk who develops and cultivates the four jhānas slant, slope, and incline towards nibbāna? Here, monks, secluded from sensual pleasures, secluded from unwholesome states, a monk enters and dwells in the first jhāna ... the second jhāna... the third jhāna... the fourth jhāna.

"It is in this way, monks, that **a monk who develops and cultivates the four jhānas slants, slopes, and inclines towards nibbāna.**

"Monks, there are these five higher fetters. What five?

"Lust for form, lust for the formless, conceit, restlessness, ignorance. These are the five higher fetters.[49] **The four jhānas are to be developed for direct knowledge of these five higher fetters, for the full understanding of them, for their utter destruction, for their abandoning.**

"What four? Here, monks, secluded from sensual pleasures, secluded from unwholesome states, a monk enters and dwells in the first jhāna... the second jhāna... the third jhāna... the fourth jhāna.

"These four jhānas are to be developed for direct knowledge of these five higher fetters, for the full understanding of them, for their utter destruction, for their abandoning."[50]

---

49 The higher fetters of the non-returner or anāgāmī are attachment to the form realms, attachment to the formless realms, conceit, restlessness and ignorance.

50 S.N., Mahā-vagga, Jhāna-saṃyutta (1), p. 1762-64, Bhikkhu Bodhi.

Sāriputta, Son of the Lord Buddha

"I have heard that at one time the Blessed One was staying in Sāvatthī at Jeta's Grove, Anāthapindika's monastery. There he addressed the monks, saying, 'Monks.'

'Yes, Lord,' the monks responded to him.

"The Blessed One said, 'Monks, Sāriputta is wise, of great discernment, deep discernment, wide... joyous... rapid... quick... penetrating discernment. For half a month, Sāriputta clearly saw insight into mental qualities one after another. This is what occurred to Sāriputta through insight into mental qualities one after another:

Dhamma in the First Jhāna

"There was the case where Sāriputta — quite secluded from sensuality, secluded from unskillful qualities — entered and remained in the first jhāna: rapture and pleasure born of seclusion, accompanied by directed thought and evaluation.

"Whatever qualities there are in the first jhāna — directed thought, evaluation, rapture, pleasure, [one-pointedness] of mind, contact, feeling, perception, intention, consciousness, desire, decision, persistence, mindfulness, equanimity, and attention — he ferreted them out one after another. Known to him they arose, known to him they remained, known to him they subsided. He discerned, 'So this is how these qualities, not having been, come into play. Having been, they vanish.' He remained unattracted and unrepelled with regard to those qualities, independent, detached, released, dissociated, with an awareness rid of barriers. He discerned that 'There is a further escape,' and pursuing it, there really was for him.

Dhamma in the Second Jhāna

"Furthermore, with the stilling of directed thoughts and evaluations, Sāriputta entered and remained in the second jhāna: rapture and pleasure born of composure, unification of awareness free from directed thought and evaluation — internal assurance.

"Whatever qualities there are in the second jhāna — internal assurance, rapture,... — he ferreted them out one after another. Known to him they arose....

Dhamma in the Third Jhāna

"Furthermore, with the fading of rapture, Sāriputta — remaining in equanimity, mindful and alert, and physically sensitive to pleasure — entered and remained in the third jhāna, of which the noble ones declare, 'Equanimous and mindful, he has a pleasant abiding.'

"Whatever qualities there are in the third jhāna — equanimity, pleasure,... — he ferreted them out one after another. Known to him they arose....

Dhamma in the Fourth Jhāna

"Furthermore, with the abandoning of pleasure and stress — as with the earlier disappearance of elation and distress — Sāriputta entered and remained in the fourth jhāna: purity of equanimity and mindfulness, neither-pleasure-nor-pain.

"Whatever qualities there are in the fourth jhāna — a feeling of equanimity, neither pleasure nor pain; an unconcern due to serenity of awareness,... — he ferreted them out one after another. Known to him they arose....

Dhamma in the Realm of Boundless Space

"Furthermore, with the complete transcending of perceptions of [physical] form, with the disappearance of perceptions of resistance, and not heeding perceptions of diversity, [perceiving] '[boundless] space,' Sāriputta entered and remained in the dimension of [boundless] space.

"Whatever qualities there are in the dimension of [boundless] space — the perception of the dimension of [boundless] space,... — he ferreted them out one after another. Known to him they arose....

Dhamma in the Realm of Boundless Consciousness

"Furthermore, with the complete transcending of the dimension of the [boundless] space, [perceiving] '[boundless] consciousness,' Sāriputta entered and remained in the dimension of [boundless] consciousness.

"Whatever qualities there are in the dimension of [boundless] consciousness — the perception of the dimension of [boundless] consciousness,... — he ferreted them out one after another. Known to him they arose....

Dhamma in the Realm of Nothingness

"Furthermore, with the complete transcending of the dimension of the [boundless] consciousness, [perceiving] 'There is nothing,' Sāriputta entered and remained in the dimension of nothingness.

"Whatever qualities there are in the dimension of nothingness — the perception of the dimension of nothingness,... — he ferreted them out one after another. Known to him they arose....

Dhamma in the Realm of Neither Perception nor Non-Perception

"Furthermore, with the complete transcending of the dimension of nothingness, Sāriputta entered and remained in the dimension of neither perception nor non-perception. He emerged mindfully from that attainment.

"On emerging mindfully from that attainment, he regarded the past qualities that had ceased and changed: 'So this is how these qualities, not having been, come into play. Having been, they vanish.' He remained unattracted and unrepelled with regard to those qualities, independent, detached, released, dissociated, with an awareness rid of barriers. He discerned that 'There is a further escape,' and pursuing it there really was for him.

Dhamma in the Realm of Cessation of Perception and Feeling

"Furthermore, with the complete transcending of the dimension of neither perception nor non-perception, Sāriputta entered and remained in the cessation of feeling and perception. Seeing with discernment, his fermentations were totally ended.

"He emerged mindfully from that attainment. On emerging mindfully from that attainment, he regarded the past qualities that had ceased and changed.... He discerned that 'There is no further escape,' and pursuing it there really was not for him.

Sāriputta, the Expert

"If a person, rightly saying it of anyone, were to say, 'He has attained mastery and perfection in noble virtue..., noble concentration..., noble discernment..., noble release,' he would be rightly saying it of Sāriputta if he were to say: 'He has attained mastery and perfection in noble virtue....'

Sāriputta, the Lord Buddha's Son

"If a person, rightly saying it of anyone, were to say, 'He is the Blessed One's son, his offspring — born of his mouth, born of the Dhamma, created by the Dhamma, his heir in the Dhamma, not his heir in material things,' he would be rightly saying it of Sāriputta if he were to say: 'He is the Blessed One's son, his offspring....' Sāriputta, monks, takes the unexcelled wheel of Dhamma set rolling by the Tathāgata, and keeps it rolling rightly.'

That is what the Blessed One said. Gratified, the monks delighted in the Blessed One's words.[51]

---

51 M.N., Anupada Sutta (111), Bhikkhu Thannisaro, ATI.

❊❊❊❊❊❊❊❊

He whose cankers are destroyed

and who is not attached to food,

whose object is the Void,

the Unconditioned Freedom —

his path cannot be traced,

like that of birds in the air.

❊❊❊❊❊❊❊❊

Calm is his mind;
Calm is his speech;
Calm is his bodily action;
Who, rightly knowing, is wholly freed,
Perfectly peaceful and equipoised.

Who so would look upon the world
Just as one would see a bubble,
And as one would view a mirage -
Him the King of Death finds not.

CHAPTER III

The One Way

Mahā Satipaṭṭhāna Sutta[52]

"Thus have I heard, on one occasion the Blessed One was staying in the Kuru country. Now there is a town of the Kurus called Kammasadhamma. There the Blessed One addressed the monks, 'Monks.'

'Lord,' the monks replied.

"The Blessed One said this: 'This is the direct path for the purification of beings, for the overcoming of sorrow and lamentation, for the disappearance of pain and distress, for the attainment of the right method, and for the realization of unbinding — in other words, the four frames of reference. Which four?'

"There is the case where a monk remains focused on the **body** in and of itself — ardent, alert, and mindful — putting aside greed and distress with reference to the world. He remains focused on **feelings... mind... mental qualities in and of themselves** — ardent, alert, and mindful — putting aside greed and distress with reference to the world.

52 The Buddha's Great Discourse on the Four Foundations of Mindfulness.

A. Mindfulness of the Body
(*Kāyānupassanā*)

"And how does a monk remain focused on the body in and of itself?

1. Mindfulness of Breathing

"There is the case where a monk — having gone to the wilderness, to the shade of a tree, or to an empty building — sits down folding his legs crosswise, holding his body erect and setting mindfulness to the fore [lit: the front of the chest]. Always mindful, he breathes in; mindful, he breathes out.

"Breathing in long, he discerns that he is breathing in long; or breathing out long, he discerns that he is breathing out long.

"Or breathing in short, he discerns that he is breathing in short; or breathing out short, he discerns that he is breathing out short.

"He trains himself to breathe in sensitive to the entire body and to breathe out sensitive to the entire body. He trains himself to breathe in calming bodily fabrication and to breathe out calming bodily fabrication. Just as a skilled turner or his apprentice, when making a long turn, discerns that he is making a long turn, or when making a short turn discerns that he is making a short turn; in the same way the monk, when breathing in long, discerns that he is breathing in long; or breathing out short, he discerns that he is breathing out short.... He trains himself to breathe in calming bodily fabrication, and to breathe out calming bodily fabrication.

"In this way he remains focused internally on the body in and of itself, or externally on the body in and of itself, or both internally and externally on the body in and of itself. Or he remains focused on the phenomenon of origination with regard to the body, on the phenomenon of passing away with regard to the body, or on the phenomenon of origination and passing away with regard to the body. Or his mindfulness that 'There is a body' is maintained to the extent of knowledge and remembrance. And he remains independent, unsustained by (not clinging to) anything in the world. This is how a monk remains focused on the body in and of itself.

2. The Four Postures

"Furthermore, when walking, the monk discerns that he is walking. When standing, he discerns that he is standing. When sitting, he discerns that he is sitting. When lying down, he discerns that he is lying down. Or however his body is disposed, that is how he discerns it.

"In this way he remains focused internally on the body in and of itself, or focused externally... unsustained by anything in the world. This is how a monk remains focused on the body in and of itself.

3. Clear Awareness in Minor Postures

"Furthermore, when going forward and returning, he makes himself fully alert; when looking toward and looking away... when bending and extending his limbs... when carrying his outer cloak, his upper robe and his bowl... when eating, drinking, chewing, and savoring... when urinating and defecating... when walking, standing, sitting, falling asleep, waking up, talking, and remaining silent, he makes himself fully alert.

"In this way he remains focused internally on the body in and of itself, or focused externally... unsustained by anything in the world. This is how a monk remains focused on the body in and of itself.

4. Reflection on the Repulsive Parts of the Body

"Furthermore... just as if a sack with openings at both ends were full of various kinds of grain — wheat, rice, mung beans, kidney beans, sesame seeds, husked rice — and a man with good eyesight, pouring it out, were to reflect, 'This is wheat. This is rice. These are mung beans. These are kidney beans. These are sesame seeds. This is husked rice.' In the same way, monks, a monk reflects on this very body from the soles of the feet on up, from the crown of the head on down, surrounded by skin and full of various kinds of unclean things: 'In this body there are head hairs, body hairs, nails, teeth, skin, flesh, tendons, bones, bone marrow, kidneys, heart, liver, pleura, spleen, lungs, large intestines, small intestines, gorge, feces, bile, phlegm, pus, blood, sweat, fat, tears, skin-oil, saliva, mucus, fluid in the joints, urine.'

"In this way he remains focused internally on the body in and of itself, or focused externally...unsustained by anything in the world. This is how a monk remains focused on the body in and of itself.

5. Contemplating the Body as Composed of the Four Elements

"Furthermore... just as a skilled butcher or his apprentice, having killed a cow, would sit at a crossroads cutting it up into pieces, the monk contemplates this very body — however it stands, however it is disposed — in terms of properties: 'In this body there is the earth property, the liquid property, the fire property, and the wind property.'

"In this way he remains focused internally on the body in and of itself, or focused externally... unsustained by anything in the world. This is how a monk remains focused on the body in and of itself.

6. The Nine Charnel Ground Contemplations

"Furthermore, as if he were to see a corpse cast away in a charnel ground — one day, two days, three days dead — bloated, livid, and festering, he applies it to this very body, 'This body, too: such is its nature, such is its future, such is its unavoidable fate...'

"Or again, as if he were to see a corpse cast away in a charnel ground, picked at by crows, vultures, and hawks, by dogs, hyenas, and various other creatures... a skeleton smeared with flesh and blood, connected with tendons... a fleshless skeleton smeared with blood, connected with tendons... a skeleton without flesh or blood, connected with tendons... bones detached from their tendons, scattered in all directions — here a hand bone, there a foot bone, here a shin bone, there a thigh bone, here a hip bone, there a back bone, here a rib, there a breast bone, here a shoulder bone, there a neck bone, here a jaw bone, there a tooth, here a skull... the bones whitened, somewhat like the color of shells... piled up, more than a year old... decomposed into a powder. He applies it to this very body, 'This body, too: such is its nature, such is its future, such is its unavoidable fate.'

"In this way he remains focused internally on the body in and of itself, or externally on the body in and of itself, or both internally and externally on the body in and of itself. Or he remains focused on the phenomenon of origination with regard to the body, on the phenomenon of passing away with regard to the body, or on the phenomenon of origination and passing away with regard to the body. Or his mindfulness that 'There is a body' is maintained to the extent of knowledge and remembrance. And he remains independent, unsustained by (not clinging to) anything in the world. This is how a monk remains focused on the body in and of itself.

B. Mindfulness of Feelings
(Vedanānupassanā)

"And how does a monk remain focused on feelings in and of themselves?

"There is the case where a monk, when feeling a painful feeling, discerns that he is feeling a painful feeling. When feeling a pleasant feeling, he discerns that he is feeling a pleasant feeling. When feeling a neither-painful-nor-pleasant feeling, he discerns that he is feeling a neither-painful-nor-pleasant feeling.

"When feeling a painful feeling of the flesh, he discerns that he is feeling a painful feeling of the flesh. When feeling a painful feeling not of the flesh, he discerns that he is feeling a painful feeling not of the flesh. When feeling a pleasant feeling of the flesh, he discerns that he is feeling a pleasant feeling of the flesh. When feeling a pleasant feeling not of the flesh, he discerns that he is feeling a pleasant feeling not of the flesh. When feeling a neither-painful-nor-pleasant feeling of the flesh, he discerns that he is feeling a neither-painful-nor-pleasant feeling of the flesh. When feeling a neither-painful-nor-pleasant feeling not of the flesh, he discerns that he is feeling a neither-painful-nor-pleasant feeling not of the flesh.

"In this way he remains focused internally on feelings in and of themselves, or externally on feelings in and of themselves, or both internally and externally on feelings in and of themselves. Or he remains focused on the phenomenon of origination with regard to feelings, on the phenomenon of passing away with regard to feelings, or on the phenomenon of origination and passing away with regard to feelings. Or his mindfulness that 'There are feelings' is maintained to the extent of knowledge and remembrance. And he remains independent, unsustained by (not clinging to) anything in the world. This is how a monk remains focused on feelings in and of themselves.

C. Mindfulness of the Mind
(Cittānupassanā)

"And how does a monk remain focused on the mind in and of itself? There is the case where a monk, when the mind has passion, discerns that the mind has passion. When the mind is without passion, he discerns that the mind is without passion. When the mind has aversion, he discerns that the mind has aversion. When the mind is without aversion, he discerns that the mind is without aversion. When the mind has delusion, he discerns that the mind has delusion. When the mind is without delusion, he discerns that the mind is without delusion.

"When the mind is restricted, he discerns that the mind is restricted. When the mind is scattered, he discerns that the mind is scattered. When the mind is enlarged, he discerns that the mind is enlarged. When the mind is not enlarged, he discerns that the mind is not enlarged. When the mind is surpassed, he discerns that the mind is surpassed. When the mind is unsurpassed, he discerns that the mind is unsurpassed. When the mind is concentrated, he discerns that the mind is concentrated. When the mind is not concentrated, he discerns that the mind is not concentrated. When the mind is released, he discerns that the mind is released. When the mind is not released, he discerns that the mind is not released.

"In this way he remains focused internally on the mind in and of itself, or externally on the mind in and of itself, or both internally and externally on the mind in and of itself. Or he remains focused on the phenomenon of origination with regard to the mind, on the phenomenon of passing away with regard to the mind, or on the phenomenon of origination and passing away with regard to the mind. Or his mindfulness that 'There is a mind' is maintained to the extent of knowledge and remembrance. And he remains independent, unsustained by (not clinging to) anything in the world. This is how a monk remains focused on the mind in and of itself.

D. Mindfulness of Mental-Qualities
(Dhammānupassanā)

"And how does a monk remain focused on mental qualities in and of themselves?

1. The Five Hindrances

"There is the case where a monk remains focused on mental qualities in and of themselves with reference to the five hindrances. And how does a monk remain focused on mental qualities in and of themselves with reference to the five hindrances? There is the case where, there being sensual desire present within, a monk discerns that 'There is sensual desire present within me.' Or, there being no sensual desire present within, he discerns that 'There is no sensual desire present within me.' He discerns how there is the arising of unarisen sensual desire. And he discerns how there is the abandoning of sensual desire once it has arisen. And he discerns how there is no future arising of sensual desire that has been abandoned. [The same formula is repeated for the remaining hindrances: ill will, sloth and torpor, restlessness and anxiety, and doubt.]

"In this way he remains focused internally on mental qualities in and of themselves, or externally on mental qualities in and of themselves, or both internally and externally on mental qualities in and of themselves. Or he remains focused on the phenomenon of origination with regard to mental qualities, on the phenomenon of passing away with regard to mental qualities, or on the phenomenon of origination and passing away with regard to mental qualities. Or his mindfulness that 'There are mental qualities' is maintained to the extent of knowledge and remembrance. And he remains independent, unsustained by [not clinging to] anything in the world. This is how a monk remains focused on mental qualities in and of themselves with reference to the five hindrances.

Just as the air that flows in
and blows out is not 'me,'
so the body that the air
flows in and out is not 'me.'

2. The Five Aggregates

"Furthermore, the monk remains focused on mental qualities in and of themselves with reference to the five clinging-aggregates. And how does he remain focused on mental qualities in and of themselves with reference to the five clinging-aggregates?

There is the case where a monk [discerns]: 'Such is form, such its origination, such its disappearance. Such is feeling.... Such is perception.... Such are fabrications.... Such is consciousness, such its origination, such its disappearance.'

"In this way he remains focused internally on the mental qualities in and of themselves, or focused externally... unsustained by anything in the world. This is how a monk remains focused on mental qualities in and of themselves with reference to the five clinging-aggregates.

3. The Six Internal and External Sense-Bases

"Furthermore, the monk remains focused on mental qualities in and of themselves with reference to the sixfold internal and external sense media. And how does he remain focused on mental qualities in and of themselves with reference to the sixfold internal and external sense media? There is the case where he discerns the eye, he discerns forms, he discerns the fetter that arises dependent on both. He discerns how there is the arising of an unarisen fetter. And he discerns how there is the abandoning of a fetter once it has arisen. And he discerns how there is no future arising of a fetter that has been abandoned. [The same formula is repeated for the remaining sense media: ear, nose, tongue, body, and mind].

"In this way he remains focused internally on the mental qualities in and of themselves, or focused externally.... unsustained by anything in the world. This is how a monk remains focused on mental qualities in and of themselves with reference to the sixfold internal and external sense media.

4. The Seven Factors of Enlightenment[53]

"Furthermore, the monk remains focused on mental qualities in and of themselves with reference to the seven factors [of enlightenment]. And how does he remain focused on mental qualities in and of themselves with reference to the seven factors [of enlightenment]? There is the case where, there being mindfulness as a factor [of enlightenment] present within, he discerns that 'Mindfulness as a factor [of enlightenment] is present within me.' Or, there being no mindfulness as a factor [of enlightenment] present within, he discerns that 'Mindfulness as a factor [of enlightenment] is not present within me.' He discerns how there is the arising of unarisen mindfulness as a factor [of enlightenment]. And he discerns how there is the culmination of the development of mindfulness as a factor [of enlightenment] once it has arisen. [The same formula is repeated for the remaining factors [of enlightenment]: investigation of states, energy, rapture, serenity, concentration, and equanimity].

"In this way he remains focused internally on mental qualities in and of themselves, or externally... unsustained by [not clinging to] anything in the world. This is how a monk remains focused on mental qualities in and of themselves with reference to the seven factors [of enlightenment].

---

53 The seven factors of enlightenment are so called because they lead one to enlightenment. The seven factors are: mindfulness, investigation of states, energy, rapture, serenity, concentration, and equanimity. They may be attained by means of the four foundations of mindfulness.

5. The Four Noble Truths

"Furthermore, the monk remains focused on mental qualities in and of themselves with reference to the Four Noble Truths. And how does he remain focused on mental qualities in and of themselves with reference to the Four Noble Truths? There is the case where he discerns, as it has come to be, that 'This is [suffering]... This is the origination of [suffering]... This is the cessation of [suffering]... This is the [path] leading to the cessation of [suffering].'

A. The Noble Truth of [Suffering]

"Now what is the noble truth of suffering? Birth is [suffering], aging is [suffering], death is [suffering], sorrow, lamentation, pain, distress, and despair are [suffering], association with the unbeloved is [suffering], separation from the loved is [suffering], not getting what one wants is [suffering]. In short, the five clinging-aggregates are [suffering].

"And what is birth? Whatever birth, taking birth, descent, coming-to-be, coming-forth, appearance of aggregates, and acquisition of [sense] spheres of the various beings in this or that group of beings, that is called birth.

"And what is aging? Whatever aging, decrepitude, brokenness, graying, wrinkling, decline of life-force, weakening of the faculties of the various beings in this or that group of beings, that is called aging.

"And what is death? Whatever deceasing, passing away, breaking up, disappearance, dying, death, completion of time, breaking up of the aggregates, casting off of the body, interruption in the life faculty of the various beings in this or that group of beings, that is called death.

"And what is sorrow? Whatever sorrow, sorrowing, sadness, inward sorrow, inward sadness of anyone suffering from misfortune, touched by a painful thing, that is called sorrow.

"And what is lamentation? Whatever crying, grieving, lamenting, weeping, wailing, lamentation of anyone suffering from misfortune, touched by a painful thing, that is called lamentation.

"And what is pain? Whatever is experienced as bodily pain, bodily discomfort, pain or discomfort born of bodily contact, that is called pain.

"And what is distress? Whatever is experienced as mental pain, mental discomfort, pain or discomfort born of mental contact, that is called distress.

"And what is despair? Whatever despair, despondency, desperation of anyone suffering from misfortune, touched by a painful thing, that is called despair.

"And what is the [suffering] of association with the unbeloved? There is the case where undesirable, unpleasing, unattractive sights, sounds, aromas, flavors, or tactile sensations occur to one; or one has connection, contact, relationship, interaction with those who wish one ill, who wish for one's harm, who wish for one's discomfort, who wish one no security from the yoke. This is called the [suffering] of association with the unbeloved.

"And what is the [suffering] of separation from the loved? There is the case where desirable, pleasing, attractive sights, sounds, aromas, flavors, or tactile sensations do not occur to one; or one has no connection, no contact, no relationship, no interaction with those who wish one well, who wish for one's benefit, who wish for one's comfort, who wish one security from the yoke, nor with one's mother, father, brother, sister, friends, companions, or relatives. This is called the [suffering] of separation from the loved.

"And what is the [suffering] of not getting what one wants? In beings subject to birth, the wish arises: 'O, may we not be subject to birth, and may birth not come to us.' But this is not to be achieved by wishing. This is the stress of not getting what one wants. In beings subject to aging... illness... death... sorrow, lamentation, pain, distress, and despair, the wish arises, 'O, may we not be subject to aging... illness... death... sorrow, lamentation, pain, distress, and despair, and may aging... illness... death... sorrow, lamentation, pain, distress, and despair not come to us.' But this is not to be achieved by wishing. This is the [suffering] of not getting what one wants.

"And what are the five clinging-aggregates that, in short, are [suffering]? Form as a clinging-aggregate, feeling as a clinging-aggregate, perception as a clinging-aggregate, fabrications as a clinging-aggregate, consciousness as a clinging-aggregate: These are called the five clinging-aggregates that, in short, are [suffering].

"This is called the noble truth of [suffering].

B. The Noble Truth of the Origination of Suffering

"And what is the noble truth of the origination of [suffering]? The craving that makes for further becoming — accompanied by passion and delight, relishing now here and now there — i.e., craving for sensuality, craving for becoming, craving for non-becoming.

"And where does this craving, when arising, arise? And where, when dwelling, does it dwell? Whatever is endearing and alluring in terms of the world: that is where this craving, when arising, arises. That is where, when dwelling, it dwells.

"And what is endearing and alluring in terms of the world? The eye is endearing and alluring in terms of the world. That is where this craving, when arising, arises. That is where, when dwelling, it dwells.

"The ear... The nose... The tongue... The body... The intellect...

"Forms... Sounds... Smells... Tastes... Tactile sensations... Ideas...

"Eye-consciousness... Ear-consciousness... Nose-consciousness... Tongue-consciousness... Body-consciousness... Intellect-consciousness...

"Eye-contact... Ear-contact... Nose-contact... Tongue-contact... Body-contact... Intellect-contact...

"Feeling born of eye-contact... Feeling born of ear-contact... Feeling born of nose-contact... Feeling born of tongue-contact... Feeling born of body-contact... Feeling born of intellect-contact...

"Perception of forms... Perception of sounds... Perception of smells... Perception of tastes... Perception of tactile sensations... Perception of ideas...

"Intention for forms... Intention for sounds... Intention for smells... Intention for tastes... Intention for tactile sensations... Intention for ideas...

"Craving for forms... Craving for sounds... Craving for smells... Craving for tastes... Craving for tactile sensations... Craving for ideas...

"Thought directed at forms... Thought directed at sounds...

Thought directed at smells... Thought directed at tastes... Thought directed at tactile sensations... Thought directed at ideas...

"Evaluation of forms... Evaluation of sounds... Evaluation of smells... Evaluation of tastes... Evaluation of tactile sensations... Evaluation of ideas... is endearing and alluring in terms of the world. That is where this craving, when arising, arises. That is where, when dwelling, it dwells.

"This is called the noble truth of the origination of [suffering].

C. The Noble Truth of the Cessation of [Suffering].

"And what is the noble truth of the cessation of [suffering]? The remainderless fading and cessation, renunciation, relinquishment, release, and letting go of that very craving.

"And where, when being abandoned, is this craving abandoned? And where, when ceasing, does it cease? Whatever is endearing and alluring in terms of the world: that is where, when being abandoned, this craving is abandoned. That is where, when ceasing, it ceases.

"And what is endearing and alluring in terms of the world? The eye is endearing and alluring in terms of the world. That is where, when being abandoned, this craving is abandoned. That is where, when ceasing, it ceases.

"The ear... The nose... The tongue... The body... The intellect...

"Forms... Sounds... Smells... Tastes... Tactile sensations... Ideas...

"Eye-consciousness... Ear-consciousness... Nose-consciousness... Tongue-consciousness... Body-consciousness... Intellect-consciousness...

"Eye-contact... Ear-contact... Nose-contact... Tongue-contact... Body-contact... Intellect-contact...

"Feeling born of eye-contact... Feeling born of ear-contact... Feeling born of nose-contact... Feeling born of tongue-contact... Feeling born of body-contact... Feeling born of intellect-contact...

"Perception of forms... Perception of sounds... Perception of smells... Perception of tastes... Perception of tactile sensations... Perception of ideas...

"Intention for forms... Intention for sounds... Intention for smells... Intention for tastes... Intention for tactile sensations... Intention for ideas...

"Craving for forms... Craving for sounds... Craving for smells... Craving for tastes... Craving for tactile sensations... Craving for ideas...

"Thought directed at forms... Thought directed at sounds... Thought directed at smells... Thought directed at tastes... Thought directed at tactile sensations... Thought directed at ideas...

"Evaluation of forms... Evaluation of sounds... Evaluation of smells... Evaluation of tastes... Evaluation of tactile sensations... Evaluation of ideas... is endearing and alluring in terms of the world. That is where, when being abandoned, this craving is abandoned. That is where, when ceasing, it ceases.

"This is called the noble truth of the cessation of [suffering].

D. The Noble Truth of the Path of Practice Leading to the Cessation of [Suffering]

"And what is the noble truth of the path of practice leading to the cessation of [suffering]? Just this very noble eightfold path: right view, right resolve, right speech, right action, right livelihood, right effort, right mindfulness, right concentration.

"And what is right view? Knowledge with regard to [suffering], knowledge with regard to the origination of [suffering], knowledge with regard to the cessation of [suffering], knowledge with regard to the way of practice leading to the cessation of [suffering]: this is called right view.

"And what is right resolve? Aspiring to renunciation, to freedom from ill will, to harmlessness: this is called right resolve.

"And what is right speech? Abstaining from lying, from divisive speech, from abusive speech, and from idle chatter: this is called right speech.

"And what is right action? Abstaining from taking life, from stealing, and from illicit sex: this is called right action.

"And what is right livelihood? There is the case where a disciple of the noble ones, having abandoned dishonest livelihood, keeps his life going with right livelihood: this is called right livelihood.

"And what is right effort? There is the case where a monk generates desire, endeavors, arouses persistence, upholds and exerts his intent for the sake of the non-arising of evil, unskillful qualities that have not yet arisen... for the sake of the abandoning of evil, unskillful qualities that have arisen... for the sake of the arising of skillful qualities that have not yet arisen... (and) for the maintenance, non-confusion, increase, plenitude, development, and culmination of skillful qualities that have arisen: this is called right effort.

"And what is right mindfulness? There is the case where a monk remains focused on the body in and of itself — ardent, alert and mindful — putting aside greed and distress with reference to the world. He remains focused on feelings in and of themselves... the mind in and of itself... mental qualities in and of themselves — ardent, alert and mindful — putting aside greed and distress with reference to the world. This is called right mindfulness.

"And what is right concentration? There is the case where a monk — quite withdrawn from sensuality, withdrawn from unskillful [mental] qualities — enters and remains in the first jhāna: rapture and pleasure born from withdrawal, accompanied by directed thought and evaluation. With the stilling of directed thought and evaluation, he enters and remains in the second jhāna: rapture and pleasure born of composure, unification of awareness free from directed thought and evaluation — internal assurance. With the fading of rapture, he remains equanimous, mindful and alert, and senses pleasure with the body. He enters and remains in the third jhāna, of which the noble ones declare, 'Equanimous and mindful, he has a pleasant abiding.' With the abandoning of pleasure and pain — as with the earlier disappearance of elation and distress — he enters and remains in the fourth jhāna: purity of equanimity and mindfulness, neither pleasure nor pain. This is called right concentration.

"This is called the noble truth of the path of practice leading to the cessation of [suffering].

"In this way he remains focused internally on mental qualities in and of themselves, or externally on mental qualities in and of themselves, or both internally and externally on mental qualities in and of themselves. Or he remains focused on the phenomenon of origination with regard to mental qualities, on the phenomenon of passing away with regard to mental qualities, or on the phenomenon of origination and passing away with regard to mental qualities. Or his mindfulness that 'There are mental qualities' is maintained to the extent of knowledge and remembrance. And he remains independent, unsustained by [not clinging to] anything in the world. This is how a monk remains focused on mental qualities in and of themselves with reference to the Four Noble Truths...

Benefits of Satipaṭṭhāna Practice

"Now, if anyone would develop these four [foundations of mindfulness] in this way for seven years, one of two fruits can be expected for him: either gnosis right here and now, or — if there be any remnant of clinging-sustenance — non-return.

"Let alone seven years. If anyone would develop these four [foundations of mindfulness] in this way for six years... five... four... three... two years... one year... seven months... six months... five... four... three... two months... one month... half a month, one of two fruits can be expected for him: either gnosis right here and now, or — if there be any remnant of clinging-sustenance — non-return.

"Let alone half a month. If anyone would develop these four [foundations of mindfulness] in this way for seven days, one of two fruits can be expected for him: either gnosis right here and now, or — if there be any remnant of clinging-sustenance — non-return.

"'This is the direct path for the purification of beings, for the overcoming of sorrow and lamentation, for the disappearance of pain and distress, for the attainment of the right method, and for the realization of Unbinding — in other words, the four [foundations of mindfulness].' Thus was it said, and in reference to this was it said."[54]

Development Process of Satipaṭṭhāna

"And when, Aggivessana, the *ariyan* [the noble person] disciple is possessed of mindfulness and clear consciousness, then the Tathāgata disciplines him further, saying: 'Come you, monk, choose a remote lodging in a forest, at the root of a tree, on a mountain slope, in a wilderness, in a hill-cave, a cemetery, a forest haunt, in the opcn or on a heap of straw.' He chooses a remote lodging in the forest... or on a heap of straw.

"Returning from alms-gathering, after the meal, he sits down cross-legged, holding the back erect, having made mindfulness rise up in front of him, he, by getting rid of coveting for the world, dwells with a mind devoid of coveting, he purifies the mind of coveting. By getting rid of the taint of ill-will, he dwells benevolent in mind, compassionate for the welfare of all creatures and beings, he purifies the mind of the taint of ill-will. By getting rid of sloth and torpor, he dwells devoid of sloth and torpor; perceiving the light, mindful, clearly conscious, he purifies the mind of sloth and torpor. By getting rid of restlessness and [anxiety], he dwells calmly, the mind subjectively tranquilized, he purifies the mind of restlessness and [anxiety]. By getting rid of doubt, he dwells doubt-crossed, unperplexed as to the states that are skillful, he purifies the mind of doubt.

54 D.N., (22), Mahā-Satipaṭṭhāna Sutta, Bhikku Thanissaro, ATI.

"He, by getting rid of these five hindrances which are defilements of the mind and weakening to intuitive wisdom, dwells contemplating the body in the body, ardent, clearly conscious [of it], mindful [of it] so as to control the covetousness and dejection in the world. He fares along contemplating the feelings... the mind... the mental states in mental states, ardent, clearly conscious [of them], mindful [of them] so as to control the covetousness and dejection in the world.

"The Tathāgata then disciplines him further, saying: 'Come you, monk, fare along contemplating the body in the body, but do not apply yourself to a train of thought connected with the body[55]; fare along contemplating the feelings in the feelings... the mind in the mind... mental states in mental states, but do not apply yourself to a train of thought connected with mental states.'

"He by allaying initial thought and discursive thought, with the mind subjectively tranquilized and fixed on one point, enters on and abides in the second [jhāna]... the third [jhāna]... the fourth [jhāna]."[56]

Mental Bondage

"Monks, there are five forms of mental bondage. What five?

"Monks, herein a monk as regards the lusts is not completely free of **passion,** nor of **desire**, nor of **fondness**, nor of **thirst**, nor of **fever**, nor of **craving**. Who so is not completely free of passion,... his heart inclines not to ardor, devotion, perseverance, nor to exertion. Where the heart does not so incline, it is the first bondage.

55 At this moment, the mind rests in the first jhāna.
56 M.N., (125), Dantabhūmi Sutta, Horner, ATI.

"So, too, when a monk as regards the **body**… as regards **shapes** is not completely free of passion...; if after eating as much as his belly can hold, he gives himself over to the ease of bed, of [lying on his] back, of **slumber**...; if he lives the godly life set on gaining some celestial body, **thinking by virtue, practice, austerity or chastity to become a deva**..., his heart inclines not to ardor, devotion, perseverance, nor to exertion.

"Monks, these are the five forms of mental bondage. Monks, when these five are put away, **four arisings of mindfulness should be made to become**. What four?

"Monks, herein a monk abides contemplating the body as body, strenuous, mindful and self-possessed, having overcome both the hankering and discontent common in the world. He abides contemplating the feelings as feelings…. He abides contemplating the mind as mind…. He abides contemplating ideas as ideas, strenuous, mindful and self-possessed, having overcome both the hankering and discontent common in the world.

Monks, when these five sources of weakness to training are put away, these four arisings of mindfulness should be made to become."[57]

Essence of Satipaṭṭhāna

1. Satipaṭṭhāna is the Buddha's most systematic explanation of the practice of mind training for the realization of truth. It also indicates the timeframe for the result of practice. Whoever follows these guidelines should reap the fruit of enlightenment (arahantship or anāgāmī) within at least seven years.

57 A.N, vol. 4, The Book of the Nines (9,8,63), p. 300, Hare.

2. Satipaṭṭhāna covers nearly all other teachings of the Buddha, including moral conduct, concentration and wisdom. **Many people still hold the misconception that the practice of mindfulness refers to vipassanā only, and does not include concentration (samādhi) or absorption concentration[58] (appanāsamādhi).** Practically and theoretically, this is incorrect.

Throughout the forty five years of Dhamma propagation, though the Buddha's teaching concerns different levels and aspects of practice, i.e. charity, observance of precepts, concentration, insight, liberation, and vision of truth gained through liberation, these various components do not contradict one another. This striking feature can be recognized by anyone who follows his teaching.

I would like to discuss briefly here the path of enlightenment focusing on the following argument. **To attain the four levels of enlightenment (four maggañāṇa[59]) necessarily requires absorption concentration at least at the level of the first jhāna.**

The meaning of the term aṭṭhaṇgikamagga[60] lies in the moment when all components of the eightfold path arise simultaneously so that the power generated from all components is strong enough to completely destroy the defilements. Therefore, any teaching of the Buddha regarding the path to enlightenment will always consist of two-fold powers, concentration at the level of absorption and wisdom.

To illustrate the point, let us take an example from the section of mindfulness on the body. It reads "Breathing in and out, one calms bodily formations." Bodily formations, which are gradually calmed down until breathing ceases. signify the mind in the level

58 See fn. 22 and fn. 28 in Chapter Two.

59 See p. 15-16 in Chapter Two.

60 See p. 16 in Chapter Two.

of absorption concentration. In the section on feelings, it reads "Experiencing pleasant feeling not related to sensual pleasure, one is mindful." In the section on mind, it reads "Experiencing the firmly fixed mind, one is mindful" (firmly fixed mind signifies mind in jhāna). In the section on mind-objects, it reads "As the concentration arises, one is fully aware."

"What is right concentration?

"A monk withdrawn from sensuality and unwholesome mental qualities enters and remains in the first, second, third and forth jhāna… He is said to have right concentration.

"On one occasion, Visākhā, a lay supporter, approached the arahant Dhammadinnā and questioned her, 'Lady, what is concentration? What is the basis of concentration? What is the equipment of concentration? What is the development of concentration?'

'Unification of mind, friend Visākhā, is concentration; **the four foundations of mindfulness are the basis of concentration;** the four right kinds of striving[61] are the equipment of concentration; the repetition, development, and cultivation of these same states is the development of concentration therein."[62]

3. Satipaṭṭhāna is the system of practice comprised of three levels:

3.1 The level for ordinary people who wish to strengthen their enlightenment faculties in order to attain the not-yet achieved liberation.

---

61 The four right efforts or strivings are 1) the effort to avoid unwholesome states, 2) to overcome unwholesome states, 3) to develop wholesome states, 4) to maintain wholesome states.

62 M.N., Mūlapaṇṇāsapāli, Cūḷavedalla Sutta (44), p. 399, Bhikkhu Ñāṇamoli and Bhikkhu Bodhi.

3.2 The level for the sekha[63] (learner or trainee) who wish to strengthen their faculties in order to attain the higher levels of enlightenment.

3.3 The level for the *asekha*[64] (adept) for their present dwelling.[65]

"Come, friends, dwell contemplating the body in the body, ardent, clearly comprehending, unified, with limpid mind, concentrated, with one-pointed mind, **in order to know the body as it really is,... in order to know feelings as they really are,... in order to know mind as it really is,... in order to know phenomena as they really are.**

"Monks, **those monks who are trainees**, who have not attained their mind's ideal, who dwell aspiring for the unsurpassed security from bondage: they too dwell contemplating the body in the body, ardent, clearly comprehending, unified, with limpid mind, concentrated, with one-pointed mind, **in order to fully understand the body... the feelings... the mind... the phenomena as they really are**.

"Monks, **those monks who are arahants,** whose taints are destroyed, who have lived the holy life, done what had to be done, laid down the burden, reached their own goal, utterly destroyed the fetters of existence, and are completely liberated through final knowledge: they too dwell contemplating the body in the body, ardent, clearly comprehending, unified, with limpid mind, concentrated, with one-pointed mind, detached from the body... detached from the feelings... **detached from the mind... detached from the phenomena."**[66]

---

63 See fn. 29 in Chapter Two.

64 One who does not require any further training or a fully enlightened person (arahant).

65 S.N.,Mahā-vagga, Satipaṭṭhāna-saṃyutta (47,1,4), p. 1630-31, Bhikkhu Bodhi.

66 Ibid.

"On one occasion the Venerable Sāriputta said to the Venerable Anuruddha: 'It is, friend, because one has partly developed the four establishments of mindfulness that one is a trainee... It is, friend, because one has completely developed the four establishments of mindfulness that one is beyond training.'[67]

4. The difference and variation of techniques in the practice of Satipaṭṭhāna are found only in the section on the body. This is because the mind of the beginner is usually under the influence of distraction and wild thoughts. The Buddha therefore laid out several techniques regarding bodily contemplation in order to fight against such strong obstacles.

Means and techniques also vary with the experience of teachers and characteristics of practitioners. Beginners should follow strictly and ardently the means and techniques on mindfulness. When their wisdom is developed up to a certain extent, they will find their own way to continue onward.

"Here, Ānanda, a monk dwells contemplating the body in the body, ardent, clearly comprehending, mindful, having removed covetousness and displeasure in regard to the world. While he is contemplating the body in the body, there arises in him, based on the body, either a fever in the body or sluggishness of mind, or the mind is distracted outwardly. **That monk should then direct his mind towards some inspiring sign. When he directs his mind towards some inspiring sign, gladness is born. When he is gladdened, rapture is born. When the mind is uplifted by rapture, the body becomes tranquil. One tranquil in body experiences happiness. The mind of one who is happy becomes concentrated.** He reflects thus: 'The purpose for the sake of which I directed my mind has been achieved. Let me now withdraw

---

67 Ibid. (47,3,26), p. 1652.

it.' So he withdraws the mind and does not think or examine. He understands: 'Without thought and examination, internally mindful, I am happy.' **It is in such a way, Ānanda, that there is development by direction.**"[68]

5. The Buddha presented the development of mindfulness successively from gross to subtler levels, i.e., body, feelings, mind and mental qualities. This gradual progression of subtlety corresponds with the nature of the mental development of the practitioner. The content of each section in the *Satipaṭṭhāna Sutta* also proceeds in the same way.

6. Those who are interested in theory and practice of Dhamma should understand that mind and mental concomitants are conditions that arise and pass away simultaneously. Mind cannot arise independently without mental concomitants and vice versa. In *Satipaṭṭhāna*, mental concomitants are divided into two components: feelings and mental qualities. Our awareness, however, can capture the rising-falling pattern of only one of these two factors at a time. Whether we are aware of the characteristics of mind or mental concomitants at any given moment depends on the conditions of our awareness. It suffices for the practitioner to simply observe whatever arises and passes away in the present moment.

A Summary of Satipaṭṭhāna Practice

1. The four bases which are the objects of contemplation in the training of mindfulness can be divided into two major categories, body and mind.

2. The **body base** refers to the six bodily contemplations in the mindfulness on body (*kāyānupassanā*).

---

68 Ibid. (47,1,10), p. 1638-9.

2.1 The breathing section (*ānāpānasati pabba*) is described only in the sitting posture. However, one can also practice breathing meditation while standing. Practitioners should try to practice mindfulness of breathing in both postures.

2.2 Another five bodily bases can be used as objects of contemplation in various postures. One can practice them while standing, walking, sitting or lying down.

2.3 Standing, walking, sitting and lying down are major bodily postures. Beginners should start training with them. Once a certain level of proficiency has been attained, mindfulness and clear comprehension will automatically diffuse into minor bodily gestures in daily activities.

2.4 As for walking and sitting postures, beginners should follow first the techniques as instructed by their teachers, since these techniques are the outcome of the teachers' accumulated experiences and fruitful experiments. For beginners who cannot capture the breathing while in sitting posture, they may try other bodily movements, such as observing the expanding or flattening movements of the abdomen. If these two strategies do not provide any results, hand movement as taught by the Venerable Tien Chittasupo[69] can be used, namely observing the moving gestures of the hands (which can be grouped under the section of mindfulness on minor gestures or *sampajañña pabba*).

2.5 Each method and technique has its own advantages and disadvantages. Practitioners should select the one which best corresponds with their own characteristics and inclinations. They should not criticize other methods without having actually practiced them.

---

69 A famous vipassanā teacher of Thailand's central plains who invented a mindfulness technique of focusing on movements of hands and arms.

2.6 *Kāyagatāsati*, or mindfulness with regard to the body, is highly recommended by the Buddha for its various benefits. It should also be noted that the six bodily bases in *Satipaṭṭhāna* are similar to kāyagatāsati.

2.7 In conclusion, any of the six bodily bases in *Satipaṭṭhāna* can enable practitioners to attain liberation and nibbāna. The time required and depth of attainment depends on each individual's characteristics and accumulated faculties.

3. The **mind bases**: feeling, mind, and mental qualities.

3.1 Mind and mental concomitants are not mutually exclusive, i.e., they depend on each other while arising and passing away. Feeling and mental qualities are mental concomitants that arise and pass away simultaneously with the mind.

3.2 As feeling, mind, and mental qualities arise and pass away together at the same time, mindfulness is able to catch only one among these various bases, depending on the conditions of awareness in that particular moment.

3.3 The bodily base provides six different locations for the establishment of mindfulness, so that one can shift the object of concentration from one location to another during each period of practice. The mind bases (feelings, mind, mental qualities), however, cannot be treated in the same way. The extremely subtle nature of the mind bases allows our awareness to catch only the most distinctive feature that appears in the present moment of practice.

4. By nature, **the rising-passing away of the bodily and mental components are always interrelated.** When the bodily states are still very gross, feelings, mind, and mental qualities are also gross. This interrelation of body and mind can be found constantly from gross up to subtler levels of mental development.

5. In each gesture or bodily posture, it is impossible for a practitioner to control his or her mindfulness so that it is fixed only on one particular base throughout the period of practice. **The object of consciousness will shift alternately between the mental base and bodily base. However, in the beginning, teachers usually focus on the bodily base**, since at the early stage of practice, the gross elements associated with the bodily base are more easily noticed than feelings or mental qualities.

6. **Once mindfulness on the bodily base has become thoroughly clear and strong, keener awareness of feeling, mind, and mental qualities will naturally follow.**

7. Please note that inhalation and exhalation are essential aspects of the bodily formation. In addition, breathing is fundamentally related to the mind. When the mind is calm, in and out breathing will become soft, gentle, and finally cease altogether when the mind attains the fourth jhāna.

8. When the mind develops up to a certain level, all deliberations and concerns about using certain techniques or methods will automatically vanish. Then, there is no need for any formal technique, as one has already attained the absolute knowledge of things as they really are (*yathābhūtañāṇadassana*).

Figure 2: The Interrelated States in *Satipaṭṭhāna*
The Interrelation of the Four Bases
(Nine-level Progress from Gross to Subtle)

	Body	Feelings	Mind	Mental Qualities
	Mindfulness of breathing			**Hindrances**
1.	Long breathing in and out	Pleasant feelings related to sensual pleasure	Lust	Sensual desire
2.	Long breathing in and out	Disagreeable feelings related to sensual displeasure	Aversion, ill-will	Ill Will
3.	Long breathing in and out	Neither-painful-nor-pleasant feeling related to the senses	Delusion	Doubt
4.	Long breathing in and out	Neither-painful-nor-pleasant feeling related to the senses	Depression	Sloth and torpor
5.	Long breathing in and out	Neither-painful-nor-pleasant feeling related to the senses	Distraction	Restlessness and anxiety
6.	Short breathing in and out, sensitive to the entire breath. Bodily formations calmed down.	Bliss or neither-painful-nor-pleasant feeling not related to the senses	Unbounded mind[A]: absorption concentration	
7	Short breathing in and out, sensitive to the entire breath. Bodily formations calmed down.	Bliss or neither-painful-nor-pleasant feeling not related to the senses	Highly concentrated mind: right concentration	
8	Short breathing in and out, sensitive to the entire breath. Bodily formations calmed down.	Bliss or neither-painful-nor-pleasant feeling not related to the senses	Surpassed mind: path and fruition	
9	Breathing in and out, sensitive to the entire breath. Bodily formations calmed down	Bliss or neither-painful-nor-pleasant feeling not related to the senses	Liberated mind	

Remark: The states of breathing described in levels six through nine depend on the level of jhāna. In the first, second and third *rūpajhāna*[70], breathing is soft, short and refined. In the fourth rūpajhāna, breathing ceases completely. As for feelings in jhāna, in the first and second rūpajhāna one experiences bliss. In the third rūpajhāna, bliss and equanimity. In the fourth rūpajhāna, only equanimity.

Continuation of figure 2:

Five Aggregates	Sense-bases	Seven Enlightenment Factors[B]	Four Noble Truths
Rising-falling of aggregates	Fetters generated from the six pairs of sense-bases	Enlightenment Factors	Noble Truths
Corporeality Feelings Perception Mental formations Consciousness	Delusion of self Doubt Adherence to rules and rituals Sensual desire Ill will Attachment to form and formless realms Conceit Distraction Ignorance	Mindfulness Investigation of states Energy Rapture (these three are powers of wisdom) Serenity Concentration Equanimity (these three are powers of concentration)	Suffering Origin of suffering Cessation of suffering Path leading to cessation of suffering

---

70 Absorption of the form realm (fine material realm or rūpajhāna) during which there is a complete, though temporary, suspension of five-fold sense activity and of the five hindrances. The four levels of the form realm absorption are: first jhāna (whose components are applied and sustained thought (see fn. 23, Chapter Two), rapture, bliss and one-pointedness), second jhāna (with rapture, bliss and one-pointedness), third jhāna (with bliss and one-pointedness), and fourth jhāna (with one-pointedness and equanimity).

A. To emphasize the progressive order of the interrelated states, the author has rearranged the enlightenment steps as follows: unbounded mind, highly concentrated mind, surpassed and liberated mind.

B. See page 95-96 for the Buddha's explanation of the seven factors of enlightenment.

The Interrelated States in *Satipaṭṭhāna*
The Interrelation of the Four Bases
(Nine-level Progress from Gross to Subtle)

From Figure 2, the interrelated states in *Satipaṭṭhāna* can be summarized as follows:

1. Bodily base:
long breathing in and out, one is clearly aware

1.1 Feeling: **Pleasant feelings**, which are a result of pleasant sensual contacts, occur. They have sensual pleasure as their foundation. One should remain constantly and clearly mindful.

1.2 Mind: When occupied by pleasant feelings, if one fails to maintain mindfulness of the rising and passing away of this phenomenon, lust and craving, which are the characteristics of **covetousness,** will arise.

1.3 Mental qualities: Pleasant feelings and covetousness are based on the five **sensual desires** (at the five sense doors: eyes, ears, nose, etc). If one is not fully aware of these three related states (pleasant feelings, covetousness, and sensual desires), **obsession with sensual pleasure** will be accumulated and will become a latent tendency.

2. Bodily base: long breathing in and out, one is clearly aware

2.1 Feeling: **Disagreeable feelings,** which are a result of unpleasant sensual contacts, occur.

2.2 Mind: When occupied by disagreeable feelings, if one fails to maintain mindfulness of this phenomenon, agitation, annoyance or anger, which are the characteristics of **dissatisfaction,** will arise.

2.3 Mental qualities: If the practitioner fails to understand this negative state as it is, it can develop further into **aversion.** Always maintain perfect mindfulness. Should one allow these three related states (disagreeable feelings, dissatisfaction and aversion) to occur without clear mindfulness, **aversion-obsession** can accumulate and become a latent tendency.

Remark: In the first and second levels described above, one's mind is engaged in past memories. Various forms of physical discomfort may appear very strongly. Pains, aches, and stiffness become acute and the body's temperature can rise.

Past memories (of the gross level) related to covetousness and dissatisfaction will come to the surface of the mind. This should be considered as positive because the accumulated negative and latent tendencies which control bodily, verbal and mental behaviors are being released and rooted out. The poison deeply ingrained in the unconscious level is being removed.

3. Bodily base: long breathing in and out, one is clearly aware

3.1 Feeling: **Neither-painful-nor-pleasant feelings,** which are a result of neutral sensual contacts, occur.

3.2 Mind: When occupied by neither-painful-nor-pleasant feelings, if one fails to maintain mindfulness of this phenomenon, delusion, which is a characteristic of **ignorance,** will arise.

3.3 Mental qualities: At this stage, **doubt** occurs. If one is not fully aware of these three related states (neither-painful-nor-pleasant feelings, ignorance, and doubt, **ignorance obsession** will be accumulated and will become a latent tendency.

"When, monks, a monk has seen **pleasant feeling as painful, painful feeling as a dart, and neither-painful-nor-pleasant feeling as impermanent**, he is called a monk who sees rightly. He has cut off craving, severed the fetters, and by completely breaking through conceit, he has made an end to suffering."[71]

"When one is touched by a **pleasant feeling**, if one delights in it, welcomes it, and remains holding to it, then the underlying tendency of **desire** lies within one.

"When one is touched by a **painful feeling**, if one sorrows, grieves and laments, weeps beating one's breast and becomes distraught, then the underlying tendency of **aversion** lies within one.

"When one is touched by a **neither-painful-nor-pleasant feeling**, if one does not understand as it actually is the origination, the disappearance, the gratification, the danger, and the escape with regard to that feeling, then the underlying tendency to **ignorance** lies within one.

---

71 S.N., Saḷāyatanavagga, Vedanāsaṃyutta (36,1,5), p. 1263, Bhikkhu Bodhi.

"Monks, that **one shall here and now make an end of suffering without abandoning the underlying tendency of desire for pleasant feeling, without abolishing the underlying tendency of aversion towards painful feeling, without extirpating the underlying tendency of ignorance in regard to neither-painful-nor-pleasant feeling, without abandoning ignorance and arousing true knowledge — this is impossible.**"[72]

4. Bodily base: long breathing in and out, one is clearly aware

4.1 Feeling: **Neither-painful-nor-pleasant feelings,** which are a result of neutral sensual contacts, occur.

4.2 Mind: **Distress** occurs. One should maintain clear awareness of it.

4.3 Mental qualities: **Sloth and torpor**. One should keep observing the rising-falling phenomenon.

Remark: The states of the first and second bodily base levels relate to **covetousness** and **dissatisfaction** in past experiences, and arc gcncrated by sensual contacts and feelings.

When mindfulness continues, covetousness and dissatisfaction will be reduced until one feels neutral to any objects occurring in consciousness. However, such a state of mind does not result from wisdom, but is the consequence of temporarily weakened stimulation of covetousness and dissatisfaction.

Devoid of stimulation, the mind is like a body that loses excitement generated from methamphetamine. A mind without

72 M.N., Uparipaṇṇāsapāḷi, Chachakha Sutta (148), p. 1134-5, Bhikkhu Ñāṇamoli and Bhikkhu Bodhi.

energy will be unable to grasp the present moment. It will become blurred and drowsy as though one is going to sleep.

At this particular stage, one may be surprised when strange images that one has never seen before appear suddenly and vividly, but they arise and pass away very rapidly too. Typically, practitioners may be able to distinguish whether emerging mental images belong to the past or the future; however, at this stage, one is not always able to differentiate between these aforementioned images in temporal terms.

When this phenomenon occurs, awareness of the present moment becomes dim, unclear, and blurred. It seems as if one is going to lose consciousness. One may try to breathe deeply to resume keen awareness, but cannot succeed because the blurred sensation keeps returning. Finally, the practitioner usually falls into sleep while sitting.

Highly experienced teachers, then, typically recommend certain techniques to prevent the mind from entering into such states. Instead of observing the breath, another five objects of contemplation (in *Satipaṭṭhāna)* can be used. Moreover, one may choose to observe hand movements or move the base of observation to other areas in the body or even change postures.

After drowsiness subsides, the characteristics of the fifth state will appear.

5. Bodily base:
long breathing in and out, one is clearly aware

5.1 Feeling: Pleasant feelings co-arise with neither-pleasant-nor-painful feelings.

5.2 Mind: Distraction predominates.

5.3 Mental qualities: Restlessness and anxiety prevails.

One should remain mindful of any noticeable changes or predominant states in the body, mind and mental concomitants.

Remark: In the first and second levels, covetousness or aversion relating to **past experiences** are predominant.

In the third and fourth levels, delusion and drowsiness dominate. One cannot clearly identify temporal dimensions of arising mental images.

In the fifth level, distraction and restlessness about the **future** occur.

Having recovered from drowsiness, the mind will again look for new objects of consciousness. Objects from the past have already been released. Remaining constantly in the present is still unfamiliar. The mind then resorts to future images based on expectations or projections that the mind previously developed. Every mental projection into the future will be retrieved and consumed.

However, the future state has not yet occurred, and therefore has no reality to serve as its base. The mind then goes back and forth between different future projections. As soon as it decides on one project, opposing issues arise. The mind then goes around in a circle of contradicting thoughts and feelings. It is like a traveler who arrives at an intersection of pathways. **Doubt**, therefore, often arises in this state.

Summary of the Previous States of Mind and Mental Concomitants

Past objects occur during the first and second levels. Predominant here are lust, covetousness, and gratification in sensual desire and their opposites, dissatisfaction, aversion and ill will.

Drowsiness prevails in the third and fourth levels where delusion, sloth, and doubt also come forth.

Future objects occur in the fifth level where distraction, agitation and doubt permeate the mind.

Every practitioner will experience these three successive states regardless of the different bodily bases being used.

The duration of each state varies from person to person depending on the practitioner's acquired spiritual faculties.

When the five hindrances temporarily cease, it signifies that the mind has passed beyond the three aforementioned stages. If the practitioner's spiritual faculties are strong enough, he or she will move on to the following subtler states.

6. Bodily base: short breathing in and out

When the mind is about to enter into jhāna, the characteristics of the breath appear as follows:

During momentary concentration (khanikasamādhi) and access concentration (upacārasamādhi) the in-and-out breaths are short.

In absorption concentration (appanāsamādhi), from the first to the second and the third jhāna, breathing becomes shorter, subtler and calmer as the mind develops into higher jhāna.

In the fourth jhāna the breath is completely extinguished.

6.1 Feeling: Pleasant feelings appear in the first, second and third jhāna. Equanimity appears in the third and fourth jhāna.

6.2 Mind: The mind in absorption concentration is unbounded *(mahaggatacitta[73])*.

6.3 Mental qualities: Rapture, serenity, concentration, and equanimity.

The mental states in absorption concentration are discussed in detail in chapter VIII.

7. Bodily base: short breathing in and out

7.1 Feeling: Feelings not associated with sensual pleasure arise.

Bliss *(sukhavedanā)* appears in the first, second and third jhānas.

Equanimity accompanies the third and fourth jhānas.

7.2 Mind: Concentrated mind (sammāsamādhi, or right concentration) signifies absorption concentration which is supported by the seven factors of enlightenment.

"Monks, develop concentration. A monk who is concentrated understands things as they really are. And what does he understand as it really is? He understands as it really is: **'This is suffering.' 'This is the origin of suffering.' 'This is the cessation of suffering.' 'This is the path leading to the cessation of suffering.'"**[74]

73 Mahaggata literally means 'grown great.' Unbounded mind is the state of developed, exalted and supernormal consciousness attained in the form and formless absorptions (jhānas).

74 S.N., Mahā-vagga, Saccasaṃyutta (56,1,1), p. 1838, Bhikkhu Bodhi.

Suffering (*dukkha*): Being able to see and understand the series of rising-falling of the five aggregates is to understand the rise and fall of suffering.

"Monks, one who sees suffering also sees the path leading to the cessation of suffering."[75]

7.3 Mental qualities: The highest level of insight (*vipassanāñāṇa*) is at work.

The five aggregates can be considered as corresponding to the four bases of satipaṭṭhāna as shown below:

Rūpakhandha (corporeality or form) — body base

Vedanākhandha (feeling) — feeling base

Viññāṇakhandha (consciousness) — mind base

Saññākhandha (perception) } — mental qualities base
Saṅkhārakhandha (mental formation) }

The stronger the power of insight becomes, the clearer one can realize the rising-falling state of the five aggregates. The practitioner has now understood the first noble truth, i.e. **suffering**.

The chain of origin of suffering mentioned in Dependent Origination reads, "*vedanā paccaya taṇhā…*" — dependent on feelings, craving arises.

The corresponding section on the chain of cessation of suffering reads, "*vedanā nirodhā taṇhā nirodho…*" — when feelings cease, the craving that is attached to them also ceases.

Therefore, **one who sees clearly the rising-falling pattern of feelings also sees the dependent rising-falling states of craving**.

75 Ibid. (56,3,30), p. 1857.

In this light, one is able to grasp the second noble truth: the **cause of suffering** (*samudaya*). **As the states of craving become clearer and clearer, so do the states of clinging to the five aggregates.**

If we look at the ten chains or fetters *(saṃyojana)*[76], with the exception of ignorance, in terms of related conditions, they can be understood through the process of craving. They are manifested in the yearning to adhere to the rising-falling of the five aggregates. Each fetter occurs on account of contact between one of the six pairs of the internal and external sense fields[77]. The cause and cessation of these fetters and the way to prevent the already ceased fetters from re-occurring will become clearer and clearer to thc practitioners depending on the strength of their enlightenment faculties and the level of their achievcment.[78]

Mindfulness developed thus far can be described as "the great mindfulness" *(satisambojjhaṅga)* which is one of the seven enlightenment factors. It will support the other six enlightenment factors, fostering them until their strength is sufficient for attaining the final goal. Before the seven factors are ripe, wisdom (which is one of the factors) will examine and evaluate the potential of the other factors and find ways to promote them. Within this process, mindfulness will always grasp each rising and falling moment thoroughly.

The person who develops the seven bojjhaṅgas is also developing the eightfold path. Therefore, the truth of the path for

76 The ten fetters that bind human being to the round of rebirth can be divided into five lower and five higher fetters. The five lower fetters are the false view or delusion of self, doubt, adherence to rules and rituals, sensual desire or lust, and ill will. The higher fetters consist of attachment to the form realms, attachment to the formless realms, conceit, restlessness and ignorance.

77 The six internal sense fields are the eyes, the ears, the nose, the tongue, the body and the mind or intellect. The six external sense fields are form, sound, odor, taste, tangible objects and mind objects.

78 See p. 75-76 for a description of the three levels of practitioners.

such a person is confirmed.

8. Bodily base: The bodily formation is calmed down

8.1 Feeling: Feeling not related to sensual pleasure.

Bliss appears in the first, second and third jhānas.

Equanimity accompanies the third and fourth jhānas.

8.2 Mind: At this level, the mind displays the feature of *sanuttaracitta*, which is the mind that is able to achieve the insight which still pertains to the worldly realm. (Whereas *anuttaracitta* refers to the mind in its excellence, which means the mind that reaches the four maggas and the four phalas.)

8.3 Mental qualities: The truth of cessation.

9. Bodily base: The bodily formation is calmed down

9.1 Feeling: Feeling not related to sensual pleasure.

Bliss appears in the first, second and third jhānas.

Equanimity accompanies the third and fourth jhānas.

9.2 Mind: The liberated mind of the four noble individuals (i.e. the stream-enterer, the once-returner, the non-returner and the fully enlightened one).

9.3 Mental qualities: Nibbānic state (the truth of cessation of suffering).

Remarks on the Four Noble Truths

The truth of suffering refers to the states of the five aggregates. The truth of origination of suffering refers to the states of the sense doors and fetters. The truth of cessation of suffering refers to the eight levels of anuttaracitta. The truth of the path refers to the states of the noble truth and the seven bojjhaṅgas.

Note: The way of practice and the successive conditions leading to the attainment of jhāna are discussed in detail in chapter VIII.

The method of practice and the successive conditions leading to the attainment of the four levels of enlightenment are discussed in detail in the subsection on *The Attainment of The Four Levels of Enlightenment* in Chapter V.

Mindfulness is Necessary in All Cases

"On an occasion, monks, when the mind becomes sluggish, it is untimely to develop the enlightenment factor of serenity, the enlightenment factor of concentration, and the enlightenment factor of equanimity. For what reason? Because the mind is sluggish, monks, and it is difficult to arouse it with those things. Suppose, monks, a man wants to make a small fire flare up. If he throws wet grass, wet cow dung, and wet timber into it, sprays it with water, and scatters soil over it, will he be able to make that small fire flare up? 'No, Venerable Sir.' So too, monks, on an occasion when the mind becomes sluggish, it is difficult to arouse it with those things.

"On an occasion, monks, when the mind becomes sluggish, it is timely to develop the enlightenment factor of investigation of states, the enlightenment factor of energy, and the enlightenment

factor of rapture. For what reason? Because the mind is sluggish, monks, and it is easy to arouse it with those things. Suppose, monks, a man wants to make a small fire flare up. If he throws dry grass, dry cow dung, and dry timber into it, blows on it, and does not scatter soil over it, will he be able to make that small fire flare up? 'Yes, Venerable Sir.' So too, monks, on an occasion when the mind becomes sluggish, it is easy to arouse it with those things.

"On an occasion, monks, when the mind becomes excited, it is untimely to develop the enlightenment factor of investigation of states, the enlightenment factor of energy, and the enlightenment factor of rapture. For what reason? Because the mind is excited, monks, and it is difficult to calm it down with those things. Suppose, monks, a man wants to extinguish a great bonfire. If he throws dry grass, dry cow dung, and dry timber into it, blows on it, and does not scatter soil over it, will he be able to extinguish that great bonfire? 'No, Venerable Sir.' So too, monks, on an occasion when the mind becomes excited, it is difficult to calm it down with those things.

"On an occasion, monks, when the mind becomes excited, it is timely to develop the enlightenment factor of serenity, the enlightenment factor of concentration, and the enlightenment factor of equanimity. For what reason? Because the mind is excited, monks, and it is easy to calm it down with those things. Suppose, monks, a man wants to extinguish a great bonfire. If he throws wet grass, wet cow dung, and wet timber into it, sprays it with water, and scatters soil over it, will he be able to extinguish that great bonfire? 'Yes, Venerable Sir.' So too, monks, on an occasion when the mind becomes excited, it is easy to calm it down with those things.

But mindfulness, monks, I say, is always useful."[79]

---

79 S.N., Mahā-vagga, Bojjhaṅga-saṃyutta (46,6,53), p. 1605-7, Bhikkhu Bodhi.

This is the only way:
None other is there for the purity of vision.
Do you enter upon this path,
Which is the bewilderment of Māra.

There is no fire like lust;
there is no grip like hatred;
there is no net like delusion;
there is no river like craving.

Long is the night to the sleepless;
long is the league to the weary.
Long is worldly existence to fools
who know not the Sublime Truth.

CHAPTER IV

Cycle And Exit

Figure 3: Dependent Origination
(Paṭiccasamuppāda)

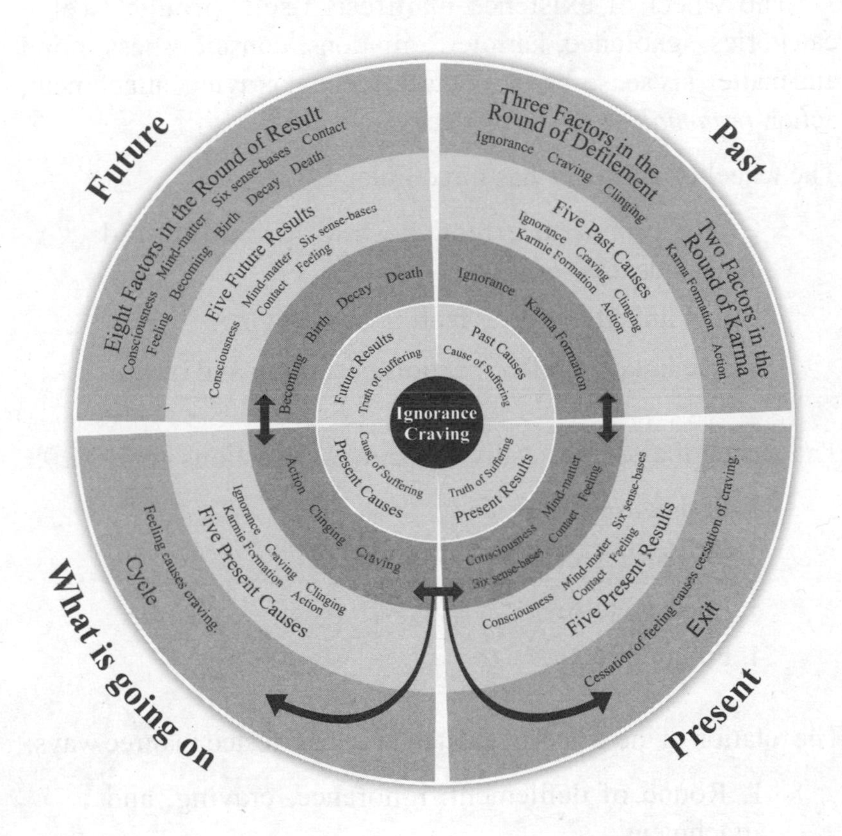

Dependent Origination

The wheel of existence (*bhavacakka*) is caused by ignorance and craving.

The wheel of existence consists of two kinds of truth: the truth of origin and the truth of suffering.

The wheel of existence manifests itself through twelve categories: ignorance, karmic formations, consciousness, mind and matter, six sense-bases, contact, feeling, craving, attachment, action *(kammabhava)*, birth, decay, and death.

The wheel of existence has three linkages:

Cause linked to effect: karmic formation and consciousness.

Effect linked to cause: feeling and craving.

Cause linked to effect: action/becoming and birth.

The wheel of existence is divided into four sections *(sangaha)*:

1. Past causes
2. Present effects
3. Present causes
4. Future effects

The rotation of the wheel of existence is manifested in three ways:

1. Round of defilement: ignorance, craving, and attachment.
2. Round of karma: karmic formations and action/becoming.

3. Round of results: consciousness, body and mind, six sense-bases, contact, feeling, process of future becoming *(uppādibhava),* birth, decay, and death.

"Whether there is an arising of Tathāgatas or no arising of Tathāgatas, that element still persists, the stableness of the Dhamma, the fixed course of the Dhamma, specific conditionality."[80]

"A Tathāgata awakens to this and breaks through to it. Having done so, he explains it, teaches it, proclaims it, establishes it, discloses it, analyses it, elucidates it. And he says: 'See! With ignorance as condition, monks, volitional formations arise.'

"Thus, monks, the actuality in this, the inerrancy, the not-otherwiseness, specific conditionality: this is called dependent origination."[81]

"One who sees dependent origination sees the Dhamma; one who sees the Dhamma sees dependent origination."[82]

"Monks, when a noble disciple thus understands as they really are the origin and the passing away of the world, he is then called a noble disciple who is accomplished in view, accomplished in vision, who has arrived at this true Dhamma, who sees this true Dhamma, who possesses a trainee's knowledge, a trainee's true knowledge, who has entered the stream of the Dhamma, a noble one with penetrative wisdom, one who stands squarely before the door to the Deathless."[83]

"But, monks, those ascetics and brahmins who understand aging-and-death, its origin, its cessation, and the way leading to

80 S.N., Nidānavagga, Nidānasaṃyutta (20), p. 551, Bhikkhu Bodhi.
81 Ibid.
82 M.N., Mūlapaṇṇāsapāḷi, Mahāhatthipadopama Sutta(1,15), p. 191, Bhikkhu Ñāṇamoli and Bhikkhu Bodhi.
83 S.N., Nidānavagga, Nidānasaṃyutta (49), p. 585-6., Bhikkhu Bodhi.

its cessation; who understand birth..., volitional formations, their origin, their cessation, and the way leading to their cessation: these I consider to be ascetics among ascetics and brahmins among brahmins, and these venerable ones, by realizing it for themselves with direct knowledge, in this very life enter and dwell in the goal of asceticism and the goal of brahminhood."[84]

"It is wonderful, Venerable Sir! It is amazing, Venerable Sir! This dependent origination is so deep and so deep in implications, yet to me it seems as clear as clear can be.

"Not so, Ānanda! Not so, Ānanda! This dependent origination is deep and deep in implications. It is because of not understanding and not penetrating this Dhamma, Ānanda, that this generation has become like a tangled skein, like a knotted ball of thread, like matted reeds and rushes, and does not pass beyond the plane of misery, the bad destinations, the nether world, saṃsāra."[85]

"I considered: 'This Dhamma that I have attained is profound, hard to see and hard to understand, peaceful and sublime, unattainable by mere reasoning, subtle, to be experienced by the wise. But this generation delights in adhesion, takes delight in adhesion, rejoices in adhesion. It is hard for such a generation to see this truth, namely, specific conditionality, dependent origination. And it is hard to see this truth, namely, the stilling of all formations, the relinquishing of all attachments, the destruction of craving, dispassion, cessation, nibbāna. If I were to teach the Dhamma, others would not understand me, and that would be wearying and troublesome for me.'"[86]

---

84 Ibid. (13), p. 542-3.
85 Ibid. (60), p. 594.
86 M.N., Mūlapaṇṇāsapāḷi, Ariyapariyesanā Sutta (3,26), p. 260, Bhikkhu Ñāṇamoli and Bhikkhu Bodhi.

What needs to be elaborated on for further practice are the three linkages of dependent origination as follows:

1. Cause Linked to Effect — Karmic Formations and Consciousness

There are five causes of the past: ignorance, craving, attachment (which belong to the round of defilement), karmic formations, and actions (which belong to the round of karma).

There are also five effects of the present: consciousness, body and mind, six sense bases, contact, and feelings. These five categories are the five aggregates that actually exist; in other words, they are the conglomeration of aggregates that have already arisen (or were born). Having arisen, they are bound to change, decay and die. These five present effects, including becoming, birth, decay and death, will make up the eight states in the round of results.

2. Effect Linked to Cause — Feeling and Craving

It is already well-known that all processes of conditionality finally converge on feeling. If we do not attempt to understand the truth of feeling, then enjoyment, addiction, and infatuation with that feeling which is the characteristic of craving and the origin of suffering will definitely arise again.

In this present lifetime, should we fail to practice and follow the noble eightfold path, the result will be ignorance of the truth of aggregates and the mind will become infatuated with, and take pleasure in, the rising and falling of aggregates. One will begin to cling to them as one's own "self," and volitionally develop and construct several kinds of mental formations, which are consequently manifested through bodily, verbal and mental behaviors. Therefore, these five present causes, namely ignorance, craving, clinging, karmic formation, and action, should be thoroughly understood.

3. Cause Linked to Effect — Action *(*kammabhava*)*and Becoming *(*uppādibhava*)*

Actions performed in the present will shape the becoming, birth, decay, and death of aggregates in the future, both in this life and future lives.

Cycle — Causes of suffering *(dukkha samudayo)*: Those who have not understood or have not had their minds trained along the lines of the noble eightfold path will not be able to grasp and penetrate the true characteristics of feeling. Due to the veil of ignorance, craving which generates suffering will create further conditions in the present. "*Vedanā paccayā taṇhā": feeling causes craving.*

Exit of the cycle — Cessation of suffering *(dukkha nirodho)*: One who possesses wisdom and comprehends the conditions of feeling as they really are (the rising-falling pattern) will not be misled and will not attach to or use them to form a "self." One's mind will develop along the path to liberation. Once comprehending clearly the rising and falling pattern of feeling, craving will lose the ability to maintain its stronghold. *"Vedanā nirodhā taṇhā nirodho": through the cessation of feeling, craving ceases.* **This is the path to liberation.**

"Monks, the uninstructed worldling feels a pleasant feeling, a painful feeling, and a neither-painful-nor-pleasant feeling. The instructed noble disciple too feels a pleasant feeling, a painful feeling, and a neither-painful-nor-pleasant feeling. Therein, monks, what is the distinction, the disparity, the difference between the instructed noble disciple and the uninstructed worldling?

"Monks, when the uninstructed worldling [feels] a painful feeling, he sorrows, grieves, and laments; he weeps beating his breast and becomes distraught. He feels two feelings — a bodily one and a mental one. Suppose they were to strike a man with a dart, and then they would strike him immediately afterwards with a second dart, so that the man would feel a feeling caused by two darts. So too, when the uninstructed worldling is being contacted by a painful feeling… he feels two feelings — a bodily one and a mental one.

"Being contacted by that same painful feeling, he harbors aversion towards it. When he harbors aversion towards painful feeling, **the underlying tendency to aversion towards painful feeling lies behind this**. Being contacted by painful feeling, he seeks delight in sensual pleasure. For what reason? Because the uninstructed worldling does not know of any escape from painful feeling other than sensual pleasure. When he seeks delight in sensual pleasure, **the underlying tendency to lust for pleasant feeling lies behind this**. He does not understand as it really is the origin and the passing away, the gratification, the danger, and the escape in the case of these feelings. When he does not understand these things, **the underlying tendency to ignorance in regard to neither-painful-nor-pleasant feeling lies behind this**.

"If he feels a pleasant feeling, he feels it attached. If he feels a painful feeling, he feels it attached. If he feels a neither-painful-nor-pleasant feeling, he feels it attached. This, monks, is called an uninstructed worldling who is attached to birth, aging, and death; who is attached to sorrow, lamentation, pain, displeasure, and despair; **who is attached to suffering**, I say.

"Monks, when the instructed noble disciple is contacted by a painful feeling, he does not sorrow, grieve, or lament; he does not weep beating his breast and become distraught. He feels one feeling — a bodily one, not a mental one. Suppose they were to strike a man with a dart, but they would not strike him immediately afterwards with a second dart, so that the man would feel a feeling caused by one dart only. So too, when the instructed noble disciple is contacted by a painful feeling… he feels one feeling — a bodily one, not a mental one.

"Being contacted by that same painful feeling, he harbors no aversion towards it. Since he harbors no aversion towards painful feeling, the underlying tendency to aversion towards painful feeling does not lie behind this. Being contacted by painful feeling, he does not seek delight in sensual pleasure. For what reason? Because the instructed noble disciple knows of an escape from painful feeling other than sensual pleasure. Since he does not seek delight in sensual pleasure, the underlying tendency to desire for pleasant feeling does not lie behind this. He understands as it really is the origin and the passing away, the gratification, the danger, and the escape in the case of these feelings. Since he understands these things, the underlying tendency to ignorance in regard to neither-painful-nor-pleasant feeling does not lie behind this.

"If he feels a pleasant feeling, he feels it detached. If he feels a painful feeling, he feels it detached. If he feels a neither-painful-nor-pleasant feeling, he feels it detached. This, monks, is called a noble disciple who is detached from birth, aging, and death;

who is detached from sorrow, lamentation, pain, displeasure, and despair; **who is detached from suffering**, I say.

"This, monks, is the distinction, the disparity, the difference between the instructed noble disciple and the uninstructed worldling."[87]

"Monks, when one knows and sees the eye as it actually is, when one knows and sees forms as they actually are, when one knows and sees eye-consciousness as it actually is, when one knows and sees eye-contact as it actually is, when one knows and sees as it actually is [the feeling] felt as pleasant or painful or neither-painful-nor-pleasant that arises with eye-contact as condition, then one is not inflamed by lust for the eye, for forms, for eye-consciousness, for eye-contact, for [the feeling] felt as pleasant or painful or neither-painful-nor-pleasant that arises with eye-contact as condition.

"When one abides uninflamed by lust, unfettered, uninfatuated, contemplating danger, then the five aggregates affected by clinging are diminished for oneself in the future; and one's craving — which brings renewal of being, and is accompanied by delight and lust, and delights in this or that — is abandoned. One's bodily and mental troubles are abandoned, one's bodily and mental torments are abandoned, one's bodily and mental fevers are abandoned, and one experiences bodily and mental pleasure.

"The view of a person such as this is right view. His intention is right intention, his effort is right effort, his mindfulness is right mindfulness, his concentration is right concentration. But his bodily action, his verbal action, and his livelihood have already been well purified earlier. Thus this noble eightfold path comes to fulfillment in him by development.

---

87 S.N., Saḷāyatana-vagga, Vedanā-saṃyutta (36,1,5), p. 1264-5, Bhikkhu Bodhi.

"When he develops this noble eightfold path, the four foundations of mindfulness also come to fulfillment in him by development, the four right kinds of striving… the four bases for spiritual power… the five faculties… the five powers… the seven enlightenment factors also come to fulfillment in him by development. **These two things — [tranquility] and insight — occur in him yoked evenly together**. He fully understands by direct knowledge those things that should be fully understood by direct knowledge. He abandons by direct knowledge those things that should be abandoned by direct knowledge. He develops by direct knowledge those things that should be developed by direct knowledge. He realizes by direct knowledge those things that should be realized by direct knowledge.

"And what things should be fully understood by direct knowledge? The answer to that is: the five aggregates affected by clinging, that is, **the material form aggregate affected by clinging, the feeling aggregate affected by clinging, the perception aggregate affected by clinging, the formations aggregate affected by clinging, the consciousness aggregate affected by clinging.** These are the things that should be fully understood by direct knowledge.

"And what things should be abandoned by direct knowledge? Ignorance and craving for being. And what things should be developed by direct knowledge? **[Tranquility] and insight**. And what things should be realized by direct knowledge? True knowledge and deliverance."[88]

"It may be, O monks, that wandering ascetics of another persuasion might ask you: 'In what are all things rooted? How

88 M.N., Upararipaṇṇāsapāḷi, Mahāsaḷāyatanika Sutta (5,149), p. 1138-9 Bhikkhu Ñāṇamoli and Bhikkhu Bodhi.

do they come to actual existence? Where do they arise? Where do they converge? What is the foremost in all things? What is their master? What is the highest of all things? What is the essence in all things? Where do all things merge? Where do they end?'

"If you are thus questioned, monks, you should reply as follows: 'All things are rooted in desire. They come to actual existence through attention, originate from contact, and **converge on feelings**. The foremost of all things is concentration. All things are mastered by mindfulness. Their peak is wisdom, their essence liberation. All things merge in the Deathless, and nibbāna is their culmination.'"[89]

Just as the howling wind will blow itself out,
and silence and calm will concurrently arise and begin,
so all fearsome states and things
are merely temporary states,
arising and ceasing in the mind.

89 A.N., The Chapter of the Tens (194), p. 250-1, Bhikku Nyanaponika and Bhikkhu Bodhi.

Like water on a lotus leaf,
or a mustard seed
on the point of a needle,
he who does not cling to sensual pleasure -
him do I call a holy man.

CHAPTER V

The Attainment of the Noble Truth

The Attainment of Nibbāna

Every object of consciousness, arising from sensory contact, converges on feeling. As practitioners keep observing the rising and falling of feeling, their wisdom will become sharper. Once they are able to understand clearly the characteristics of feeling, they will also be able to realize the true characteristics of craving - how it is conditioned and manifested. **Since feeling is the state which craving entwines and clings to, when feeling ceases, craving no longer has any footing or stronghold, and therefore must also cease.**

On reaching such a state, one is able to experience very clearly and strongly the taste of freedom from craving (which is actually our own cruel master). One can also begin realizing subtler truths at this time. Indeed, because of ignorance, which opens the door for craving, one has so far enjoyed and been satisfied with the rising-falling flow of aggregates. When attachment to aggregates grows, one ends up creating a "self" out of such rising-falling patterns. Now, the true state of "self" reveals itself and the illusion of attachment dissolves. One is able to realize that suffering, or any uncomfortable mental state, originates from the yearning to attach. One suffers because one acts against the law of nature: "It is undesirable that this state of affairs exists. Be the way I want, not the other way around. Things must remain like this forever; I don't want them to change."

All conditioned states occur because of related causes and effects. They emerge, persist, and finally fall apart. Knowledge of the three characteristics of **impermanence, suffering and selflessness** appears very clearly while passion, likes and dislikes, covetousness and dissatisfaction become weaker and weaker and finally subside.

The mind remains neutral (*upekkhāsambojjhaṅga* - equanimity - or *saṅkhārupekkhā ñāṇa*[90]) towards the rising and falling phenomenon. Whenever one remains focused on the rising and falling of feeling, one will also realize the ceasing of craving. The force of attachment will gradually weaken. Keep practicing and developing this. **This is the right path to liberation.**

When the potentials of **concentration** and **insight** are well-balanced and developed to the point that they can enable a breakthrough, one will be able to capture clearly every detail of the rising and falling of phenomenon. Whoops!… One's feeling is drawn towards the conscious element at the heart. It is like something is pressing hard there, and the heart is being squeezed, causing an uncomfortable feeling. **This is the characteristic of the mind at the turning point or at the door of change.** The mind is about to be liberated from the gravitational grip and the pulling force of craving… whoops!… whoops! Rising and falling… rising and falling. Finally, **the state of rising and falling ceases**… no more continuation, no more rising and falling of aggregates. This condition, which is void of the rising and falling of phenomenon, is the state of **nibbāna**.

Throughout the course of this unending cycle of saṃsāra, the rising and falling flow of aggregates has continuously overwhelmed

90 Knowledge of equanimity towards all formations. It is one important step in the successive development of vipassanā insight.

us like an endless wave. But now it comes to an end. The mind has now realized that the wave has run its course. How would one feel? "Whatever is of the nature to uprise, all that is of the nature to [fall apart]."[91]

The one who experiences the cessation of the rising and falling for the first time is known as the "stream-enterer." In the case of Upatissaparipājaka (who later became Ven. Sāriputta), he attained the first stage of enlightenment after listening to the Dhamma taught by Ven. Assaji. After the moment of enlightenment, the retrospective knowledge (*paccavekkhana ñāṇa*) occurred to him: "If this is indeed dhamma, you have penetrated as far as the sorrowless path, unseen, neglected for many myriads of aeons."[92]

During the period of cessation of the rising-falling state, the pulling force of craving also ceases completely. One feels extremely light and free, dwelling beyond every kind of thought, beyond feeling (heart) and any kind of perception (brain). One remains free. Such a state of being can be experienced only by those who have attained it. It is very difficult to explain, to find words capable of describing it. One has to experience this for oneself.

At the very moment when phalacitta[93] occurs successively after maggacitta[94], one feels at the eyelids an unlimited volume of light. Both eyelids are palpitating. It seems that one is opening the eyes, although one is not. This will last until the mind releases itself from the appreciation of such a state. This kind of light, if occurring

---

91 The Book of Discipline, Mahāvagga 1 (24,1-3), p. 54, Horner..

92 Ibid.

93 Phalacitta is the successive moments of supermundane consciousness which flash forth immediately after the moment of path consciousness. See the detailed explanation on p. 15-16 of Chapter Two.

94 Maggacitta is the very instant when the mind attains one of the four states of liberation.

in the case of the attainment of arahantship or Buddhahood, will become immensely strong and far reaching. In those cases, it shines throughout the entire universe.

"Monks, on the manifestation of a Tathāgata... then an infinite, glorious radiance is manifested, surpassing the deva-majesty of the devas. Even the gloom of space between the worlds, the fathomless darkness, the murk of darkness, where even the radiance of our moon and sun, though of such wondrous power and majesty, cannot be manifested — even there an infinite, glorious radiance is spread abroad, surpassing the deva-majesty of the devas. Likewise, those creatures that have come into being there, becoming aware of each other through that radiance, exclaim: 'It seems, friends, that there be other creatures also that have come into being here.'"[95]

After attaining nibbāna, some meditators are unable to sleep for a few days. There are also certain bodily cleansing conditions which occur to clear out the crude and coarse elements in the body. These are also states which are accessible only to those who have attained enlightenment.

Characteristics of Maggacitta: Some Metaphors

… It is as if one is running at very high speed and suddenly being wrenched backwards by a tremendously strong power.

… It is as if one has always suffered carrying a heavy object… and suddenly... whoops!… the object drops and immediately disappears.

… It is as if a rope which has been fully stretched is abruptly cut in the middle.

95 A.N., vol. 2, The Book of the Fours, Marvels (4,8,127), p. 134, Woodward.

... It is as if an aerated balloon is put into a bucket and one is pouring water into it. When the water overflows the bucket's rim, the balloon then falls out of the bucket.

... It is as if one is watching pictures on a screen and they suddenly all disappear.

... It is as if one is weightless, beyond any boundary, dimensionless and timeless.

Omens Occurring Before the Attainment of Enlightenment

One or two days before attaining enlightenment, omens usually come in the form of a dream. A kind of dream occurs which has never appeared before. However, it will happen to everyone who is about to be liberated.

... Some dream that they are running and being chased by a demon or monster who is rapidly gaining on them. Then, they arrive at a river bank which is very large and wide. As the demon jumps to grab them, a miracle happens. They find themselves flying safely over the water and across the river to the other side. They have escaped the clutches of the demon.

... Some dream that they are correctly answering Dhamma questions. Each time they finish an answer, angels bless them by playing harps and scattering divine flowers around them.

Omens of the Buddha's Enlightenment

"Monks, before the Tathāgata, the Arahant, the Fully Enlightened One attained enlightenment, while he was still a *bodhisatta*[96], five great dreams appeared to him. What five?

"1. He dreamt that this mighty earth was his great bedstead; the Himālaya, king of mountains, was his pillow; his left hand rested on the eastern sea, his right hand on the western sea; his two feet on the southern sea. This, monks, was the first dream that appeared to the Tathāgata while he was still a bodhisatta... This first dream was a sign that he would awaken to unsurpassed, perfect enlightenment.

"2. Again, he dreamt that from his navel arose a kind of grass called tiriyā and continued growing until it touched the clouds. This, monks, was the second great dream... This second great dream was a sign that he would fully understand the noble eightfold path and would proclaim it well among devas and humans.

"3. Again, he dreamt that white worms with black heads crawled on his legs up to his knees, covering them. This, monks, was the third great dream... This third great dream was a sign that many white-clad householders would go for refuge to the Tathāgata until the end of their lives.

"4. Again, he dreamt that four birds of different colors came from the four directions, fell at his feet and turned all white. This, monks, was the fourth great dream… This fourth great dream was a sign that members of the four castes — nobles, brahmins, commoners and menials — would go forth into homelessness in the Doctrine and Discipline taught by the Tathāgata and would realize the unsurpassed liberation.

---

96 A being destined for Buddhahood, a future Buddha.

"5. Again, he dreamt that he climbed up a huge mountain of dung without being soiled by the dung. This, monks, was the fifth great dream.... This fifth great dream was a sign that the Tathāgata would receive many gifts of robes, almsfood, dwellings and medicines, and he would make use of them without being tied to them, without being infatuated with them, without being committed to them, seeing the danger and knowing the escape."[97]

Insight in Concentration (*Samādhibala*)

"I tell you, the ending of the mental fermentations depends on the first jhāna... the second jhāna... the third... the fourth... the dimension of the [boundless] space... the dimension of [boundless] consciousness... the dimension of nothingness. I tell you, the ending of the mental fermentations depends on the dimension of neither perception nor non-perception.

"'I tell you, the ending of the mental fermentations depends on the first jhāna.' Thus it has been said. In reference to what was it said? There is the case where a monk, secluded from sensuality, secluded from unskillful qualities, enters and remains in the first jhāna: rapture and pleasure born of seclusion, accompanied by directed thought and evaluation. He regards whatever phenomena there that are connected with form, feeling, perception, fabrications, and consciousness, as inconstant, stressful, a disease, a cancer, an arrow, painful, an affliction, alien, a disintegration, an emptiness, not-self. He turns his mind away from those phenomena, and having done so, inclines his mind to the property of deathlessness: 'This is peace, this is exquisite — the resolution of all fabrications; the relinquishment of all acquisitions; the ending of craving; dispassion; cessation; unbinding.'

---

97 A.N., The Chapter of the Fives, The Five Dreams of the Bodhisatta, (113) p. 147-8, Bhikkhu Nyanaponika and Bhikkhu Bodhi.

"Suppose that an archer or archer's apprentice were to practice on a straw man or mound of clay, so that after a while he would become able to shoot long distances, to fire accurate shots in rapid succession, and to pierce great masses. In the same way, there is the case where a monk... enters and remains in the first jhāna... He regards whatever phenomena there that are connected with form, feeling, perception, fabrications, and consciousness, as inconstant, stressful, a disease, a cancer, an arrow, painful, an affliction, alien, a disintegration, an emptiness, not-self. He turns his mind away from those phenomena, and having done so, inclines his mind to the property of deathlessness: 'This is peace, this is exquisite — the resolution of all fabrications; the relinquishment of all acquisitions; the ending of craving; dispassion; cessation; unbinding.'

"Staying right there, he reaches the ending of the mental fermentations. Or, if not, then — through this very Dhamma-passion, this very Dhamma-delight, and from the total wasting away of the first five of the fetters — he is due to be reborn [in the pure abodes][98], there to be totally unbound, never again to return from that world.

"'I tell you, the ending of the mental fermentations depends on the first jhāna.' Thus was it said, and in reference to this was it said. [Similarly with the second, third, and fourth jhāna].

"'I tell you, the ending of the mental fermentations depends on the dimension of [boundless] space.' Thus it has been said.

98 The pure abodes are a group of five heavens belonging to the form realm, where only non-returners are reborn, and in which they attain arahatship and nibbāna.

"In reference to what was it said? There is the case where a monk, with the complete transcending of perceptions of [physical] form, with the disappearance of perceptions of resistance, and not heeding perceptions of diversity, [perceiving boundless] space,' enters and remains in the dimension of [boundless] space. **He regards whatever phenomena there that are connected with feeling, perception, fabrications, and consciousness, as inconstant, stressful, a disease, a cancer, an arrow, painful, an affliction, alien, a disintegration, an emptiness, not-self.** He turns his mind away from those phenomena, and having done so, inclines his mind to the property of deathlessness: 'This is peace, this is exquisite — the resolution of all fabrications; the relinquishment of all acquisitions; the ending of craving; dispassion; cessation; unbinding.'

"... Staying right there, he reaches the ending of the mental fermentations. Or, if not, then — through this very Dhamma-passion, this very Dhamma-delight, and from the total wasting away of the first five of the fetters — he is due to be reborn [in the Sublime Abodes], there to be totally unbound, never again to return from that world.

"'I tell you, the ending of the mental fermentations depends on the dimension of the boundless space.' Thus was it said, and in reference to this was it said. [Similarly with the realm of boundless consciousness and the realm of nothingness].

"Thus, as far as the perception-attainments [the realm of neither perception-nor-non-perception] go, that is as far as gnosis-penetration [the cessation of perception and feeling] goes. As for these two spheres — the attainment of the [realm] of neither perception nor non-perception and the attainment of the cessation of feeling and perception[99] — I tell you that they are to be rightly explained by those monks who are meditators, skilled in attaining, skilled in attaining and emerging, who have attained and emerged in dependence on them."[100]

Successive Steps of Insight Knowledge (paññābala)

1. *Nāmarūpaparicccheda ñāṇa*: Knowledge of the states of mind and body.

2. *Paccayapariggaha ñāṇa*: Knowledge of the relationship and conditions of mind and body.

3. *Sammasana ñāṇa*: Knowledge of mind and body as they really are (impermanent, unsatisfactory and non-self, always rising and passing away).

4. *Udayabbaya ñāṇa*: Knowledge of clear realization of the rise and fall of aggregates.

5. *Bhaṅga ñāṇa*: Knowledge of the dissolution of aggregates.

6. *Bhayatūpattāna ñāṇa*: Knowledge which perceives the appearance of aggregates as terror or executioners.

7. *Ādīnavānupassañā ñāṇa*: Knowledge of danger inherent in the aggregates and danger of attachment to the self.

8. *Nibbidā ñāṇa:* Knowledge of dispassion and boredom with the aggregates that rise and fall… nothing except the everlasting flow of rising and falling. Nothing else except suffering.

99 The realm of neither perception-nor-non-perception, because of its ambiguous status, cannot be the basis for attaining the path (magga). However, it is the necessary basis for attaining a higher stage of the cessation of feeling and perception. Please see Chapter Nine for further detail.

100 A.N., The Book of the Nines (9.36), Jhāna Sutta, Bhikkhu Thanissaro, ATI.

9. *Muccitukamyatā ñāṇa*: Knowledge of very strong desire for deliverance.

10. *Paṭisankhā ñāṇa*: Knowledge of reflective contemplation to find the way of escape.

11. *Saṅkhārupekkhā ñāṇa*: Knowledge of equanimity towards all formations, finally finding the escape from suffering, acknowledging the law of cause and effect, stopping the push and pull of the fruits of karma, abandoning rejection of the rise and fall of aggregates, remaining equanimous, being neither covetous nor dissatisfied towards all phenomena. This knowledge will not lead to creating new causes.

12. **Anuloma ñāṇa: After observing continuously the incessant rising-falling wave, up to a certain point, suddenly all feelings move to the conscious element at the heart which is the main door of all perceptions and consciousness. One feels as if there is a strong pressure over the heart, so suffocating that one can hardly breathe. After a while, there are mental formations arising and falling away — three times for people with moderate wisdom, two times for those with stronger wisdom. This is a special type of rising and falling pattern, as it happens and falls apart much more quickly than usual... whoops... whoops... whoops, suddenly the continuity of rising-falling flow of aggregates comes to an end.**

13. *Gotrabhū ñaṇa*: Mental state at the moment of the "Change-of-lineage."[101] The mind is released from the gravity of *bhava* (the state of being) to the state of **non-rising and non-falling (it transcends all kinds of dualism)**.

101 The turning point at which an ordinary person becomes a noble (ariya) person.

14. *Magga ñāṇa:* The state of mind in nibbāna. There is no formation of thoughts. Fetters are destroyed according to the power of the wisdom of the path.

15. *Phala ñāṇa*: Mental state during which the mind continues experiencing nibbāna for two or three instants.

16. *Paccavekkhana ñāṇa*: The cessation of aggregates can be grasped only by those who have already reached that state. Paccavekkhana ñāṇa is the knowledge occurring after the cessation, when the rising and falling of aggregates reappears again. One begins to review all previous processes of being and becoming, how many lives, how many births, how many aeons have passed without experiencing the termination of aggregates. **"Whatever is of the nature to uprise, all that is of the nature to [fall apart]."**[102]

When the moment of attaining nibbāna has passed, *bhavaṅgacitta*[103] appears for an interval. After that, the five paccavekkhana ñāṇa occur. This is the knowledge that contemplates and reviews the enlightenment process, i.e. the characteristics of maggacitta, phalacitta, nibbāna. It reconsiders the fetters already destroyed and the remaining or yet to be eradicated fetters. As for those who attain arahantship, there is no need to contemplate the remaining defilements as they have been completely eradicated. No single particle of fetters or mental fermentation of defilement remains to be destroyed.[104]

---

102 The Book of Discipline, Mahā-vagga 1 (24,1-3), p. 54., Horner.

103 The mental passive state during which the mind does not respond to external objects. Its flow will be interrupted when objects enter the mind.

104 *Buddhadhamma* (Thai version), p. 364.

Through many a birth in saṃsāra
Have I wandered in vain,
Seeking the builder of this house.
Repeated birth is indeed suffering.

O House-builder, you are seen!
You will not build this house again.
For your rafters are broken,
And your ridgepole shattered.
My mind has reached the Unconditioned;
I have attained the destruction of craving.

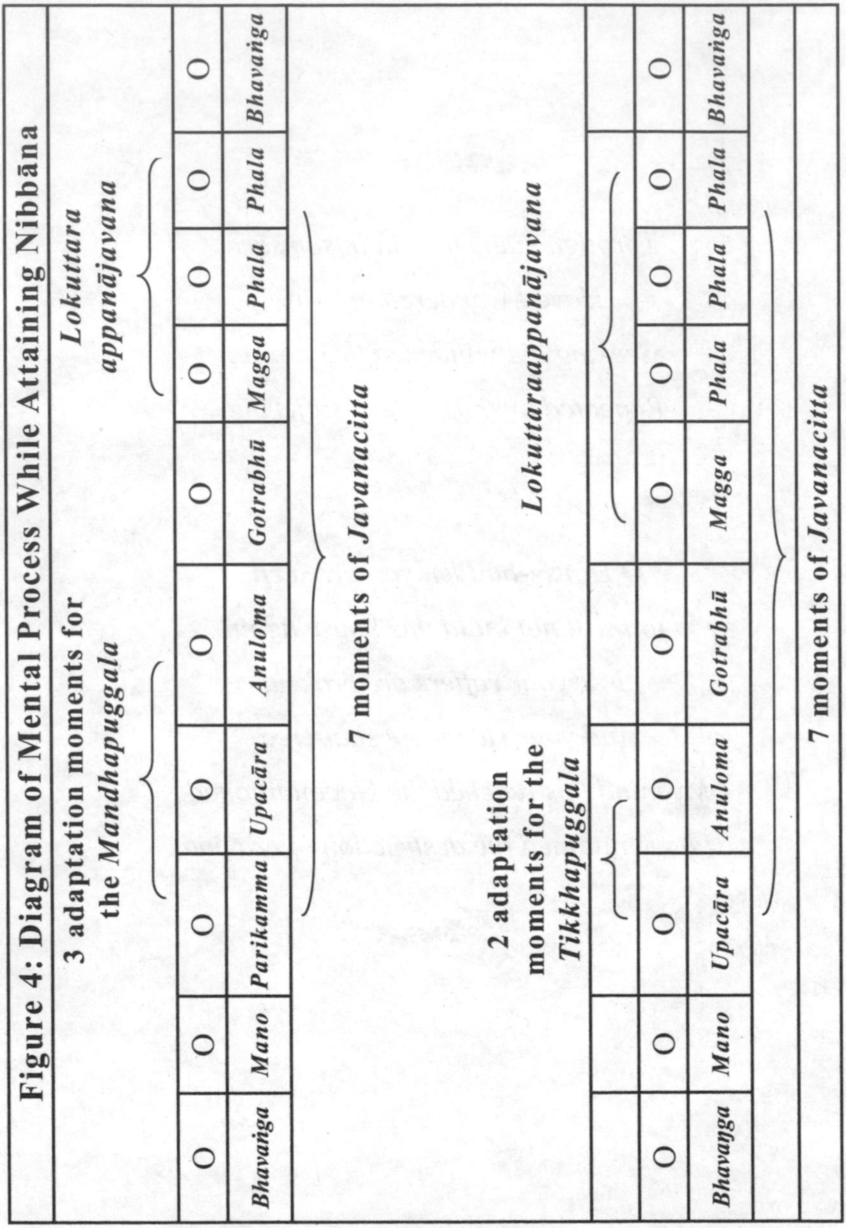

Figure 4: Diagram of Mental Process While Attaining Nibbāna

3 adaptation moments for the *Mandhapuggala* (*Parikamma*, *Upacāra*, *Anuloma*)

Lokuttara appanājavana (*Magga*, *Phala*, *Phala*)

O	O	O	O	O	O	O	O	O	O
Bhavaṅga	*Mano*	*Parikamma*	*Upacāra*	*Anuloma*	*Gotrabhū*	*Magga*	*Phala*	*Phala*	*Bhavaṅga*

7 moments of *Javanacitta* (*Parikamma* to second *Phala*)

2 adaptation moments for the *Tikkhapuggala* (*Upacāra*, *Anuloma*)

Lokuttaraappanājavana (*Magga*, *Phala*, *Phala*, *Phala*)

O	O	O	O	O	O	O	O	O	O
Bhavaṅga	*Mano*	*Upacāra*	*Anuloma*	*Gotrabhū*	*Magga*	*Phala*	*Phala*	*Phala*	*Bhavaṅga*

7 moments of *Javanacitta* (*Upacāra* to third *Phala*)

* Dhammasangani (Atthasālini) 359, Visuddhimagga 3/316-324 (Thai version).

Explanation of Terms:

Mandhapuggala: people with moderate wisdom experience three thought-occurences in the adaptation[105] phase, and two in the fruition phase.

Tikkhapuggala: people with stronger wisdom experience two thought-occurences in the adaptation phase, and two in the fruition phase.

Bhavaṅga: the passive state of mind which does not respond to external objects.

Manodavāravajana: mind-door cognition or the moment of consciousness which turns the mind towards a mental object.

Anuloma: adaptation or thought-moment when the mind qualifies itself for nibbāna.

Parikamma: preparation.

Upacāra: access.

Gotrabhū: change of lineage.

Lokuttaraappanājavana: sequences of thought-occurences in nibbāna.

Magga: path.

Phala: fruition.

Javanacitta: the active state of mind.

105 Adaptation moment of consciousness denotes the moments of impulsion flashing up immediately before reaching either the absorptions or the paths of enlightenment.

Remark: Even for those who have never experienced jhāna before, at the moment of attaining nibbāna, their concentration power must escalate to the level of absorption concentration. This is the meaning of right concentration in the noble eightfold path.

Attainment of the Four Levels of Enlightenment[106]

It has been widely accepted that the attainment of enlightenment requires both the power of established concentration (absorption concentration or appanāsamādhi) — and the power of wisdom. Both faculties have to be developed to the point that they can lead to the eradication of defilement. **Enlightenment arises when these two faculties are well-developed and equal in strength and balance**. However, on the path to enlightenment, each practitioner may develop these faculties in different ways. **For those who have accumulated a tendency towards concentration, the concentrative power will precede the power of wisdom, whereas for those who tend more towards insight meditation, wisdom will precede concentration**.

"Friends, whatever monks or nuns declare before me that they have attained the final knowledge of arahantship, all these do so in one of four ways. What four?

"Here, friends, a monk develops insight preceded by tranquility. While he thus develops insight preceded by tranquility, the path arises in him. He now pursues, develops and cultivates that path, and while he is doing so the fetters are abandoned and the underlying tendencies eliminated.

106 See the detailed explanation of the four levels of enlightenment on page 15-16 of Chapter Two.

"Or again, friends, a monk develops tranquility preceded by insight. While he thus develops tranquility preceded by insight, the path arises in him. He now pursues, develops and cultivates that path, and while he is doing so the fetters are abandoned and the underlying tendencies eliminated.

"Or again, friends, a monk develops tranquility and insight joined in pairs. While he thus develops tranquility and insight joined in pairs, the path arises in him. He now pursues, develops and cultivates that path, and while he is doing so the fetters are abandoned and the underlying tendencies eliminated.

"Or again, friends, a monk's mind is seized by agitation caused by higher states of mind. But there comes a time when his mind becomes internally steadied, composed, unified and concentrated; then the path arises in him. He now pursues, develops and cultivates that path, and while he is doing so the fetters are abandoned and the underlying tendencies eliminated."[107]

Wisdom of the Path of the Stream-Enterer (Sotāpattimaggañāṇa)

The last element of the noble eightfold path, right concentration, refers to the four absorptions of the form realms (rūpajhānas).[108] The last element of the seven factors of enlightenment is equanimity. The last element of vipassanā knowledge before the mind attains enlightenment is the knowledge ripe with equanimity.

107 A.N., The Chapter of the Fours (83), p. 114, Bhikkhu Nyanaponika and Bhikkhu Bodhi.

108 See fn. 70 on p. 83 in Chapter Three.

The mind in this state is unwavering, very firm yet relaxed, and remains neutral to any rising-falling phenomena. This is the wisdom at the level of saṅkhārupekkhā ñāṇa ("equanimity towards all formations" - see p. 121 above). One should enhance it, develop it and turn it into an instrument for observing the endless series of rising and falling patterns. **This is the mental state leading to enlightenment.**

The rising-falling waves emerge one after another and the mind moves into the path of absorption concentration (appanājavanavithī) of the first jhāna. In the first jhāna, the one-pointedness of mind arises and remains for a period of time. Then the mind moves on to observe the rising-falling occurrence of the sixteen mental concomitants that co-arise with the first jhāna (as described below).

"Here, monks, quite secluded from sensual pleasures, secluded from unwholesome states, Sāriputta entered upon and abided in the first jhāna, which is accompanied by applied and sustained thought, with rapture and pleasure born of seclusion.

"And the states in the first jhāna — the applied thought, the sustained thought, the rapture, the pleasure, and the unification of mind; the contact, feeling, perception, volition, and mind; the zeal, decision, energy, mindfulness, equanimity, and attention — these states were defined by him one by one as they occurred; known to him those states arose, known they were present, known they disappeared.

"He understood thus… 'So indeed, these states, not having been, come into being; having been, they vanish.' Regarding those states, he abided unattracted, unrepelled, independent, detached, free, dissociated, with a mind rid of barriers. He understood: there is an escape beyond, and with the cultivation of that [attainment], he confirmed that there is."[109]

---

109 M.N., Uparipaṇṇasapāḷi, Anupada Sutta (111), p. 899, Bhikkhu Ñāṇamoli and Bhikkhu Bodhi.

Having experienced clearly the rising-falling of mental concomitants, the mind is released from the first jhāna and moves on to the conscious element at the heart. A certain kind of force pins the mind to the state of one-pointedness at that area. It appears as if the heart is pressed so hard that one can hardly breathe or as if this is going to be one's last breath. The mind is void of any thoughts and mental formations. After a while, the rising-falling of aggregates reappears two or three times, but they appear much faster than usual. One…two…three… whoops…whoops… whoops! Then a **complete cessation of the rising-falling continuity** happens. The mind is now free from the gravitational force of all craving, going into the state void of any rising-falling of aggregates, going beyond dimension, beyond the realm of form, beyond time and space. It is not the state of emptiness, as it transcends the polarity of either existing or non-existing, beyond all conventional truth.

This phase, while the mind is fixed to the conscious element at the heart and the rising-falling states occur two or three times, is called the period of **anuloma ñāṇa** (see diagram on p. 124). The first moment of rising-falling is characterized as **parikamma** (preparatory), the second one is called **upacāra** (access), and the third one is distinguished as **anuloma** (adaption). Then, the continuity of rising-falling states ceases and the mind is released from the gravitational force. This is the state of **gotrabhū ñāṇa** (maturity-knowledge; knowledge of having attained change-of-lineage).

The mind, which is beyond any dimension, boundary, space or time, and beyond any conventional truth, is called the state of **maggañāṇa** (knowledge of the path). After maggañāṇa has ceased, **phalañāṇa** (knowledge of fruition) arises two or three times and has nibbāna as its sole object (as in the state of maggañāṇa*)*, without any interruption of bhavaṅgacitta (life continuum consciousness).

As soon as the last occurrence of phalañāṇa (the seventh maggajavanacitta [impulsive path consciousness]) ceases, bhavaṅgacitta arises and passes away. Then, **paccavekkhana ñāṇa** (retrospective knowledge) appears and performs five tasks: which are: contemplating the states of maggañāṇa, phalañāṇa, nibbāna, defilements that are eradicated completely and the remaining defilements.

Flash of Lightning

The speed of the rising-falling patterns one experiences upon entering maggañāṇa can be compared with a flash of lightning.

1. The last rising-falling occurrence ceases.
2. The mind is released from the pulling force of craving.
3. **The mind enters into the state of non rising-falling phenomena,** which transcends the realm of dimension, shape, boundary, space and all conventional truth.

These three successive rising-falling moments happen like a flash of lightning. In experiential terms, all four levels of enlightenment will always be based on one of the four levels of rūpajhāna. The moment of entering such a state is called *appanājavanamaggavāravithi*.

If the first rūpajhāna accompanies the entering into the state of stream-enterer (the first attainment has the first jhāna as its base), then the first jhāna will not later arise simultaneously with the other higher three levels of enlightenment. This is because the characteristics of the special types of aggregates (the force of concentration and wisdom at the

moment of enlightenment) that rise and fall at the turning point of change-of-lineage will take place only once. Hence, they will not co-arise with the other higher three levels.

This means that the greater the power of enlightenment faculties of the practitioner, the more refined the aggregates that co-arise with each level of enlightenment will be.

Concentration Bases at the Attaining Moment of Enlightenment

Sotāpattimagga (path of stream-enterer) is based on the first jhāna, which acts as the component of right concentration in the eightfold path.

Sakadāgāmimagga (path of once-returner) is based on the second or other higher jhānas, which act as the component of right concentration in the eightfold path.

Anāgāmimagga (path of non-returner) is based on the third or other higher jhānas, which act as the component of right concentration in the eightfold path.

Arahattamagga (path of the fully-enlightened) is based on the fourth or other higher jhānas, which act as the component of right concentration in the eightfold path.

Arūpajhāna consists of the same components as the fourth rūpajhāna except it has formless objects as the base of contemplation. The first, second and third arūpajhānas can also be the foundation for all levels of enlightenment. As for the fourth arūpajhāna, its temporal characteristics and the feature of its rising-falling of aggregates are not appropriate as the foundation of any level of enlightenment.

Three Aspects of Liberation

There are three aspects of the rising and falling of aggregates that are the focus of contemplation before the mind attains enlightenment.

1. The feature of impermanence *(aniccalakkhana)*. The wisdom of the practitioner develops as the result of focusing upon the characteristics of change, seeing the continuous rising-falling flow as impermanent, until it finally ceases completely. This is characteristic of liberation by signlessness *(animittavimokkha)* (eradication of attachment to signs as permanent things).

2. The feature of suffering *(dukkhalakkhana)*. Shortly before the mind enters anuloma ñāṇa, physical pain appears clearly on certain parts of the body. Then, the last moment of the rising-falling of aggregates occurs. Finally, the rising and falling state ceases, and the pain ceases as well. This is characteristic of liberation by **desirelessness** (*appanihitavimokkha*) (eradication of the desire to go beyond pain).

3. The feature of non-self *(anattalakkhana)*. Wisdom occurs by seeing the rising-falling phenomenon as having neither any intrinsic essence nor any "self," until at last it ceases completely. This is characteristic of liberation by voidness *(suññatavimokkha)* (eradication of attachment to essence or self).

Figure 5: Functions of the Three Knowledges Concerning the Four Noble Truths

Three Knowledges / Four Noble Truths	*Saccañāṇa* (Knowledge about the truth of suffering)	*Kiccañaṇa* (Knowledge about the functions of wisdom)	*Katañāṇa* (Knowledge about what has been achieved with regards to the Four Noble Truths)
Suffering	Knowledge of the five aggregates as they really are.	The rising-falling of aggregates appears clear and prominent.	The characteristics and states of aggregates are clearly acknowledged.
Cause of suffering	Realization of the characteristics of craving as clinging to the rising-falling of feeling. One understands thus: "Feeling causes craving."	By clear realization of the rising-falling of feeling, one also realizes the rising-falling of craving. Thus, craving has no more footing. "Cessation of feeling causes cessation of craving."	Clear realization of the nature of craving, which is now without footing.
Cessation of suffering	The longtime continuity of rising-falling states comes to an end. Maggañāṇa occurs.	Maggañāṇa occurs with nibbāna as its object, destroying fetters according to one's power of the path.	Paccavekkhana ñāṇa occurs and performs a contemplative function, after maggañāṇa and phalañāṇa have ceased successively.
Path leading to cessation of suffering	Right speech, right action, right livelihood: powers that purify action Right view, right thought: powers of wisdom Right effort, right mindfulness, right concentration: powers of concentration.	All components of the eightfold path are enhanced to the level of enlightenment and are functioning simultaneously.	Wisdom clearly realizes the complete function of the eightfold path.

Remarks: *Related to the above chart, the Four Noble Truths and three kinds of knowledge function simultaneously, like a candle, once lit, achieving four different functions at the same time:*

1. Burning the candlewick

2. Wiping away darkness

3. Shining brightly

4. Finishing off the wax

The Buddha's words in *Satipaṭṭhāna Sutta, Nīvaraṇapabba* sub-section, read: "He discerns how there is the abandoning of unarisen doubt once it has arisen. And he discerns how there is no further appearance in the future of doubt that has been abandoned."

Āyatanapabba sub-section reads: "He discerns how there is the abandoning of unarisen lower fetters (personality belief, doubt, adherence to mere rules and rituals) once they have arisen. And he discerns how there is no further appearance in the future of fetters that have been abandoned."[110] Contemplation of mind-objects as mentioned herein will appear clearly and fully to the wisdom of those noble stream-enterers.

110 D.N., 22, Mahā-Satipaṭṭhāna Sutta, Bhikkhu Thanissaro, ATI

Wisdom Leading to the State of the Once-Returner (Sakadāgāmimaggañāṇa)

The stream-enterer who seeks to attain a higher level of peace must develop the higher state of his or her controlling faculties using satipaṭṭhāna. During the satipaṭṭhāna practice of such a person, certain types of mental formations such as consciousness rooted in greed *(lobhamūlacitta)* accompanied by the four components of false view, and consciousness rooted in delusion *(mohamūlacitta)* accompanied by doubt, have already been abandoned completely and will never arise again. Such an unwholesome mind and its mental concomitants, which lead to lower rebirths, are completely destroyed by the wisdom of the stream-enterer. For the noble person, the rising-falling phenomenon appears more refined and subtler than for ordinary people. Such wisdom is therefore called *asāthārana ñāṇa* i.e., a wisdom that appears only to the noble one, not to an ordinary person.

The path leading to the state of the once-returner is similar to that of the stream-enterer except for the much subtler rising-falling of aggregates and the stronger controlling faculties. Those who are entering sakadāgāmimagga are already enlightened ones, whereas those entering sotāpattimagga are still ordinary people. Therefore, for the three higher levels of enlightenment, the thirteenth of the sixteen vipassanā insights, gotrabhū ñāṇa, is described as *vodāna,* which means "higher subtlety."

If the force of the two enlightenment components, tranquility and insight, is equally balanced, and the continuous flow of rising and falling of aggregates that appears clearly has finally ceased for the second time, wisdom leading to the attainment of sakadāgāmī (once-returner) occurs. It will eradicate the same lower fetters as in the case of sotāpatti (stream-enterer). The additional quality of the once-returner is the ability to further reduce desire, ill-will and ignorance, making those defilements much weaker.

Wisdom leading to the State of the Non-Returner (Anāgāmimaggañāṇa)

For those noble ones whose vehicle is solely vipassanā, or "insight meditation," their attainment of jhāna will happen only when maggañāṇa occurs. In other words, they attain jhāna at the very moment they attain enlightenment. Then, after having reached the enlightenment level of the once-returner, the systematic development of jhāna will gradually become established. As the mind keeps practicing until it becomes fully proficient in the first jhāna, the second, third and fourth jhāna will be attained respectively without difficulty. Thus, for the once-returners, the rising and falling of the aggregates that are the objects of their contemplation also include the rising-falling of the components of rūpajhānas.

When the once-returner has fully cultivated the four rūpajhānas to the point where both powers of tranquility and wisdom are equal in strength and well-balanced for the purpose of enlightenment, the continuity of the rising-falling aggregates **ceases completely** for the third time. Wisdom leading to the state of the non-returner (anāgāmimaggañāṇa) occurs and completely destroys two more fetters, namely lust and ill-will — these hindrances will be uprooted and disappear forever.

When both maggañāṇa and phalañāṇa have come to an end, subliminal consciousness (bhavaṅgacitta) arises and passes away. Finally the reviewing wisdom (paccavekkhana ñāṇa) of the anāgāmī occurs... and one realizes that one will never return to this world again!

The concentration power and faculty of a noble person of this third level is fully developed. When the four rūpajhānas have been perfected, attaining the other four absorption concentrations of the formless realm is easier.

As the lower fetters *(orambhāgiyasaṃyojana)* which bend and bind the mind to cling to and crave for sensual pleasure, i.e, form, sound, odor, taste and tangible objects, by now have been completely destroyed due to the power of anāgāmimaggañāṇa, the rise and fall of aggregates which appear consists mostly of components of rūpajhāna and arūpajhāna.

The Buddha's words in the *Satipaṭṭhāna Sutta*, *Nīvaraṇapabba* sub-section reads: "He discerns clearly how there is the abandoning of the arisen sensual desires, repulsion and remorse once they have arisen. And he discerns how there is no further appearance in the future of unarisen sensual desires, repulsion and remorse."[111]

This above mentioned contemplation of Dhamma appears vividly to an anāgāmī by direct knowledge.

111 Ibid.

Wisdom Leading to the State of the Fully Enlightened (Arahattamaggañāṇa)

Any remaining defilements and cravings which still draw the mind of the anāgāmī to enjoy the rising-falling aggregates are those elements pertaining to the realms of form and formlessness, since defilements and cravings at the level of sensuality have been completely destroyed. Therefore, if a noble person of this level fails to attain the final state of enlightenment within the present lifetime, he or she is bound to be reborn in *suddhāvāsabhūmi,* which is the pure abode in the realm of form (see footnote 98 in this chapter) where non-returners are reborn, and will attain the final state of enlightenment there.

The aggregates pertaining to the form and formless spheres that keep rising and falling are the objects of contemplation for the anāgāmī. When the power of concentration and wisdom for enlightenment reaches its culmination, the continuity of the rising and falling of aggregates ceases for the fourth and final time. Wisdom leading to the state of the fully-enlightened (arahattamaggañāṇa) arises to destroy all the higher fetters. Any remaining defilements which had not yet been eradicated by the previous maggañāṇas are now destroyed completely. The enlightened noble person of the fourth category is the one who can maintain perfect mindfulness in the real sense of the term.

The Wheel and Wisdom of Liberation
(Chakrabhava — Vimuttiñāṇadassana)

After the mind emerges from the state of enlightenment, subliminal consciousness (bhavaṅgacitta) continues to rise and fall away. Even though the mind has come out from the nibbānic state, its transcending characteristics still remain very distinct when external objects contact the internal sense doors. A wave of light contacting the nerves at the eyes, a wave of sound with the nerves at the ears, a wave of odor with the nerves at the nose, a wave of taste with the nerves at the tongue, a wave of cold, heat, hardness and softness with the nerves at the body, a wave of mental formations with the heart. All these waves of cognizable objects which meet the corresponding contact point of the nerves will dash to the heart consciousness. There and then, they simply cease, evaporating into emptiness. Then new waves occur in the same manner — making contact and then melting away. These waves of cognizable objects appear like a wheel or chakra revolving around the contact points of the nerves and heart consciousness.

During the period in which the state of the wheel distinctly occurs, the mind remains beyond all mental formations and all conventional truth. At a certain point, even the state of the wheel itself ceases. Wisdom which does not depend on thought occurs. **The round of rebirth is now finished, Holy-faring is complete, there is no further task for one to do, one has now fully attained liberation which is beyond all defilements, beyond the loop of Māra and Death**. Thunder roars with the power of celestial beings.

The Buddha's sayings in *Anguttaranikāya*, *Pārichattaka Sutta* reads: "What time the Ariyan disciple, by destroying the cankers… enters and abides in full realization… his flowers are in full bloom, like the celestial coral tree of the devas of the Thirty."

"Then the earth devas utter a shout: 'This reverend sir called so and so, living the life of faith of such a reverend one, gone forth from such a village or market-town, has destroyed the cankers… and dwells in full realization…!'

"Hearing the shout of the earth devas, the company of the four royal devas… the devas of the Thirty… the Yāma devas… the Tusita devas… the devas who delight in creating… the devas who have power over others' creations… and the devas of Brahmā's retinue roll back the shout: 'This reverend sir, living the life of faith, gone forth from such a village or from such a market-town into the homeless life, has, by the destruction of the cankers, entered and there abides in that state of emancipation of the mind and wisdom which is free of the cankers, having come to know and realize this state fully for himself, even in this present life.'

"Thus in an instant, thus in a moment, the sound soars up to Brahmā's heaven.

"This is the progressive power of a monk who has destroyed the cankers."[112]

Sea of Saṃsāra

The round of rebirth (saṃsāra), of which the beginning and the end cannot be found, is the world of the perpetual cycle of dying and becoming on various planes of existence.

Those beings who have been born are all struggling in the sea of pleasure, suffering, hope, disappointment, parting, illness, aging, and finally death. If the causes and effects are not finished off, there will still be a further rebirth. One then has to encounter

---

112 A.N., vol. 4, The Book of the Sevens (7,7,65), p. 78-80, Hare.

further a great storm in the sea of suffering. Such is the endless cycle.

It is as if all beings are floating in the middle of a great sea. Every single life struggles to reach the shore to avoid perils. However, they cannot find the shore as their eyes are covered by years of ignorance. From one life to another, going through so many deaths and births, they are still struggling in the sea.

Amidst the great sea full of darkness and dangers, only the light of wisdom can lead beings safely to the shore.

Satipaṭṭhāna is the training for the mind to develop wisdom. It is the only vchicle, the marvelous and perfect vehicle, which releases beings from the whirlpool of suffering where they have been struggling for so long.

In *Abhidhammapiṭaka*, under the section of *Puggalapaññatti*, volume 36, item 203, *Sattapuggala*, the Buddha classified people into seven groups:[113]

1. **Those who have drowned under the water, and remain under the water.** This refers to those who are full of unwholesome deeds, or dominated mainly by darkness.

2. **Those who emerge to the surface of the water and later sink down again.** This refers to those who practice the five wholesomc dccds, i.e., faith, moral shame, moral dread, effort and wisdom. These five factors cnable a person to reap the culmination of benefits. However, unable to maintain them, they are faced with decadence.

---

113 Translated from *Abhidhamma Piṭaka* (in Thai), Puggalapaññatti, vol. 36, no. 203, The Recitation of Tipiṭaka under the Royal Patronage, B.E. 2530, Department of Religious Affair, Ministry of Education, Bangkok.

3. **Those who emerge to the surface of the water and stay still.** This refers to those who practice the five wholesome deeds and then stop short there, not going higher or lower.

4. **Those who emerge to the surface of the water and look around.** This refers to those whose minds are born of the five wholesome deeds and who are able to improve themselves and achieve the higher transcendental state, namely the state in which one is able to destroy defilements and fetters completely, and attain stream-entry. They will surely attain the highest level of enlightenment where all suffering ceases. They will be reborn, not exceeding seven times. Though still bound to the cycle of rebirths, they will not go down to the lower states of existence since the door to these states has been shut completely to them.

The analogy has it that amidst the darkness of ignorance, a bolt of lightning appears, for the first time enabling one to know the location of the shore.

5. **Those who emerge to the surface and swim to the shore.** This refers to the once-returners who experience the second lightning of wisdom, see clearly the shore of nibbāna and struggle towards it. At this level, like the stream-enterer, they can destroy three fetters and are able to extinguish lust, ill-will, and ignorance of the coarse level. This kind of person will remain in the cycle of rebirth one more time before reaching the shore safely.

6. **Those who emerge to the surface and swim to the shallow area where their feet can reach the ground.** This refers to the non-returners who have attained the third enlightenment or have experienced the third lightning of wisdom. They have destroyed the five lower fetters entirely, and if they do not attain arahantship in this lifetime, they will be born on the suddhāvās plane where they will attain the final enlightenment.

7. **Those who emerge to the surface, swim to the shore and reach the land.** This refers to the fully enlightened. Arahattamaggañāṇa appears like a bolt of lightning, eradicating completely all remaining defilements. The veil of ignorance is removed. The wheel of saṃsāra is absolutely destroyed. One has now fully attained liberation by the culmination of both concentrative power and wisdom.

Those Who Transcend the States of Misery

"Once, when the Exalted One was staying near Sāvatthī at Jeta Grove.., the Ven. Sārīputta dressed before noon and, with bowl and robe, went towards Sāvatthi. Then thought he: 'Too early is it yet to go about for alms...suppose I were to go and visit the park of the wanderers of other views.' So the Ven. Sārīputta went to their park and, after exchanging with them the usual compliments, sat down at one side.

"Now at that time this happened to be the topic of their talk: 'All who die with some attached remainder are not altogether freed from hell, rebirth in the womb of an animal, the realm of ghosts, nor from the untoward way, the ill way, the abyss, hell.'

"Ven. Sārīputta neither applauded, nor disparaged their speech, but without comment rose from his seat and departed, saying to himself, 'I will learn the truth of the matter from the Exalted One.'

"So, the Ven. Sārīputta...when he had returned therefrom and eaten his meal, visited the Exalted One and, after saluting, sat down at one side. So seated, [he told the Exalted One all that had taken place].

"Sārīputta, some of these wanderers of other views are fools and without understanding...'

"Sārīputta, there are these nine persons, who, when they die with some attached remainder, are altogether freed from hell, rebirth in the womb of an animal, the realm of ghosts, the untoward way....hell. What nine?'

"Consider, Sārīputta, the person who is accomplished in the precepts, accomplished in concentration, but not in wisdom-he destroys the five lower fetters and becomes **[the non-returner who is destined to enter nibbāna before his middle age]**. This, Sārīputta, is the first person, who, dying with some attached remainder, is altogether freed from hell..."

"Again, Sārīputta, consider the person who is accomplished in the precepts, accomplished in concentration, but not in wisdom - he destroys the five lower fetters and becomes **[the non-returner who is destined to enter nibbāna after his middle age and before his departure]**. This, Sārīputta, is the second person, who, dying with some attached remainder, is altogether freed from hell..."

"Again, Sārīputta, consider the person who is accomplished in the precepts, accomplished in concentration, but not in wisdom - he destroys the five lower fetters and becomes **[the non-returner who will enter nibbāna without great effort]**. This, Sārīputta, is the third person, who, dying with some attached remainder, is altogether freed from hell..."

"Again, Sārīputta, consider the person who is accomplished in the precepts, accomplished in concentration, but not in wisdom - he destroys the five lower fetters and becomes **[the non-returner who will enter nibbāna with great effort]**. This, Sārīputta, is the fourth person, who, dying with some attached remainder, is altogether freed from hell..."

"'Again, Sārīputta, consider the person who is accomplished in the precepts, accomplished in concentration, but not in wisdom - he destroys the five lower fetters and becomes **[the non-returner who is likely to enter the akaniṭṭhabrahma, the realm of the highest heaven of the supreme brahmas]**. This, Sārīputta, is the fifth person, who, dying with some attached remainder, is altogether freed from hell..."

"Again, Sārīputta, consider the person who is accomplished in the precepts, but not in concentration, nor in wisdom-by destroying the three fetters and reducing lust, hatred and delusion, **he becomes a once-returner, who returns to this world again only once** and makes the end of ill. This, Sārīputta, is the sixth person...

"Again, Sārīputta, consider the person who is accomplished in the precepts, but not in concentration, nor in wisdom - by destroying the three fetters he becomes a once-issuer **[stream enterer born again only once]**, and on being born into the state of man just once, he makes an end of ill. This, Sārīputta, is the seventh person...

"Again, Sārīputta, consider the person who is accomplished in the precepts, is moderately successful in concentration, is moderately successful in wisdom - by destroying the three fetters **he becomes a [stream-enterer] running on, faring on through two or three clans,** [and] makes an end of ill. This, Sārīputta, is the eighth person...

"Again, Sārīputta, consider the person who is accomplished in the precepts, and is moderately successful in concentration, moderately successful in wisdom - by destroying the three fetters, **he becomes one who will be reborn seven times at most,** and running on, faring on among devas and men for seven times at most, he makes an end of ill. This, Sārīputta, is the ninth person, who, dying with some attached remainder, is altogether freed from hell...

"Not until now, Sārīputta, has this Dhamma discourse been declared to monk or nun, to layman or laywoman. And why? Lest after hearing this Dhamma discourse, they bring on themselves the habit of idleness. Moreover, Sārīputta, this Dhamma discourse was only declared by me because of my being questioned."[114]

❁❁❁❁❁❁❁❁❁

Better than sole sovereignty over the earth,
better than going to heaven,
better even than lordship over all the worlds
is the supramundane
Fruition of Stream Entrance.

❁❁❁❁❁❁❁❁❁

114 A.N., vol. 4, The Book of the Nines, p. 252-254, Hare.

Better it is to live
one day seeing the rise and fall of things
than to live a hundred years
without ever seeing
the rise and fall of things.

Swans fly on the path of the sun,

Magicians pass through the air.

The wise go forth out of the world

Having conquered Māra with all his troops.

CHAPTER VI

The State of Nibbāna

The State of Nibbāna

"Venerable Sir, it is said, 'the removal of lust, the removal of hatred, the removal of delusion.' Of what now, Venerable Sir, is this the designation?"

"This, monk, is a designation for **the element of nibbāna: the removal of lust, the removal of hatred, the removal of delusion.** The destruction of the taints is spoken of in that way."[115]

The End of Suffering

"For him who clings, there is wavering; for him who clings not, there is no wavering. Wavering not being, there is calm; calm being, there is no bending. Bending not being, there is no coming-and-going [to birth]; coming and going not being, there is no decease-and-rebirth. Decease-and-rebirth not being, there is no 'here' or 'yonder' nor anything between the two. This indeed is the end of ill."[116]

115 S.N., Mahāvagga, Maggasaṃyutta (45,1,7), p. 1528, Bhikkhu Bodhi.
116 The Minor Anthologies, Udāna, Pāṭaligāma (8,4), p. 68, Woodward.

Two Conditions of Nibbāna

"This was said by the Exalted one...

"Monks, there are these two conditions of nibbāna. What two? The condition of nibbāna with the basis still remaining and that without basis. Of what sort, monks, is the condition of nibbāna which has the basis still remaining? Herein, monks, a monk is arahant, one who has destroyed the cankers, who has lived the life, done what was to be done, laid down the burden, won the goal, worn out the fetter of becoming, one released by perfect knowledge. In him the five sense-faculties still remain, through which, as they have not yet departed, he experiences sensation pleasant and unpleasant, undergoes pleasure-and-pain. In him, the end of lust, malice and delusion, monks, is called 'the condition of nibbāna with the basis still remaining.'

"And of what sort, monks, is the condition of nibbāna that is without basis?

"Herein a monk is arahant...released by perfect knowledge, but in him in this very life all things that are sensed have no delight for him, they have become cool. This is called 'the condition of nibbāna without basis.' So, monks, these are two conditions of nibbāna."[117]

---

117 The Minor Anthologies, Itivuttaka, The Twos (2,2,6), p. 143-4, Woodward.

Figure 6: Classification of Noble Ones[118]

Types of Noble people	Achieved training	Eradicated fetters	Eradicated hindrances
Sotāpanna	Perfect moral conduct Adequate concentration Adequate wisdom	Delusion of self Doubt Adherence to rules and rituals	Doubt
Sakadāgāmī	Perfect moral conduct Adequate concentration Adequate wisdom	Lust reduced Aversion reduced Delusion reduced	Sensual desire reduced Ill will reduced
Anāgāmī	Perfect moral conduct Perfect concentration Adequate wisdom	Lust Aversion	Sensual desire Ill will Restlessness and anxiety
Arahant	Perfect moral conduct Perfect concentration Perfect wisdom	Attachment to the form realms Attachment to the formless realms Conceit Restlessness Ignorance	Sloth and torpor Restlessness and anxiety

118 Adapted from A.N. , The Book of the Threes (3.88,3.89), Sikkha Sutta 1 and 2, Bhikkhu Thanissaro, ATI.

Two Types of Fully Enlightened Ones: *Paññāvimutti* and *Ubhatobhāgavimutti*

"Regarding the classification of the fully enlightened ones, we should understand that the term 'paññāvimutti,' despite being generally understood as liberation resulted from wisdom only, actually includes *'cetovimutti'* or liberation generated from concentrative power. To attain liberation through wisdom necessarily includes attaining concentrative power. But 'paññāvimutti' types rely only on a sufficient degree of concentration necessary for liberation."[119]

Therefore, every fully enlightened person must attain both paññāvimutti and cetovimutti. These two terms always appear together in many texts dealing with the attainment of liberation. For example "by destroying the cankers, [one] enters and abides in the canker-free mind-emancipation [cetovimutti], insight-emancipation [paññāvimutti], realizing this here and now entirely by his own knowledge."[120] Cetovimutti is the result of concentration while paññāvimutti is the outcome of vipassanā[121] According to the commentaries, these two factors must occur simultaneously both at the magga and phala level.[122]

"Monks, these two are *vijjābhāgiyadhamma* [dhammas supporting knowledge], namely samatha and vipassanā."[123]

"Two things, O monks, partake of supreme knowledge. What two? Tranquility and insight.

---

119 *Buddhadhamma* (Thai version), p. 311.

120 A.N., vol. 3, The Book of The Sixes (6,1,2), p. 203, Hare.

121 Commentaries on Khuddhaka Nikāya, Itivuttaka, Paramatthadipani (Thai version) p. 322.

122 Commentaries on Khuddhaka Nikāya, Udāna, Paramatthadipani (Thai version) p. 221.

123 Commentaries on Anguttara Nikāya, Manorathapurani, (Thai version) 2/33.

"If tranquility is developed, what benefit does it bring? The mind becomes developed. And what is the benefit of a developed mind? All lust is abandoned.

"If insight is developed, what benefit does it bring? Wisdom becomes developed. And what is the benefit of developed wisdom? All ignorance is abandoned.

"A mind defiled by lust is not freed, and wisdom defiled by ignorance cannot develop. Thus, monks, **through the fading away of lust there is liberation of mind [cetovimutti], and through the fading away of ignorance there is liberation by wisdom [paññāvimutti]**."[124]

In conclusion, both paññāvimutti and cetovimutti must arise to make liberation complete.

Before mentioning ubhatobhāgavimutti, it is appropriate to provide a good example from the Pāli Canon of one who is a bodily witness (from *Kāyasakkhī Sutta*) and one who is wisdom-freed (from *Paññāvimutti Sutta)*.

The Bodily Witness
(Kāyasakkhi)

"'Bodily witness, bodily witness,' it is said. To what extent is one described by the Blessed One as a bodily witness?

"There is the case, my friend, where a monk, withdrawn from sensuality, withdrawn from unskillful qualities, enters and remains in the first jhāna: rapture and pleasure born from withdrawal, accompanied by directed thought and evaluation. He remains touching with his body in whatever way there is an opening

124 A.N.,The Chapter of the Twos (14), p. 42, Bhikkhu Nyanaponika and Bhikkhu Bodhi.

there.[125] It is to this extent that one is described by the Blessed One as a **bodily witness**, though with a sequel.

"Furthermore, with the stilling of directed thoughts and evaluations, he enters and remains in the second jhāna... the third jhāna... the fourth jhāna... the [realm] of [boundless]space... the [realm] of [boundless] consciousness... the [realm] of nothingness... the [realm] of neither perception nor non-perception. He remains **touching with his body** in whatever way there is an opening there. It is to this extent that one is described by the Blessed One as a bodily witness, though with a sequel."[126]

The Released through Discernment (Paññāvimutti)

"'Released through discernment, released through discernment,' it is said. To what extent is one described by the Blessed One as released through discernment?

"There is the case, my friend, where a monk, withdrawn from sensuality, withdrawn from unskillful qualities, enters and remains in the first jhāna: rapture and pleasure born from withdrawal, accompanied by directed thought and evaluation. And he **knows it through discernment.** It is to this extent that one is described by the Blessed One as released through discernment, though with a sequel."[127]

---

125 Refined bodily experiences are dominant in the case of a bodily witness when he or she attains higher successive levels of jhāna and enlightenment, whereas for a paññāvimutti person, wisdom is dominant.
126 A.N., The Book of The Nines (9.43), Bhikkhu Thanissaro, ATI.
127 Ibid (9.44).

The Released Both Ways (Ubhatobhāgavimutti)

"'Released both ways, released both ways,' it is said. To what extent is one described by the Blessed One as released both ways?

"There is the case, my friend, where a monk, withdrawn from sensuality, withdrawn from unskillful qualities, enters and remains in the first jhāna: rapture and pleasure born from withdrawal, accompanied by directed thought and evaluation. He remains **touching with his body** in whatever way there is an opening there, and he **knows it through discernment**. It is to this extent that one is described by the Blessed One as released both ways, though with a sequel.

"Furthermore, with the stilling of directed thoughts and evaluations, he enters and remains in the second jhāna... the third jhāna... the fourth jhāna... the [realm] of [boundless] space... the [realm] of [boundless] consciousness... the [realm] of nothingness..."[128]

Two Kinds of Genius

"Thus have I heard. On one occasion the Venerable Mahācunda was dwelling at Sāhajāti among the Ceti people. There he addressed the monks thus:

"Friends, there are monks who are keen on Dhamma and they disparage those monks who are meditators, saying: 'Look at those monks! They think, **'We are meditating, we are meditating!'** And so they meditate to and meditate fro, meditate up and meditate down! **What, then, do they meditate about and why do they meditate?'** Thereby neither these monks keen on Dhamma nor the meditators will be pleased, and they will not be practicing for

128 Ibid (9.45).

the welfare and happiness of the multitude, for the good of the multitude, for the welfare and happiness of devas and humans.

"Then, friends, there are meditating monks who disparage the monks who are keen on Dhamma, saying: 'Look at those monks! They think 'We are Dhamma-experts, we are Dhamma-experts!' And therefore they are conceited, puffed up and vain; they are talkative and voluble. They are devoid of mindfulness and clear comprehension, and they lack concentration; their thoughts wander and their senses are uncontrolled. **What then makes them Dhamma-experts, why and how are they Dhamma-experts?'** Thereby neither these meditating monks nor those keen on Dhamma will be pleased, and they will not be practicing for the welfare and happiness of the multitude, for the good of the multitude, for the welfare and happiness of devas and humans.

"There are Dhamma-experts who praise only monks who are also Dhamma-experts but not those who are meditators. And there are meditators who praise only those monks who are also meditators but not those who are Dhamma-experts. Thereby neither of them will be pleased, and they will not be practicing for the welfare and happiness of the multitude, for the good of the multitude, for the welfare and happiness of devas and humans.

"Therefore, friends, you should train yourselves thus: 'Though we ourselves are Dhamma-experts, we will praise also those monks who are meditators.' And why? **Such outstanding persons are rare in the world who have personal [bodily] experience of the deathless element [nibbāna].**

"And the other monks, too, should train themselves thus: 'Though we ourselves are meditators, we will praise also those monks who are Dhamma-experts.' And why? **Such outstanding**

persons are rare in the world who can by their wisdom clearly understand a difficult subject."[129]

The Present Dwelling of the Enlightened One

"There are, O monks, these ten noble abodes where the noble ones abided in the past, where they abide at present, and where they will abide in the future. What ten?

Here, monks, a monk has abandoned five factors, possesses six factors, has a single guard, has a fourfold support, has driven away the many separate truths, has given up seeking, has clarified his thoughts, has calmed down the bodily formation, and has become well liberated in mind and well liberated by wisdom.

(1) And how has **a monk abandoned five factors**? Here, monks, a monk has abandoned sensual desire, ill-will, sloth and torpor, restlessness and worry, and doubt. Thus he has abandoned five factors.

(2) And how does **a monk possess six factors**? Here, monks, having seen a form with the eye, a monk is neither elated nor dejected but dwells equanimous, mindful and clearly comprehending. And so too when he hears a sound with the ear, smells an odor with the nose, savors a taste with the tongue, contacts a tactile object with the body, or cognizes a mind-object with the mind. In this way he possesses six factors.

(3) And how does **a monk have a single guard**? Here, monks, a monk possesses a mind guarded by mindfulness. In this way he has a single guard.

(4) And how does **a monk have a fourfold support**? Here,

129 A.N., The Chapter of the Sixes (125), p. 163-4, Bhikkhu Nyaponika and Bhikkhu Bodhi.

monks, a monk uses some things after reflection, endures some things after reflection, avoids some things after reflection, and dispels some things after reflection. In this way a monk has a fourfold support.

(5) And how has **a monk driven away the many separate truths**? Here, monks, there are many separate truths held by divers ascetics and brahmins, such as: 'The world is eternal' or 'The world is not eternal'; 'The world is finite' or 'The world is infinite'; 'The soul is one thing and the body another' or 'The soul and the body are the same'; 'The Tathāgata exists after death' or 'The Tathāgata does not exist after death' or 'The Tathāgata both exists and does not exist after death' or 'The Tathāgata neither exists nor does not exist after death.' A monk has discarded all these, driven them away, renounced and rejected them, released, abandoned and relinquished them. In this way a monk has driven away the many separate truths.

(6) And how has **a monk given up seeking**? Here, monks, a monk has abandoned the search for sensual pleasures and the search for becoming and has suspended the search for a holy life. In this way a monk has given up seeking.

(7) And how has **a monk clarified his thoughts**? Here, monks, a monk has abandoned sensual thoughts, thoughts of ill-will and thoughts of violence. In this way a monk has clarified his thoughts.

(8) And how has **a monk calmed down the bodily formation**? Here, monks, with the abandoning of pleasure and pain, and with the previous passing away of joy and sadness, a monk enters and dwells in the fourth jhāna, which is neither painful nor pleasant and includes the purification of mindfulness by equanimity. In this way a monk has calmed down the bodily formation.

(9) And how is **a monk well liberated in mind**? Here, monks, a monk's mind is liberated from lust, hatred and delusion. In this way a monk is well liberated in mind.

(10) And how is **a monk well liberated by wisdom**? Here, monks, a monk understands: 'Lust, hatred and delusion have been abandoned by me, cut off at the root, made barren like palm-tree stumps, obliterated so that they are no more subject to arise in the future.' In this way a monk is well liberated by wisdom.

"Whatever noble ones in **the past**, O monks, abided in noble abodes, all abided in just these ten noble abodes. Whatever noble ones in **the future** will abide in noble abodes, all will abide in just these ten noble abodes. Whatever noble ones **at present** abide in noble abodes, all abide in just these ten noble abodes.

These, monks, are the ten noble abodes in which the noble ones abided in the past, abide at present, and will abide in the future."[130]

130 A.N. The Chapter of the Tens (187), p. 241-2, Bhikkhu Nyaponika and Bhikkhu Bodhi.

The fever of passion
exists not for him
who has completed the journey,
who is sorrowless and wholly set free,
and has broken all ties.

The sun shines by day,
the moon shines by night.
The warrior shines in armor,
the holy man shines in meditation.

CHAPTER VII

Major Dhamma

The One Thing

"There is, Ānanda, one thing which, when developed and cultivated, fulfills four things; and four things which, when developed and cultivated, fulfill seven things; and seven things which, when developed and cultivated, fulfill two things.

"Concentration by mindfulness of breathing, Ānanda, is the one thing which, when developed and cultivated, fulfills the four establishments of mindfulness. The four establishments of mindfulness, when developed and cultivated, fulfill the seven factors of enlightenment. The seven factors of enlightenment, when developed and cultivated, fulfill true knowledge and liberation."[131]

"Therefore, if a monk wishes 'May I enters and dwell in the first…,second…third…and fourth jhāna… if a monk wishes 'May I completely transcend the [realm of boundless] space… the [realm of boundless] consciousness…the realm of nothingness… enter and dwell in the realm of neither-perception-nor-non-perception…then completely transcend it, **this same concentration by mindfulness of breathing should be closely attended to.**"[132]

---

131 S.N., Mahāvagga, Ānāpānasaṃyutta (54,2,13), p. 1780-81, Bhikkhu Bodhi.
132 Ibid. (54,1,8), p. 1770-71.

Mindfulness of Breathing Highly Acclaimed by the Buddha

"Monks, this concentration by mindfulness of breathing, when developed and cultivated, is peaceful and sublime, an ambrosial pleasant dwelling, and it disperses and quells right on the spot evil unwholesome states whenever they arise.

"Just as, monks, in the last month of the hot season, when a mass of dust and dirt has swirled up, a great rain cloud out of season disperses it and quells it on the spot, so too concentration by mindfulness of breathing, when developed and cultivated, is peaceful and sublime, an ambrosial pleasant dwelling, and it disperses and quells on the spot evil unwholesome states whenever they arise."[133]

"If anyone, monks, speaking rightly could say of anything: 'It is a noble dwelling, a divine dwelling, the Tathāgata's dwelling,' it is of concentration by mindfulness of breathing that one could rightly say this.

"Monks, those **monks who are trainees**, who have not attained their mind's ideal, who dwell aspiring for the unsurpassed security from bondage: for them concentration by mindfulness of breathing, when developed and cultivated, leads to the destruction of the taints. Those **monks who are arahants**, whose taints are destroyed, who have lived the holy life, done what had to be done, laid down the burden, reached their own goal, utterly destroyed the fetters of existence, those completely liberated through final knowledge: for them concentration by mindfulness of breathing, when developed and cultivated, leads to a pleasant dwelling in this very life and to mindfulness and clear comprehension."[134]

---

133 Ibid. (54,1,9), p. 1774.
134 Ibid. (54,2,11), p. 1778-9.

Dwelling Prior to Enlightenment

"I too, monks, before my enlightenment, while I was still a bodhisatta, not yet fully enlightened, generally dwelt in this dwelling. While I generally dwelt in this dwelling, neither my body nor my eyes became fatigued and my mind, by not clinging, was liberated from the taints.

"Therefore, monks, if a monk wishes: 'May neither my body nor my eyes become fatigued and may my mind, by not clinging, be liberated from the taints,' this same concentration by mindfulness of breathing should be closely attended to."[135]

After the Enlightenment

"On one occasion the Blessed One was dwelling at Icchānangala in the Icchānangala Wood. There the Blessed One addressed the monks thus:

"Monks, I wish to go into seclusion for three months. I should not be approached by anyone except the one who brings me almsfood.

"Then, when those three months had passed, the Blessed One emerged from seclusion and addressed the monks thus:

"Monks, if wanderers of other sects ask you: 'In what dwelling friends, did the Blessed One generally dwell during the rains residence?' Being asked thus, you should answer those wanderers thus: 'During the rains residence, friends, **the Blessed One generally dwelt in the concentration by mindfulness of breathing**.'"'[136]

---

135 Ibid. (54,1,8), p. 1770.
136 Ibid. (54,2,11), p. 1778.

❊❊❊❊❊❊❊❊

Rāhula, that is how mindfulness of breathing
is developed and cultivated,
so that it is of great fruit and great benefit.

When mindfulness of breathing
is developed and cultivated in this way,
even the final in-breaths and out-breaths
are known as they cease, not unknown.

Benefits of Mindfulness of Breathing

"When, monks, mindfulness of breathing has been developed and cultivated in this way, one of two fruits may be expected: either final knowledge in this very life or, if there is a residue of clinging, the state of non-returning."[137]

Dhamma Supporting Mindfulness of Breathing

"Endowed with...[these] qualities, a monk pursuing mindfulness of breathing will in no long time penetrate the Unprovoked [release].

"He lives in the wilderness, in an isolated dwelling place.

"He is a person who imposes only a little [on others]: one of few duties and projects, easy to support, easily contented with the requisites of life.

"He is a person who eats only a little food, committed to not indulging his stomach.

"He is a person of only a little sloth, committed to wakefulness.

"He gets to hear at will, easily and without difficulty, talk that is truly sobering and conducive to the opening of awareness: talk on modesty, contentment, seclusion, non-entanglement, arousing persistence, virtue, concentration, discernment, release, and the knowledge and vision of release.

"He is a person of much learning, who has retained what he has heard, has stored what he has heard. Whatever teachings are admirable in the beginning, admirable in the middle, admirable in the end, that — in their meaning and expression — proclaim the holy life that is entirely complete and pure: those he has listened to often, retained, discussed, accumulated, examined with his mind, and well-penetrated in terms of his views.

---

137 S.N., Mahāvagga, Ānāpānasaṃyutta (54,1,5), p. 1767, Bhikkhu Bodhi.

"He reflects on the mind as it is released.

"Endowed with these...qualities, a monk pursuing mindfulness of breathing will in no long time penetrate the Unprovoked." [138]

Discourse on Mindfulness of Breathing *(Ānāpānasati Sutta)*

"Thus have I heard. On one occasion the Blessed One was living at Sāvatthī in the Eastern Park, in the Palace of Migāra's Mother, together with many very well-known elder disciples - the venerable Sāriputta, the venerable Mahā Moggallāna, the venerable Mahā Kassapa, the venerable Mahā Kaccāna, the venerable Mahā Kotthita, the venerable Māha Kappina, the venerable Maha Cunda, the venerable Anuruddha, the venerable Revata, the venerable Ānanda, and other very well-known elder disciples.

"Now on that occasion elder monks had been teaching and instructing new monks; some elder monks had been teaching and instructing ten new monks, some elder monks had been teaching and instructing twenty... thirty... forty new monks. And the new monks, taught and instructed by the elder monks, had achieved successive stages of high distinction.

"On that occasion - the *uposatha*[139] day of the fifteenth, on the full-moon night of the *pavāranā*[140] ceremony - the Blessed One was seated in the open surrounded by the *sangha* of monks. Then,

138 A.N., The Book of the Fives (5.96,5.97,5.98), Sutadhara Sutta, Kathā Sutta, Araññа Sutta, Bhikkhu Thanissaro, ATI.

139 The day for special meetings of the order and for the recitation of *pātimokkha* (the 227 disciplinary rules binding monks).

140 The ecclesiastical ceremony at the end of the rains retreat, in which monks invite one another to speak of any offenses or unbecoming behavior they have seen, heard or suspected to have been committed during the rains.

surveying the silent sangha of monks, he addressed them thus:

"Monks, I am content with this progress. My mind is content with this progress. So arouse still more energy to attain the unattained, to achieve the unachieved, to realize the unrealized. I shall wait here at Sāvatthī for the komudī (lotus flower) full moon of the fourth month.

"The monks of the countryside heard: 'The Blessed One will wait there at Savatthī for the komudī full moon of the fourth month.' And the monks of the countryside left in due course for Savatthī to see the Blessed One.

"And elder monks still more intensively taught and instructed new monks; somc elder monks taught and instructed ten new monks, some elder monks taught and instructed twenty... thirty... forty new monks. And the new monks, taught and instructed by the elder monks, achieved successive stages of high distinction.

"On that occasion - the uposatha day of the fifteenth, the full-moon night of the komudī full moon of the fourth month, the Blessed One was seated in the open surrounded by the sangha of monks. Then, surveying the silent sangha of monks, he addressed them thus:

"Monks, **this assembly is free from prattle, this assembly is free from chatter. It consists purely of heartwood**. Such is this sangha of monks, such is this assembly. Such an assembly as is worthy of gifts, worthy of hospitality, worthy of offerings, worthy of reverential salutation, an incomparable field of merit for the world - such is this sangha of monks, such is this assembly. Such an assembly that a small gift given to it becomes great and a great gift greater - such is this sangha of monks, such is this assembly. Such an assembly as is rare for the world to see - such is this sangha of monks, such is this assembly. Such an assembly as would be worth journeying many leagues with a travel-bag to see - such is this sangha of monks, such is this assembly.

"In this sangha of monks there are monks who are arahants with taints destroyed, who have lived the holy life, done what had to be done, laid down the burden, reached the true goal, destroyed the fetters of being, and are completely liberated through final knowledge - such monks are there in this sangha of monks.

"In this sangha of monks there are monks who, with the destruction of the five lower fetters, are due to reappear spontaneously [in the Pure Abodes] and there attain final nibbāna, without ever returning from that world - such monks are there in this sangha of monks.

"In this sangha of monks there are monks who, with the destruction of three fetters and with the attenuation of lust, hate, and delusion, are once-returners, returning once to this world to make an end of suffering - such monks are there in this sangha of monks.

"In this sangha of monks there are monks who, with the destruction of the three fetters, are stream-enterers, no longer subject to perdition, bound [for deliverance], headed for enlightenment - such monks are there in this sangha of monks.

"In this sangha of monks there are monks who abide devoted to the **development of the four foundations of mindfulness -** such monks are there in this sangha of monks. In this sangha of monks there are monks who abide devoted to the **development of the four right kinds of striving...of the four bases for spiritual power...of the five faculties...of the five powers**...of the **seven enlightenment factors...of the noble eightfold path** - such monks are there in this sangha of monks.

"In this sangha of monks there are monks who abide devoted to the **development of loving-kindness**...**of compassion**...**of appreciative joy**...of **equanimity**...of **the meditation on foulness**... of **the perception of impermanence** - such monks are there in this sangha of monks. In this sangha of monks there are monks who abide devoted to the **development of mindfulness of breathing.**

Mindfulness of Breathing

"Monks, when mindfulness of breathing is developed and cultivated, it is of great fruit and great benefit. When mindfulness of breathing is developed and cultivated, it fulfills the four foundations of mindfulness. When the four foundations of mindfulness are developed and cultivated, they fulfill the seven enlightenment factors. When the seven enlightenment factors are developed and cultivated, they fulfill true knowledge and deliverance.

"And how, monks, is mindfulness of breathing developed and cultivated, so that it is of great fruit and great benefit?

"Here a monk, gone to the forest or to the root of a tree or to an empty hut, sits down; having folded his legs crosswise, set his body erect, and established mindfulness in front of him, ever mindful he breathes in, mindful he breathes out.

Section One:
Contemplation on Body

"Breathing in long, he understands: 'I breathe in long'; or breathing out long, he understands: 'I breathe out long.' Breathing in short, he understands: 'I breathe in short'; or breathing out short, he understands: 'I breathe out short.' He trains thus: 'I shall breathe in experiencing the whole body of [breath]'; he trains thus: 'I shall breathe out experiencing the whole body [of breath].' He trains thus: 'I shall breathe in tranquilizing the bodily formation'; he trains thus: 'I shall breathe out tranquilizing the bodily formation.'

Section Two:
Contemplation on Feeling

"He trains thus: 'I shall breathe in experiencing rapture'; he trains thus: 'I shall breathe out experiencing rapture.' He trains thus: 'I shall breathe in experiencing pleasure'; he trains thus: 'I shall breathe out experiencing pleasure.' He trains thus: 'I shall breathe in experiencing the mental formation'; he trains thus: 'I shall breathe out experiencing the mental formation.' He trains thus: 'I shall breathe in tranquilizing the mental formation'; he trains thus: 'I shall breathe out tranquilizing the mental formation.'

Section Three:
Contemplation on the Mind

"He trains thus: 'I shall breathe in experiencing the mind'; he trains thus: 'I shall breathe out experiencing the mind.' He trains thus: 'I shall breathe in gladdening the mind'; he trains thus: 'I shall breathe out gladdening the mind.' He trains thus: 'I shall breathe in concentrating the mind'; he trains thus: 'I shall breathe out concentrating the mind.' He trains thus: 'I shall breathe in liberating the mind"; he trains thus: 'I shall breathe out liberating the mind.'

Section Four: Contemplation on Mind-Objects

"He trains thus: 'I shall breathe in contemplating impermanence'; he trains thus: 'I shall breathe out contemplating impermanence.' He trains thus: 'I shall breathe in contemplating fading away'; he trains thus: 'I shall breathe out contemplating fading away.' He trains thus: 'I shall breathe in contemplating cessation'; he trains thus: 'I shall breathe out contemplating cessation.' He trains thus: 'I shall breathe in contemplating relinquishment'; he trains thus: 'I shall breathe out contemplating relinquishment.'

"Monks, that is how mindfulness of breathing is developed and cultivated, so that it is of great fruit and great benefit.

Fulfillment of the Four Foundations of Mindfulness

"And how, monks, does mindfulness of breathing, developed and cultivated, fulfill the four foundations of mindfulness?

"1. Monks, on whatever occasion a monk, breathing in long, understands: 'I breathe in long' or breathing out long, understands: 'I breathe out long'; breathing in short, understands: 'I breathe in short' or breathing out short, understands: 'I breathe out short'; trains thus: 'I shall breathe in experiencing the whole body [of breath]'; trains thus: 'I shall breathe out experiencing the whole body [of breath]'; trains thus: 'I shall breathe in tranquilizing the bodily formation'; trains thus: 'I shall breathe out tranquilizing the bodily formation' - on that occasion a monk abides contemplating the body as a body, ardent, fully aware, and mindful, having put away covetousness and grief for the world. **I say that this is a certain body among thc bodies, namely, in-breathing and out-breathing**....

"2. Monks, on whatever occasion a monk trains thus: 'I shall breathe in experiencing rapture'; trains thus: I shall breathe out experiencing rapture'; trains thus: 'I shall breathe in experiencing pleasure'; trains thus: 'I shall breathe out experiencing pleasure'; trains thus: 'I shall breathe in experiencing the mental formation'; trains thus: 'I shall breathe out experiencing the mental formation'; trains thus: 'I shall breathe in tranquilizing the mental formation'; trains thus: 'I shall breathe out tranquilizing the mental formation' - on that occasion a monk abides contemplating feelings as feelings, ardent, fully aware, and mindful, having put away covetousness and grief for the world. **I say that this is a certain feeling among the feelings, namely, giving close attention to in-breathing and out-breathing....**

"3. Monks, on whatever occasion a monk trains thus: 'I shall breathe in experiencing the mind'; trains thus: 'I shall breathe out experiencing the mind'; trains thus: 'I shall breathe in gladdening the mind'; trains thus: 'I shall breathe out gladdening the mind'; trains thus: 'I shall breathe in concentrating the mind'; trains thus: 'I shall breathe out concentrating the mind'; trains thus: 'I shall breathe in liberating the mind'; trains thus: 'I shall breathe out liberating the mind' - on that occasion a monk abides contemplating mind as mind, ardent, fully aware, and mindful, having put away covetousness and grief for the world. I do not say that there is the development of mindfulness of breathing for one who is forgetful, who is not fully aware. **That is why on that occasion a monk abides contemplating mind as mind**, ardent, fully aware, and mindful, having put away covetousness and grief for the world.

"4. Monks, on whatever occasion a monk trains thus: 'I shall breathe in contemplating impermanence'; trains thus: 'I shall breathe out contemplating impermanence'; trains thus: 'I shall breathe in contemplating fading away'; trains thus: 'I shall breathe out contemplating fading away'; trains thus: 'I shall breathe in contemplating cessation'; trains thus: 'I shall breathe out contemplating cessation'; trains thus: 'I shall breathe in contemplating relinquishment'; trains thus: 'I shall breathe out contemplating relinquishment' - on that occasion **a monk abides contemplating mind-objects as mind-objects,** ardent, fully aware, and mindful, having put away covetousness and grief for the world.

"Having seen with wisdom the abandoning of covetousness and grief, he closely looks on with equanimity. That is why on that occasion a monk abides contemplating mind-objects as mind-objects, ardent, fully aware, and mindful, having put away covetousness and grief for the world.

"Monks, that is how mindfulness of breathing, developed and cultivated, fulfills the four foundations of mindfulness.

Fulfillment of the Seven Enlightenment Factors

"And how, monks, do the four foundations of mindfulness, developed and cultivated, fulfill the seven enlightenment factors?

"Monks, on whatever occasion a monk abides contemplating the body as a body, feelings as feelings, mind as mind, mind-objects as mind-objects, ardent, fully aware, and mindful, having put away covetousness and grief for the world - on that occasion unremitting mindfulness is established in him. On whatever occasion unremitting mindfulness is established in a monk - on that occasion the mindfulness enlightenment factor is aroused in him, and he develops it, and by development, it comes to fulfillment in him.

"Abiding thus mindful, he investigates and examines that state with wisdom and embarks upon a full inquiry into it. On whatever occasion, abiding thus mindful, a monk investigates and examines that state with wisdom and embarks upon a full inquiry into it - on that occasion the investigation-of-states enlightenment factor is aroused in him, and he develops it, and by development it comes to fulfillment in him.

"In one who investigates and examines that state with wisdom and embarks upon a full inquiry into it, tireless energy is aroused. On whatever occasion tireless energy is aroused in a monk who investigates and examines that state with wisdom and embarks upon a full inquiry into it - on that occasion the energy enlightenment factor is aroused in him, and he develops it, and by development it comes to fulfillment in him.

"In one who has aroused energy, unworldly rapture arises. On whatever occasion unworldly rapture arises in a monk who has aroused energy - on that occasion the rapture enlightenment factor is aroused in him, and he develops it, and by development it comes to fulfillment in him.

"In one who is rapturous, the body and the mind become serene. On whatever occasion the body and the mind become serene in a monk who is rapturous - on that occasion the serenity enlightenment factor is aroused in him, and he develops it, and by development it comes to fulfillment in him.

"In one whose body is serene and who feels pleasure, the mind becomes concentrated. On whatever occasion the mind becomes concentrated in a monk whose body is serene and who feels pleasure - on that occasion the concentration enlightenment factor is aroused in him, and he develops it, and by development it comes to fulfillment in him.

"He closely looks on with equanimity at the mind thus concentrated. On whatever occasion a monk closely looks on with equanimity at the mind thus concentrated - on that occasion the equanimity enlightenment factor is aroused in him, and he develops it, and by development it comes to fulfillment in him.

"Monks, that is how the four foundations of mindfulness, developed and cultivated, fulfill the seven enlightenment factors.

Fulfillment of True Knowledge and Deliverance

"And how, monks, do the seven enlightenment factors, developed and cultivated, fulfill true knowledge and deliverance?

"Here, monks, a monk develops the mindfulness enlightenment factor, which is supported by seclusion, dispassion, and cessation, and ripens in relinquishment. He develops the investigation-of-states enlightenment factor...the energy enlightenment factor...the rapture enlightenment factor...the serenity enlightenment factor...the concentration enlightenment factor...the equanimity enlightenment factor, which is supported by seclusion, dispassion, and cessation, and ripens in relinquishment.

"Monks, that is how the seven enlightenment factors, developed and cultivated, fulfill true knowledge and deliverance.

"That is what the Blessed One said. The monks were satisfied and delighted in the Blessed One's words."[141]

141 M.N., Uparipaṇṇāsapāḷi, Ānāpānasati Sutta (2,118), p. 941-948, Bhikkhu Ñāṇamoli and Bhikkhu Bodhi.

To avoid all evil,

To cultivate good,

And to cleanse one's mind -

This is the teaching of all the Buddhas.

Figure 7: Dimensions of Mind

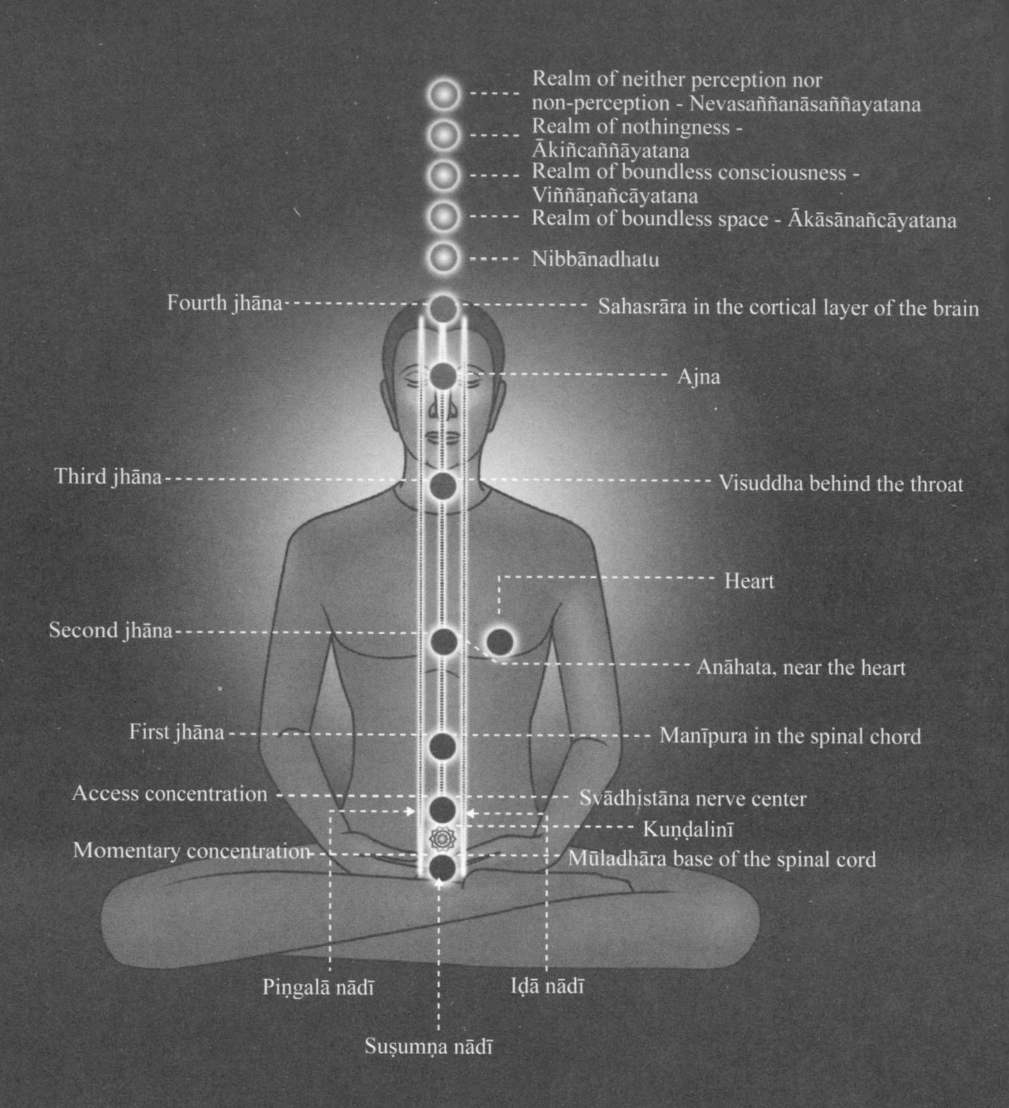

Remark : - Mind in the four arūpajhānas has the same components as mind in the fourth rūpajhāna. The only difference is that the objects of arūpa concentration are formless elements.

- **iḍā nāḍī** : Mind perceives past objects.
  Inner energy moves within the left channel.
- **piṇgalā nāḍī** : Mind perceives future objects.
  Inner energy moves within the right channel.
- **suṣumṇa nāḍī** : Mind perceives present objects.
  Inner energy moves within the middle channel.

CHAPTER VIII

Breathing Meditation: The Practice

Dimensions of Mind

Chakra.[142] A chakra is a central point of inner energy within the human body. Chakra energy is so subtle and refined that people in their normal state are unable to feel or recognize it. There are many chakras throughout the body, with seven of them being the most important. The chakras at different parts of the body control the functioning and balance of different inner organs.

In addition, our body is controlled by various endocrine glands which send different kinds of hormones directly to our blood and lymph glands. Hormones are essential for the proper functioning of our bodies. They control the balance of various systems, e.g. the body's growth, digestion, levels of inner energy, sexual energy and the liquids in the body. All of these glands relate to the seven chakras.

142 Chakra is a concept originating from Hindu text and practices. Its name derives from the Sanskrit word for "wheel" or "turning" (cakraṃ in Sanskrit and cakka in Pāli). Here in this text, we decide to spell it as 'chakra' according to the popular usage in English. Chakra refers to wheel-like vortices which, according to traditional Indian medicine, exist in the subtle body of human beings. It is considered the focal point for the reception or transmission of various energies.

Chakras in the Science of Yoga

There are electrical currents running through our bodies. The anode energy pole is located at the top of the head and the cathode energy pole is located at the base of the spinal cord. Life's energy exists between these two poles.

Ancient Yoga philosophy calls the anode pole at the top of the head *Viṣṇu's castle* and the cathode pole *Queen Kuṇḍalinī's throne*.

The light that glows from Viṣṇu urges Queen Kuṇḍalinī to come to unite with him, and she has always been more than eager to go up to unite with the mighty god. In Buddhist and scientific terms, however, if the cathode wave goes up to join the anode pole, we will be able to achieve the highest state of bliss, both physically and mentally.

In order to reach Viṣṇu's castle, the cathode wave, or kuṇḍalinī, has to travel upward through various important spots in the body. In Sanskrit, these spots are called *cakraṃ* or *padmas* (lotus).

The position of kuṇḍalinī's throne at the bottom of the spinal cord is called *mūladhāra*, which is symbolized by a lotus with four petals. The next chakra upward is *svādhistāna* at the nerve center slightly above the genital organs, symbolized by a lotus with six petals. At the navel is the position of *maṇīpūra,* shown in the form of a lotus with ten petals. *Anāhata,* the twelve petalled lotus, is the chakra at the level of the heart. Around the throat at the thyroid gland is *visuddha,* symbolized by a lotus with sixteen petals. *Ajna* is the chakra between the eyebrows, shown in the form of the twenty petalled lotus. At the top of the head is *sahasrāra,* or Viṣṇu's castle, symbolized by a lotus with one thousand petals.

Within the spinal cord, there are three channels of energy called *nāḍīs*. The left channel, or *iḍā nāḍī,* is for the cathode wave and the right channel, or *piṇgalā nāḍī*, is for the anode wave. The middle channel, or *suṣumṇa nāḍī*, is the passageway for the kuṇḍalinī wave.

Normally, kuṇḍalinī dwells dormant at the bottom of the spinal cord. With the concentrated power of meditation, the yogi can awaken and pull the kuṇḍalinī wave upward, through the various chakras respectively. When kuṇḍalinī conjoins firmly at each chakra, it will enhance the strength of one's mental power, which will increase successively from the lower chakras to the upper ones. The increased mental power can yield special forms of knowledge, e.g. the faculty of divine eyes (*dibbacakkhu*), penetration into another's mind, recollection of former lives, and insight into future lives. Finally, when the energy reaches sahasrāra, one can achieve utmost power and the highest form of knowledge (according to *rājayoga*), namely the complete union with *ātman*.

The awakening and the pull of kuṇḍalinī as described above can be called concentration meditation. The Chinese call it the practice of inner energy flow. According to *rājayoga*, this is the correct way to train the mind. All these are cited herein for the reader's benefit. In the past, knowledge about the mind was highly developed. Nevertheless, in comparison with Buddhism, the highest development of Yoga is equivalent only to the level of the fourth jhāna. It has also been claimed that in this state, one becomes united with ātman, the permanent self. However, this actually characterizes the attachment to *bhava* (being).

States of Body and Mind in Absorption Concentration (Appanāsamādhi)

Over the years, there have been different attitudes towards concentration. On the one hand, the science of Yoga emphasizes bodily changes in different chakra positions. On the other hand, The Buddhist Theravāda tradition ascribes importance to the mental concomitants (*cetasika).* However, from an experiential perspective, body and mind relate very closely to each other, from coarse to refined levels, in the development of concentration. This chapter discusses chakras, kuṇḍalinī energy and the attainment of different jhānas in the hope of guiding and inspiring practitioners who seek spiritual development.

Introduction to the Practice: Holistic Truth about the Mind

Various kinds of knowledge about different levels of mind, e.g. the theory of Universal Energy, the energy of kuṇḍalinī, the energy of chakras, sahajayoga or rājayoga, actually explain the same thing, namely the power of concentration. However, as time has passed, practices of various levels of deep concentration have deviated from the true principle of practice and have become inaccurate. For example, certain later practices hold that one can enter into any level of deep concentration that one wishes, without passing through the previous levels. This is incorrect and impossible.

Such deviation of mental development techniques of later practices in rājayoga, Universal Energy, and sahajayoga results from the lack of foundational knowledge about the components of mind and mental concomitants. Therefore, the result of these modern practices is not as complete and effective as it was in the earlier stages of the discovery of this knowledge.

Buddhism describes various levels of mental power in deep concentration as **mind in jhāna** (jhānacitta). Knowledge about the jhānas existed before the emergence of Buddhism. Prince Siddhatta also learned and achieved the eight levels of jhāna. However, the knowledge of jhāna alone is not sufficient to lead one to the final extinction of suffering. The Buddha realized that in so far as the continuous flow of arising and passing away of the aggregates still remains, there is the persistence of suffering.

In the state of the fourth arūpajhāna, or nevasaññānāsaññāyatana, the aggregates arc almost extinguished. But since the root of desire and attachment still remains, **the continuity of aggregate flows persists**. The Buddha therefore sought seclusion in order to discover a higher form of knowledge which is called vipassanā.

It is important to remember that the Buddha praised the knowledge of jhāna as a component of the noble eight-fold path, namely as one among the eight pieces of vital knowledge which will lead to final liberation. With Prince Siddhatta's long-accumulated spiritual force, all the components of supreme insight came to their completion and the seven supporting states[143] emerged to uplift the normal power of concentration, thus turning it into the higher state of **right concentration,** which was the basis of the three-fold knowledge *(vijjā sam)*[144] on the night of his enlightenment.

---

143 Bojjhaṅga or the seven factors of enlightenment are mindfulness, investigation of states, rapture, energy, serenity, concentration and equanimity.

144 The three-fold knowledge is recollection of past lives, knowledge of the death and rebirth of beings and knowledge of the destruction of all mental defilements.

The Noble Right Concentration (Ariyasammasamādhi)

"Monks, I shall teach you noble right concentration with its supports and its requisites. Listen and attend closely to what I shall say….What, monks, is noble right concentration with its supports and its requisites, that is, right view, right intention, right speech, right action, right livelihood, right effort, and right mindfulness? Unification of mind equipped with these seven factors is called noble right concentration with its supports and its requisites."[145]

Cycle of the Mind in the Wheel of Rebirth

Every kind of energy in the universe moves systematically in a circular shape. The mind is no exception, moving in an endless wave of rising and falling rhythm. The mass of energy emerging from this rising-falling also moves within the cycle of existence and rebirth. The rising-falling mind is always accompanied by its concomitants (cetasikas). When the coarse components disappear, the mind moves to more refined and subtler levels, namely from the realm of attachment to worldly sensations (*kāmābhumi*), to the realm of attachment to form (rūpajhāna) and the realm of attachment to the formless (arūpajhāna) successively. Finally, however, it has to come back to the worldly realm again. This is the cycle of the mind moving within the wheel of rebirth.

---

145 M.N., Uparipaṇṇāsapāḷi, Mahācattārīsaka Sutta, p. 934, Bhikkhu Ñāṇamoli and Bhikkhu Bodhi.

Figure 8: Cycle of the Mind in the Wheel of Rebirth

Saṃsāra

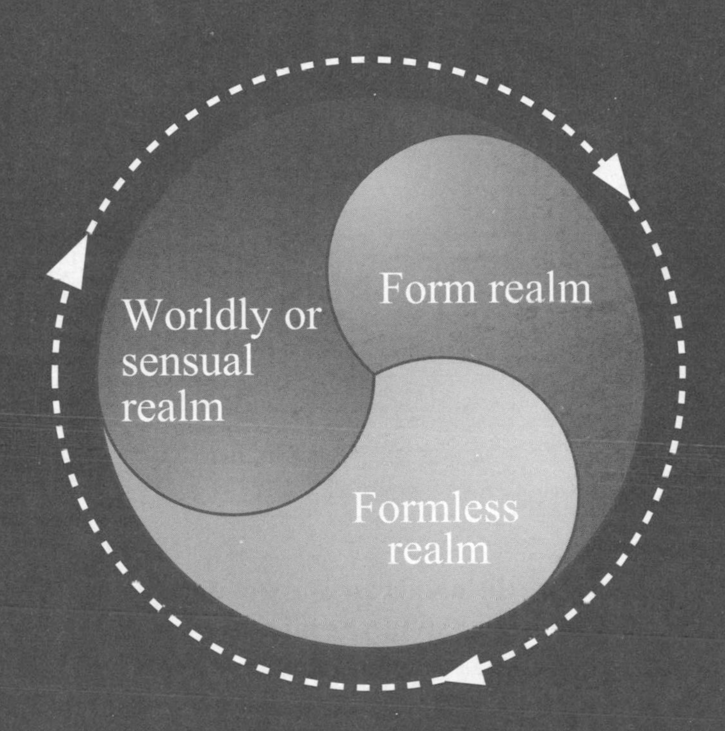

Figure 9: Concentration in Buddhism and Rājayoga

Level of Concentration	**Rājayoga**	**Position of the Concentrated Mind**
Momentary Concentration	mūladhāra	Base of the spinal cord
Access Concentration	svādhistāna	Nerve center located slightly above the genital organs
First jhāna	maṇīpūra	In the spinal cord, at the level of the navel
Second jhāna	anāhata	Level of the heart
Third jhāna	visuddha	Behind the throat
Fourth jhāna	sahasrāra	Cortical layer of the brain

In summary, before the mind can move to the upper and more refined levels of concentration, the mental concomitants must first be extinguished. If the mental concomitants still remain, no matter how hard one tries to build up the intention to move one's mind to the different chakras, this will only be one's own mental construction. The mind will remain within the level of worldliness (kāmābhumi), not able to move up to the higher realms.

Figure 10: Dimensions of Mind

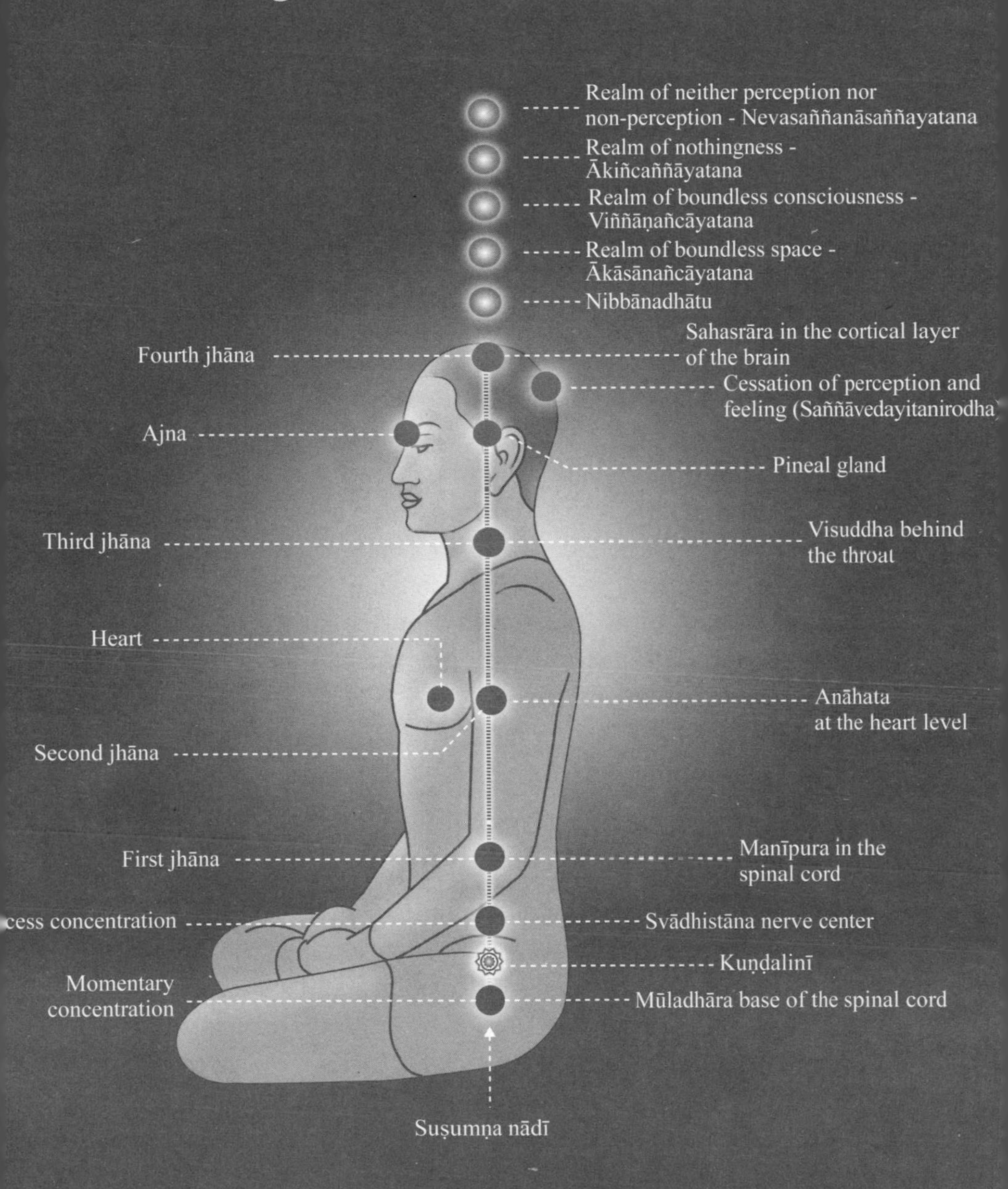

Beginning of the World of Phenomena and Time

"All things are rooted in desire. They come to actual existence through attention, **originate from contact,** and converge on feelings. The foremost of all things is concentration. All things are mastered by mindfulness. Their peak is wisdom, their essence libcration. All things merge in the Deathless, and nibbāna is their culmination."[146]

The waves of light, sound, odor, taste and physical contact which are perceived through the five senses will disappear and dissolve into emptiness, not having any further impact on the mind. However, the process of perception does not end there. Every contact at the nerves will move further to the heart and the heart consciousness (*manodhātu*). Only here does perception embrace the realm of meaning of contact. In Pāli, it is called *phassa* (contact). **Phassa in the law of dependent origination (paṭiccasamuppāda) actually means the contact at the heart consciousness (manosaṃphassa).**

Dualism is the characteristic of our perception of things. It is the realm of the constructed world in which the mind roams: good-bad, true-false, love-hate, win-lose, far-near. Dualism is the force of the positive and negative poles.

This binary opposition of meanings of every perception is the cause of vedanā or feeling, which is a reaction to every contact. Between these two opposite poles of all meanings exists the dimension of time, past and future. If one can locate the mind precisely at the center point of these opposite poles, the contact there will become neutral, and the balance of the state of things can be maintained. Therefore, in order to train the mind to

---

146 A.N., The Chapter of the Tens, p. 251, Bhikkhu Nyanaponika and Bhikkhu Bodhi.

transcend all kinds of opposing forces, one should find the way to get into this balancing point at the center.

Anusaya (latent negative dispositions) is a habit of mind that is deeply ingrained and rooted at the deepest level. Ignorant mind cannot understand the fact that the rising-falling flow of feelings are but the result of contacts. Therefore, such minds tend to be misled, and to attach themselves to those feelings. The attachment results in accumulation, and the accumulated defilement is called anusaya.

A mind that clings to pleasant feelings will accumulate *rāganusaya* or lustful temperament. If clinging more to unpleasant feelings, *paṭighanusaya* or ill-will and aversion will be accumulated. The mind that does not understand the impermanence of feelings results in the accumulation of *avijjānusaya* (ignorance).

Āsava (defilement accumulation). Every time the mind clings to feelings, our body produces a natural chemical which diffuses to different parts of the body. The energy flow of this chemical has a pulling force which makes the mind attach to feelings over and over again.

Taṇhā (desire) and **upādāna** (attachment). Anusaya urges the mind to continually seek out new objects. The nature of desire is to hold fast and wrap around different objects of consciousness. It absorbs the mind by constantly supplying new things for the mind to consume. Old accumulated anusaya in deeper layers also helps to construct the Ego and the sense of self (*upādānakhandha*). Therefore, the cycle of the rising-falling of desire and attachment increases in frequency and strength. Such accumulation creates an energy field or network of defiled mental concomitants around the heart consciousness. It is such defiled layers that prevent the mind from being free of suffering.

The knowledge which moves the mind up to different chakras until reaching the final and permanent liberation has to take into account the whole structure of this defiled energy field that encircles the heart consciousness. Such understanding is a precondition for discovering the way to freedom. For this reason, before the mind moves from a lower to a higher chakra, it must first make an intermediary stop at the heart consciousness. If one keeps concentrating more and more on the here-and-now, the wisdom of the continuity of the present moment will enable one to realize the truth of one's body and mind, or *rūpa* and *nāmā.* One can discern that behind the body and mind, there is but the flow of mere moments which rise and dissolve one after another in an unceasing chain.

With the force of accumulated wisdom, the flow of volitional impulses and mental formations will be weakened and cut off. The strength of the torrent will decrease and become more feeble until it is unable to draw the mind into its orbit. The mind can then move closer to the center point of the bipolar energy field. At that center point the energy will become completely neutral. The mind will be less and less affected by the binary poles of perception. Even the dimension of time (roaming into the past and future) will become shorter and shorter (since one dwells more and more in the present moment). The pulling force of each defiled layer will lessen, while the concentrative power increases more and more until the mind is able to free itself from the defiled force of that layer. It can then move up to the more refined, higher chakra successively.

Mindfulness of Breathing: Practice Section

"Monks, when mindfulness of breathing is developed and cultivated, it is of great fruit and great benefit. When mindfulness of breathing is developed and cultivated, it fulfills the four foundation of mindfulness.

"And how, monks, is mindfulness of breathing developed and cultivated, so that it is of great fruit and great benefit?

"Here, a monk, gone to the forest or to the root of a tree or to an empty hut, sits down; having folded his legs crosswise, set his body erect, and having established mindfulness in front of him, ever mindful, he breathes in, mindful he breathes out."[147]

Sixteen Levels of Mindfulness of Breathing

The following is a description of the various levels of ānāpānasati practice:

A. Mindfulness of the inhalation and of the exhalation. The meaning here refers to persistent awareness of breathing in and breathing out, which covers the content and description of the first to the fourth level of ānāpānasati practice. (See detail on all sixteen levels in Chapter VII).

B. Mindfulness of different features of the mental phenomena and mental concomitants which accompany every breath. This covers the content of the Ānāpānasati Sutta from the fifth to the sixteenth level.

---

147 M.N., Uparipaṇṇāsapāḷi, Ānāpānasati Sutta, p. 943, Bhikkhu Ñāṇamoli and Bhikkhu Bodhi.

Three Breath-Touching Points

The three breath-touching areas are the nostrils, the chest and the abdomen. One can choose any of these three positions to be the focus point of awareness, according to one's own inclination, habit, or advice from one's teacher.

Remark: One should maintain equanimity in observing the breath. Just remain fully aware of the in and out breaths. Then, the breath will become very clear, deep, soft and refined. One will feel very light and comfortable, and all uneasy feelings will vanish.

Section One: Contemplation of the Body

1. Breathing in long, one knows: "I am breathing in long"; Breathing out long, one knows: "I am breathing out long."

1.1. Long in and out breathing signifies that the bodily elements are still coarse, which results in corresponding coarse mental elements.

1.2. The coarse bodily elements will be removed in the form of heat, pain, numbness, sweat, heaviness in the head, dizziness, vomiting, upset stomach and fever.

1.3. All of the above mentioned features will appear distinctly if the practitioner makes continuous efforts both in walking and sitting meditation alternately. Each sitting or walking meditation should last at least forty minutes.

1.4. The mind will not enter into subtler and more refined states if the bodily elements are still coarse.

1.5.Thirty or forty minutes of daily practice will not enable the practitioner to observe any physical irregularities (as mentioned in 1.2).

1.6. There are three kinds of mental objects: thoughts, imaginations and feelings of the past, thoughts, imaginations and feelings of the future, and the awareness of the present. In daily life, the mind tends to adhere to constructed thoughts and feelings in every bodily posture, whether walking, sitting, standing or lying down. Without attentive observation, the restless mind is obsessed with irrelevant and disturbing thoughts.

1.7. Most of such thoughts and imaginations are pointless and a waste of time and energy.

1.8. The mind which is obsessed with those thoughts will lose its balance. One is prone to the defilements of life, namely stress, strain and anxiety.

1.9. If one allows these defilements into one's home, they will sooner or later take over the house and the owner will become their servants.

1.10. In order to return to the original basis of life which is full of beauty and freedom, one needs to restore the balance of mind.

1.11. The method of bringing balance back to the mind is to increasingly train the mind to live in the present moment. One can begin with the body, by being mindful of every posture, be it walking, standing, sitting, or lying down.

1.12. In order to be fully and clearly aware, the new practitioner has to know a **trick**, namely to choose the form of practice that best suits his or her characteristics and disposition.

1.13. In daily life, each time the mind becomes conscious of an object, pleasant or unpleasant feelings always accompany each contact. **Covetousness** *(abhijjhā)* and **dissatisfaction** *(domanassa)* are forms of energy which do not dissolve but are kept and stored in the form of attachment (upādāna).

1.14. Abhijjhā and domanassa which have been stored in the form of attachment are referred to by the Buddha as **the fuel of suffering** or **the fire of defilement.**

1.15. This state of affairs can be compared to a life boat captain who lacks the mindfulness to steer a straight and steady course. Therefore, he is unconsciously accumulating suffering with each passing day.

1.16. Given the accumulated fires of attachment and suffering, even a small flame ignited from daily contact can cause a violent emotional outburst which can spread dangerously. Therefore, it is not surprising that many people react aggressively when aroused by even a small amount of dissatisfaction.

1.17. Outside fires are inevitable. However, they can have no impact if the inner fire has been extinguished. Consequently, through whichever sense-door the fire sparks enter, one can immediately extinguish them.

1.18. The eulogy that reads "*The Buddha is the arahat who extinguished completely the fires of defilement and suffering*" should now become clearer for some readers.

1.19. Clean water cleanses pollution. If the mind is trained to dwell in the present moment, different sorts of mental formations in the form of attachments will be released. Some practitioners who do not understand this process will become discouraged, and may even give up the practice.

1.20. As mindfulness is developed, the coarse elements in both body and mind are decreased.

1.21. When the state of the body and mind is coarse, sensual desire and ill-will or aversion will be the most distinct hindrances to appear.

1.22. For the beginner, if physical pain or mental suffering become too strong or too much to bear, one should resort to other bodily bases as the object of mindfulness, such as contemplation on bodily impurity, contemplation on the body as composed of four fundamental elements, or contemplation on the body as a deserted corpse in a cemetery.

1.23. If one keeps contemplating one of these three bodily bases, attachment to the self will be diminished, and the object of contemplation will gradually become subtler and more refined. The more refined the mind, the less coarse the body will become.

1.24. Another bodily base is mindfulness of the bodily movements (sampajañña pabba). This method makcs use of different forms of bodily movement, e.g. a rhythmic hand movement as an object of contemplation. The practitioner can experiment with this technique if he or she wishes.

1.25. If all of the above mentioned techniques prove fruitless, and the mind remains very confused, or if the more one practices, the stronger the storm of emotion and pain becomes, then the practitioner should sit cross-legged (do not lean against the wall), and dismiss every attempt to concentrate. Do not even focus on the breath. Just sit there. If the mind wants to roam about, let it go. Do not try to control or prevent it. Do not reject or refuse any emotion or thought. With this method, the coarse objects of consciousness will pour out and be cleaned away. Let this process be fully developed.

1.26.**The emergence of strange mental objects**. After the coarse elements have been released up to a certain point, various unfamiliar and strange images which have never appeared before will emerge very clearly one after another. Their rising-falling cycle is, however, quicker than usual. One cannot identify exactly to which dimension of time they belong, past or future. Also, one cannot help wondering how such unfamiliar images emerge. Not long after this, the mind enters a state of drowsiness, and finally, the consciousness disappears as one falls asleep in the sitting posture. After waking, one will feel very fresh and light and ready to go back to the practice.

1.27. Such methods of releasing the coarse mental elements are recommended for those who cling tightly to the inner streams of thought, and whose emotions are influenced by anxiety and confusion and who may depend on sleeping pills. If using this method of practice before going to bed, they will be able to fall asleep easily without resorting to pills.

1.28 If we put in order the appearance of mental objects from coarse to refined levels, the sequence will be as follows:

- **Past objects** (coarse level). the clearest hindrances here are desire and aversion.

- **Drowsiness**. When coarse elements are largely removed, and uneasy and unpleasant feelings both in body and mind are lessened, if mindfulness is not maintained clearly, sloth and drowsiness (*thīnamiddha*) will intervene and take over.

- **Future object**s. After drowsiness fades away, future objects will emerge in its place. Here, restlessness, unfocused wild thoughts and anxieties will show up distinctly and become dominant. If one can pass this step, the mind will become more and more refined until it reaches the turning point of entering into absorption concentration (appanājavanavaravithī).

The pleasure of absorption
is never what we expect or imagine it to be;
absorption will only arise
when expectation and imagination have ceased to be.

Just as a stone, lying still, shows no motion,
so the mind in its natural state
is totally still and empty of emotion.

Figure 11: Visualized image (uggahanimitta) Conceptualized image (paṭibhāganimitta)

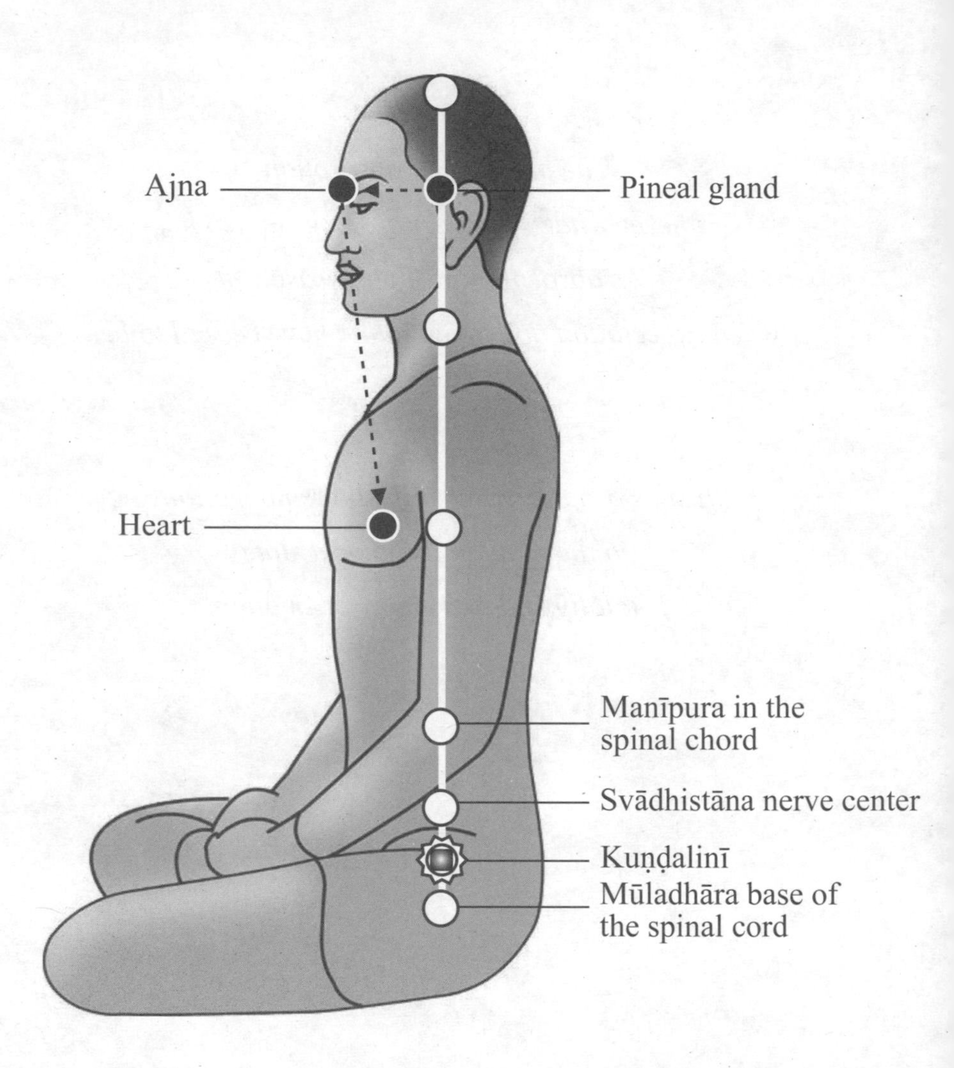

2. Breathing in short, one knows "I am breathing in short"; Breathing out short, one knows "I am breathing out short."

Uggahanimitta and Paṭibhāganimitta

Within the circle of practitioners and Dhamma scholars, there is still an incomplete and inaccurate understanding about the relationship between a visualized image *(uggahanimitta)* and a conceptualized image *(paṭibhāganimitta)* in concentration. It is generally understood that a visualized image is the emergence of a certain mental image which will become the object of concentration. A conceptualized image is the next step of enlarging that image or making it crystal clear according to one's wish. These two steps of practice are indispensable for achieving the higher level of concentration. Incomplete knowledge of these steps results in difficulty in achieving absorption concentration.

Uggahanimitta Nimitta means the object of perception. Uggahanimitta is a special form of mind which emerges when the mind is about to move from the realm of worldly sensations (kāmabhumi) to the realm of form (*rūpabhumi*). **The main difference of the characteristic of mind in these two realms is the feature of one-pointedness of mind (ekaggatā)**. One-pointedness of mind in jhāna is firmly secured at different chakras on the body. **Pineal[148] is the position at which uggahanimitta emerges, and momentary concentration (khanikasamādhi) the stage at which it is further developed.**

---

148 The pineal gland is located near the center of the brain. It produces melatonin, a hormone that affects the modulation of waking and sleeping patterns. It is also important for the postures in the science of Yoga.

Paṭibhāganimitta is characterized by the expansion of one-pointedness. This expansion becomes clear from the stage of upacārasamādhi (access concentration) onward. The higher the level of absorption concentration (jhāna), the lesser the components of mental concomitants, and hence the greater the expansion of one-pointedness. All these stages also relate to each chakra point on the body, beginning from the pineal.

The pineal and the cessation of mind and body. There is a very crucial transition point between the coarse (long) breath and the subtler (short) breath. The relationship between the changes in mind and the changes in body becomes very clear to the practitioner. While one is fully focused on the in-and-out long breath, one can also clearly discern the special rising-falling of mental objects (mental formations). Such rising-falling happens very quickly. And then the long breath suddenly vanishes.The mind moves up to the pineal and secures itself very deeply and firmly there. The body becomes very light, as if weightless. One experiences pleasant feelings throughout the body and mind. The stream of thoughts is now weak and diluted, and cannot disturb the mind any longer. A shining light emanates around the head and gradually becomes more and more distinct.

3. "I shall be aware of the entire breath, breathing in and out."

The in and out breaths are even and consistent, refined and very soft. One clearly feels the breath as being deep and subtle. All these are characteristics of the breath one can observe and feel. Here, one should maintain equanimity and just be aware of present phenomena. Permeate equanimity deep into the breath rhythm.

At this point, the breath becomes so soft and refined that some practitioners feel as if their breath has vanished and thus do not know on what object they should concentrate. The mind must maintain perfect equanimity to be able to sense the delicate breath.

Ajna. The mind moves from the pineal to ajna between the eyebrows. Maintain equanimity and anchor it deep down into the breath, which becomes more and more refined.

The Heart. The mind moves from ajna to the center of the heart. Thoughts and breath become more and more weakened, and softer. The mind seems to be drawn into the center point of the heart. The feeling of peace and firmness of mind is so strong and powerful that it conducts, draws and fixes the mind to become one and the same with the center point of the heart. The horizon of darkness gradually draws back and the ray of light becomes brighter and brighter.

Figure 12: Cetasika

5. Hindrances: sensual desire (kāmmacchanda), ill will (vyāpāda), sloth and torpor (thīnamiddha) restlessness and anxiety (uddhacca-kukkucca), doubt (vicikicchā)
4. First jhāna: applied thought, sustained thought, rapture, bliss, one-pointedness
3. Second jhāna: rapture, bliss, one-pointedness
2. Third jhāna: bliss, one-pointedness
1. Fourth jhāna: equanimity, one-pointedness

The energy fields of mental concomitants (cetasika). The energy fields of mental concomitants encircle the heart consciousness in many layers. Can the mind free itself from the pulling force of its orbit? At the center point of the heart, all past remembrances stop their function. They cannot become the object of consciousness.

Therefore, this center point of the heart is very important for the practitioner, since one can use this point to test whether the mind has already passed into the realm of jhāna or not. One can check by trying to remember events or things in the past. One will find that all dimension of past remembrance cannot emerge. The more one makes the effort, the more violent the vibration in the brain will become, which in turn results in a tense contraction and pain in the head. But if one shifts to the realm of the future, the mind can start to function again. After becoming contented, one should stop testing, and refrain from any intention to perceive things. Then the mind will become very quiet and will immerse itself into becoming one and the same at this particular center point of the heart.

Figure 13: Mūladhāra - Momentary Concentration (The Awakening of Kuṇḍalinī)

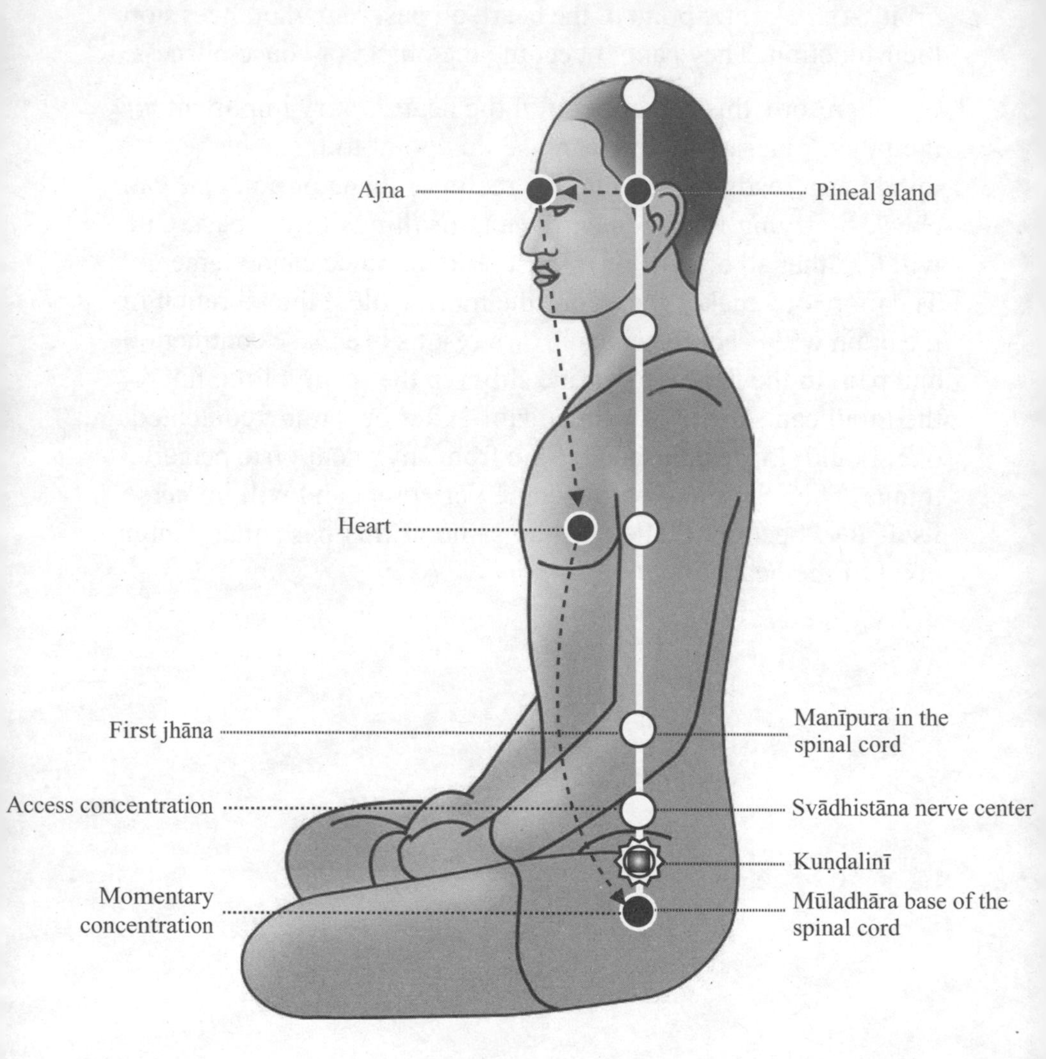

4. "I shall calm the body, breathing in...and out."

The extinction of kāmabhumi (the realm of worldliness). Before the extinction of the realm of worldliness, the past objects of consciousness come up automatically. This is a special type of rising-falling rhythm. It is powerful and happens very quickly, only two or three times (two times for one whose wisdom is powerful, three times for those whose wisdom is less powerful) Precisely at the last moment of this special rising-falling, the pulling force of the realm of worldliness vanishes. At the same time, all negative mental concomitants, namely the five hindrances, also stop functioning momentarily.

Mūladhāra and momentary concentration (khanikasamādhi). The mind moves from the center of the heart down to the root chakra (mūladhāra). The breath becomes more refined, the shining light becomes brighter. The one-pointedness of mind increases, becomes more secure and fixes the mind wholly and completely with mūladhāra. In momentary concentration, the level of one-pointedness is about 80% of that of absorption concentration (appanāsamādhi).

Figure 14: Svādhistāna - Access Concentration (The kuṇḍalinī force is driven towards chakra)

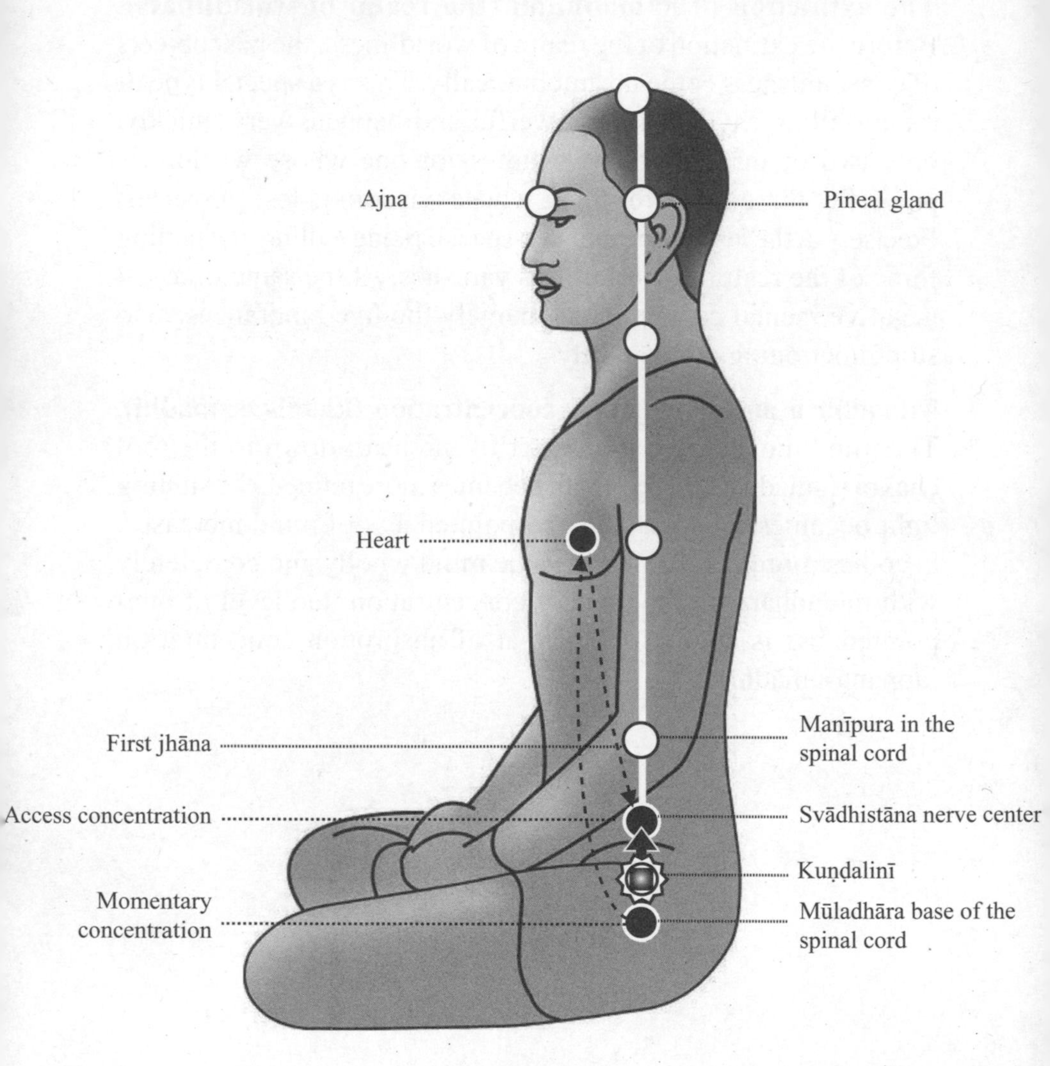

The awakening of kuṇḍalinī. At the bottom of the spinal cord, a mass of energy emerges. Warmth from this energy gradually permeates throughout the body. One can clearly feel the rising bodily temperature. **This energy is kuṇḍalinī. Finally, it is awakened!**

Svādhistāna and access concentration. Though the breath becomes very subtle, the one-pointedness of mind can still feel it and can clearly sense the in and out movement of the breath. The mind moves from mūladhāra up to the heart and then down to svādhistāna.

The movement of kuṇḍalinī. The mind moves from the heart down to svādhistāna. The whole body (specifically the trunk and neck) suddenly straightens automatically. Kuṇḍalinī energy moves from mūladhāra up to svādhistāna through the middle channel (suṣumṇa nāḍī).

The breath becomes more and more refined, the shining light brighter and brighter. The one-pointedness increases, predominating the mind and fixing it firmly at svādhistāna.

The level of one-pointedness in access concentration is about 90% of that of absorption concentration.

Figure 15: Manīpura - First Jhāna

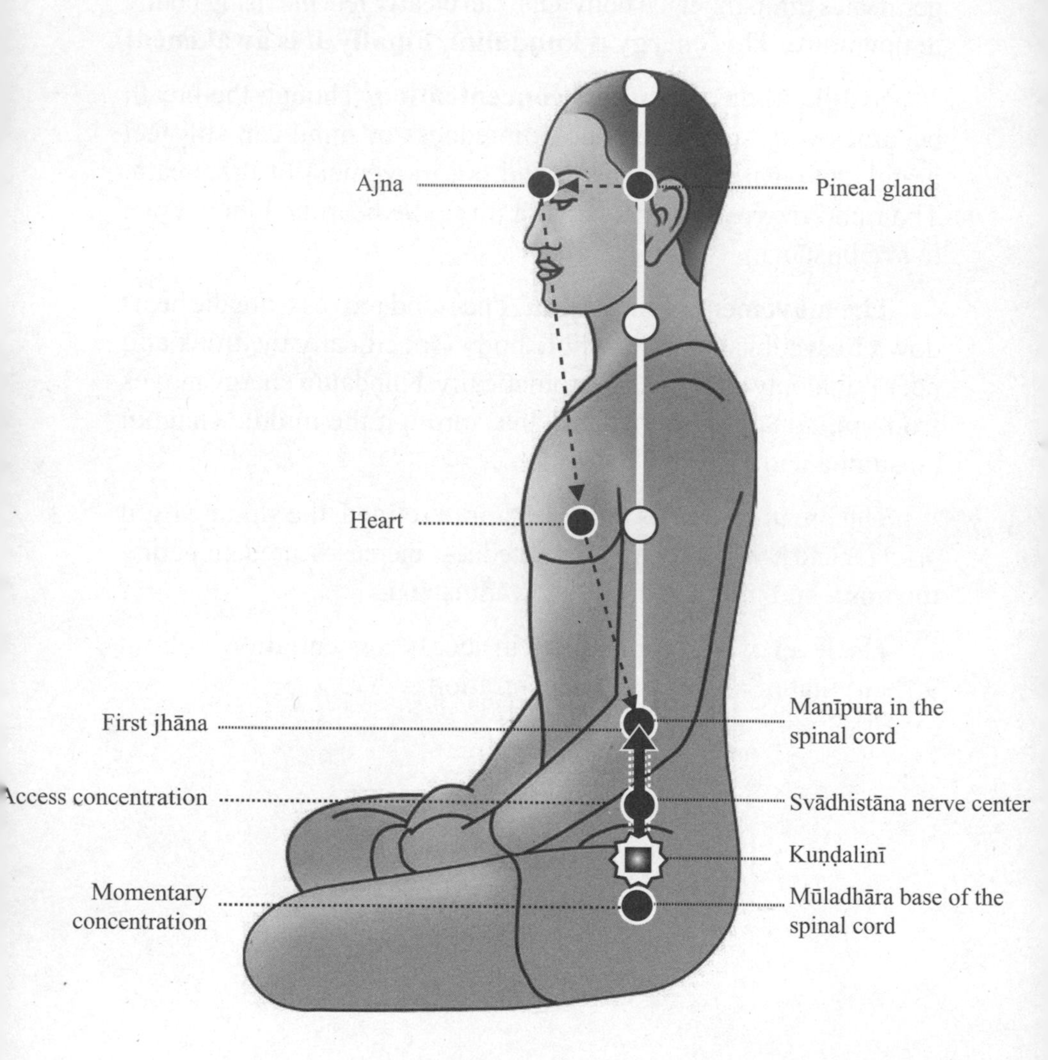

Manīpura and the first jhāna. The mind moves up from svādhistāna back to the pineal, then forward to ajna and then to the heart. Past remembrances come up automatically, in a special form of rising-falling, very powerfully and very quickly. The rising-falling happens only two or three times (two times for those whose wisdom is powerful, three times for those whose wisdom is less powerful).

There are three steps of mind movement to the chakra. Firstly, the mind moves from the heart down to manīpura, secondly the body (the trunk and the neck) become straightened automatically, and thirdly, kuṇḍalinī energy moves from svādhistāna up to manīpura through the middle channel of the spinal cord.

Manīpura is the position of the first jhāna. The mind has completely and successfully shifted from the realm of worldliness into the realm of form. The negative waves of mental formations caused by the five hindrances have ceased. The positive energy field of mental concomitants which encircles the mind emanates glowing bright light like the luminosity of the divine beings in the realm of form (*rūpabrahma*).

The five components of the first jhāna are as follows: applied thought (vitakka), sustained thought (vicāra), rapture (piti), bliss (sukha) and one-pointedness (ekaggatā)[149].

Ekaggatā and the life span in the realms of form and formlessness (rūpabrahma and arūpabrahma). One-pointedness is the necessary and most distinct component of every level of jhāna. The duration of one-pointedness can be incredibly long. In fact, it is the length or duration of one-pointedness which determines the **lifetime** of beings in both the realms of form and formlessness.

---

149 See fn. 23 in chapter II and p. 91-94 in chapter III.

The period of one-pointedness corresponds with the duration of certain kinds of positive feelings which accompany the mind and jhāna at every level. These feelings are very strong and **permeate the entire body.** They are as follows:

> **The first jhāna**: The feeling of bliss and rapture caused by detachment from the perceptions of sensual pleasure and the five hindrances.
>
> **The second jhāna:** Bliss and rapture caused by the power of concentration (and the extinction of applied and sustained thought).
>
> **The third jhāna**: Bliss accompanied by equanimity.
>
> **The fourth jhāna:** Equanimity which accompanies the unblemished and radiant mind.

The more powerful the one-pointedness is and the longer it remains, the stronger are the accompanying pleasant feelings of bliss and equanimity**. These feelings spread throughout the entire body.** Precisely at the position of the first jhāna, a pleasant stream of coolness and a glowing light emanating from manīpura permeate the body, especially at the ends of the hands and feet.

"Monks, take the case of a monk, who, aloof from sensuous appetites, enters and abides in the first [jhāna]; he steeps and drenches and fills and suffuses this body with zest and ease, born of solitude, so that there is not one particle of the body that is not pervaded by this lone-born zest and ease.

"Monks, just as a handy bathman or attendant might strew bath-powder in some copper basin and, gradually sprinkling water, knead it together so that the bath-ball gathered up the moisture, became enveloped in moisture and saturated both in and out, but did not ooze moisture; even so a monk steeps, drenches, fills and suffuses this body with zest and ease, born of solitude, so that there is not one particle of the body that is not pervaded by this lone-born zest and ease. Monks, this is firstly how to make become the five-limbed Ariyan right concentration."[150]

For the practitioner who attains the first jhāna for the first time, the mind in jhāna will be experienced only for an instant. Later, as one gains more proficiency, the concentrative mind in jhāna will appear in a successive cycles of rising and falling without the interruption of the passive states of mind (bhavaṅgacitta) or any other kinds of mental concomitants. Moreover, the practitioner can also determine the length of duration of the jhānic state to be as long as he or she wishes. This is called "meditative attainment" (jhānasamāpatti) because of the unlimited and unbounded quality of mind in absorption concentration.

150 A.N., vol.3, The Book of The Fives, p. 17-8, Hare.

Concentrative Proficiency
(Jhānavasī)

Jhānavasī consists of the five proficiencies in jhāna attainment.

1. *Āvajjanavasi*: Proficiency in rccalling the characteristics of jhāna
2. *Samāpajjanavasi:* Proficiency in entering jhāna
3. *Athisthānavasi*: Proficiency in remaining in jhāna as long as one wishes
4. *Wuddhānavasi*: Proficiency in leaving jhāna
5. *Paccavekkhanavasi*: Proficiency in identifying the components of each jhāna[151]

One should follow Ven. Sāriputta in maintaining the mind in the first jhāna and contemplating its enlightening factors.

"And the states in the first jhāna known to him those states arose, known they were present, known they disappeared. He understood thus: 'So indeed, these states, not having been, come into being; having been, they vanish.' Regarding those states, he abided unattracted, unrepelled, independent, detached, free, dissociated, with a mind rid of barriers. He understood: 'There is an escape beyond,' and with the cultivation of that [attainment], he confirmed that there is."[152]

151 Sujin Borihanwanakhet, *The Concise Paramatthadhamma.* (in Thai), p. 518-9.
152 M.N.,Uparipaṇṇāsapāḷi, Anupada Sutta, p.899, Bhikkhu Ñāṇamoli and Bhikkhu Bodhi.

Figure 16: Anāhata - Second Jhāna

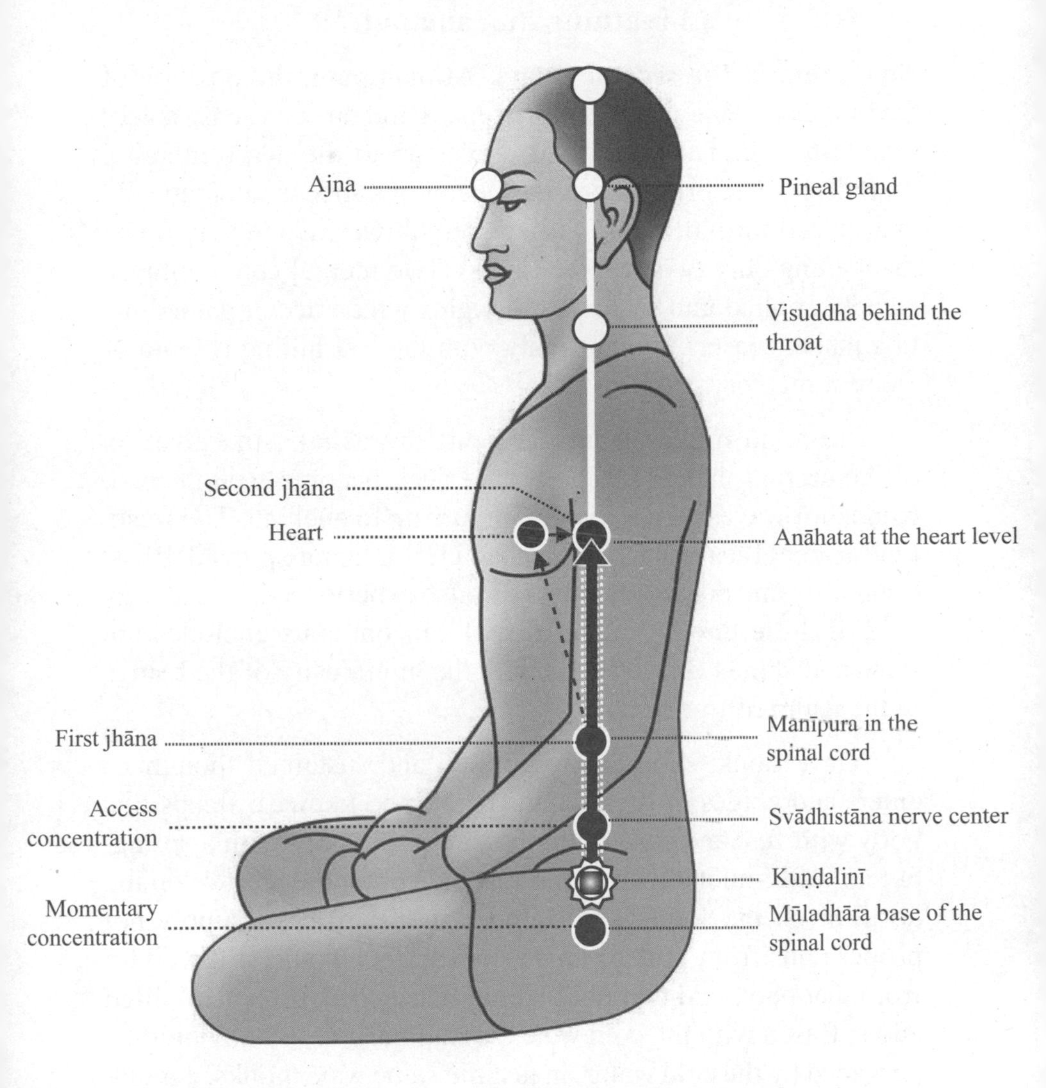

Section Two: Contemplation of Feelings
5. "I shall be aware of rapture, breathing in... and out."

Anāhata and the second jhāna. At manīpura, the position of the first jhāna, one-pointedness deepens and one can sense a very refined breath. Then the mind moves up to the heart, merging itself deeply and firmly there. Past memories appear automatically in a special form of rising-falling, very powerful and very quick (happening only two or three times). Two mental concomitants, namely applied and sustained thoughts which accompanied the first jhāna, cease simultaneously with the last falling rhythm of the past memory.

The mind moves from the heart to anāhata, the position of the second jhāna. The body and neck become straightened. Kuṇḍalinī waves move from manīpura up to anāhata. The fresh, light and cool sensations which characterize rapture prevail. Bliss, tranquility and one-pointedness are also experienced. The energy field of these three positive mental concomitants encircles the mind and shines very brightly, like the luminiosity of the beings in the realm of form.

"Or a monk, suppressing applied and sustained thought… enters and abides in the second [jhāna]; he likewise steeps this body with zest and ease…Monks, imagine a pool with a spring, but no water-inlet either on the east side or on the west or on the north or on the south, and suppose the [rain-]deva supply not proper rains from time to time - cool waters would still well up from that pool, and that pool would be steeped, drenched, filled and suffused with the cold water so that not a drop but would be pervaded by the cold water; in just the same way, monks, a monk steeps his body with zest and ease…Monks, this is secondly how to make become the five-limbed ariyan right concentration."[153]

One should follow the example of Ven. Sariputta in maintaining the mind in the second jhāna and contemplating its enlightening factors.

"And the states in the second jhāna - the self-confidence, the rapture, the pleasure, and the unification of mind; the contact, feeling, perception, volition, and mind; the zeal, decision, energy, mindfulness, equanimity, and attention - these states were defined by him one by one as they occurred; known to him those states arose, known they were present, known they disappeared. Regarding those states, he abided unattracted, unrepelled, independent, detached, free, dissociated, with a mind rid of barriers. He understood: 'There is an escape beyond,' and with the cultivation of that [attainment], he confirmed that there is."[154]

153 A.N., vol.3, The Book of the Fives, p.17-18, Hare.
154 M.N., Uparipaṇṇāsapāḷi, Anupada Sutta, p. 900, Bhikkhu Ñāṇamoli and Bhikkhu Bodhi.

Figure 17: Visuddha - Third Jhāna

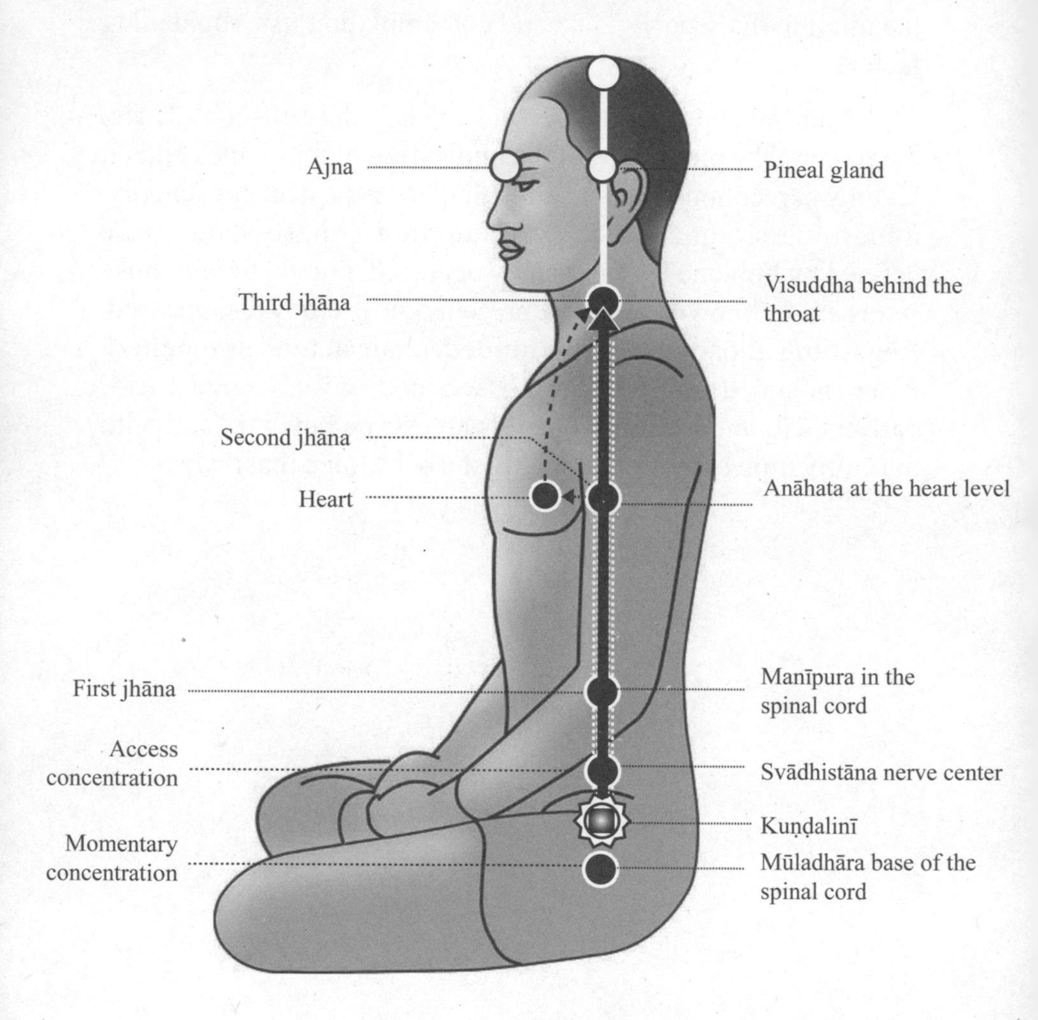

6. "I shall be aware of bliss, breathing in...and out."

Vissuddha and the third jhāna. At anāhata, which is the position of the second jhāna, the one-pointedness deepens so that one can sense even the very refined breath. The mind moves to the heart, merges itself there, and remains very still and firm at that point. Past memories appear automatically in a special form of rising-falling, very powerful and very quick (happening only two or three times). As the last falling ceases, so does rapture.

The mind moves from the heart up to vissuddha (the throat chakra), which is the position of the third jhāna. The body and neck become straightened. Kuṇḍalinī waves move up from anāhata to vissuddha. Very refined bliss and one-pointedness are distinct mental concomitants that encircle the mind, emanating a glowing light which covers the whole body. **One who achieves this jhāna is one who abides with body attuned in bliss**.

"Again, a monk, free from the fervour of zest,... enters and abides in the third [jhāna]; he steeps and drenches and fills and suffuses this body with a zestless ease so that there is not one particle of the body that is not pervaded by this zestless ease.

"Monks, just as in a pond of blue, white and red water-lilies, the plants are born in water, grow in water, come not out of the water, but, sunk in the depths, find nourishment, and from tip to root are steeped, drenched, filled and suffused with cold water so that not a part of them is not pervaded by cold water; even so, monks, a monk steeps his body in zestless ease.... Monks, this is thirdly how to make become the five-limbed ariyan right concentration."[155]

155 A.N., vol.3, op.cit, Hare.

One should follow Ven. Sāriputta in maintaining the mind in the third jhāna and contemplating its enlightening factors.

"And the states in the third jhāna - the equanimity, the pleasure, the mindfulness, the full awareness, and the unification of mind; the contact, feeling, perception, volition, and mind; the zeal, decision, energy, mindfulness, equanimity, and attention - these states were defined by him one by one as they occurred; known to him those states arose, known they were present, known they disappeared. Regarding those states, he abided unattracted, unrepelled, independent, detached, free, dissociated, with a mind rid of barriers. He understood: 'There is an escape beyond,' and with the cultivation of that [attainment], he confirmed that there is."[156]

The subtlety of breath. The mental and physical characteristics described in the three topics above (topics four through six) belong to the first, second and third jhāna respectively. Breath is one of the physical components of the body. The higher the level of jhāna, the softer, more refined and more delicate the breath becomes.

---

156 M.N., Uparipaṇṇāsapāḷi, Anupada Sutta, op.cit., Bhikkhu Ñāṇamoli and Bhikkhu Bodhi.

Figure 18: Sahasrāra - Fourth Jhāna

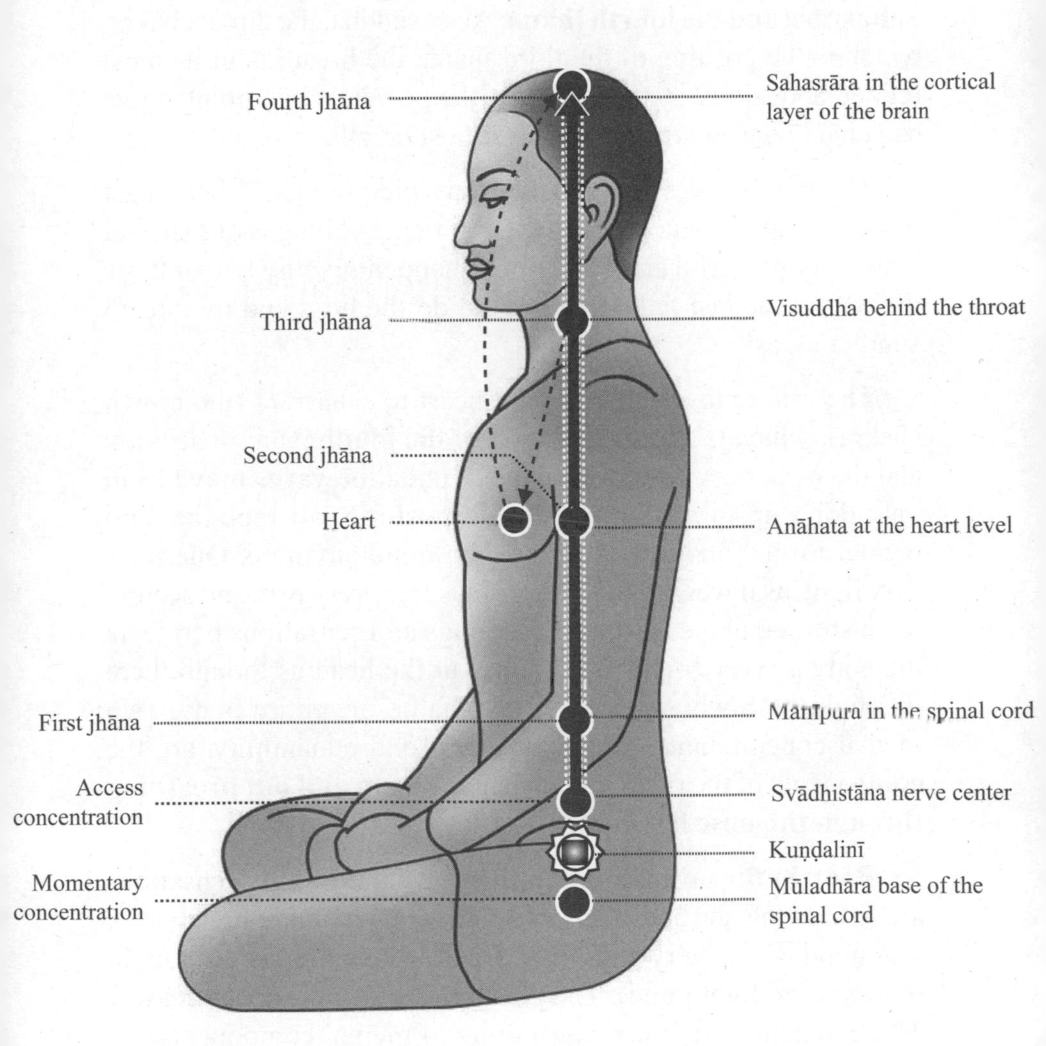

7. "I shall be aware of mental formations, breathing in...and out."

Sahasrāra and the fourth jhāna. At vissuddha, the throat chakra, which is the position of the third jhāna, the breath is in its most refined and softest state. However, the power of one-pointedness can enable one to sense even the softest breath.

The mind moves down to the heart, merging itself there. Past memories appear automatically. Their rising-falling is of a special kind, very powerful and very quick (happening only two or three times). As the last falling ceases, so do the bliss and the breath simultaneously.

The mind moves up from the heart to sahasrāra (the crown chakra), which is also the position of the fourth jhāna. The body and the neck become straightened. Kuṇḍalinī waves move from vissuddha up to sahasrāra. At this position, all thoughts and mental formations cannot disturb the mind anymore. One feels very light, as if weightless. The mind is free, very firm and secure, not disturbed in the least. Such feelings and sensations permeate the body. A very bright light shines at the head as though there is a light bulb whose glowing rays bathe the entire body. Two mental concomitants, one-pointedness and equanimity, are the components of the mind in this jhāna. **The in and out breathing through the nose has ceased.**

Body in the mind, mind in the body. The bodily sensations are so light that the body feels like cotton (*kāyalahuta*: light body). The mind is also very still, light, freed from all kinds of thought (*cittalahuta*: light mind). The physical rising-falling has ceased. There remains only the rising-falling of mental components.

"Again, a monk, putting away ease...enters and abides in the fourth (jhāna); seated, he suffuses his body with purity by the pureness of his mind so that there is not one particle of the body that is not pervaded with purity by the pureness of his mind. Monks, just as a man might sit with his head swathed in a clean cloth so that not a portion of it was not in contact with that clean cloth; even so a monk sits suffusing his body with purity...Monks, this is fourthly how to make become the five-limbed ariyan right concentration."[157]

One should follow Ven. Sāriputta in maintaining the mind in the fourth jhāna and contemplating its enlightening factors.

"And the states in the fourth jhāna - the equanimity, the neither-painful-nor-pleasant feeling, the mental unconcern due to tranquility, the purity of mindfulness and the unification of mind... these states were defined by him one by one as they occurred, known to him those state arose, known they were present, known they dissappeared. Regarding those states, he abided unattracted, unrepelled, independent, detached, free, dissociated, with a mind rid of barriers. He understood: 'There is an escape beyond,' and with the cultivation of that [attainment], he confirmed that there is."[158]

One-pointedness in absorption concentration (jhāna). At chakra positions in absorption concentration, the one-pointedness is very powerful and very secure in its stillness. Such overwhelming force **retains and focuses the mind** very firmly at the chakra positions. While the mind remains quiescent in this one-pointedness, no thoughts or mental formations can intervene. After remaining still for quite a long while, the mind

157 A.N., op.cit., Hare.
158 M.N., op.cit., Bhikkhu Ñāṇamoli and Bhikkhu Bodhi.

gradually removes itself from absorption concentration and begins again to be conscious of the rising and the falling rhythm of the mental components in each jhāna. Then, the mind will be drawn back again to the stillness of one-pointedness.

The characteristics of the mind moving up and down or staying still at different chakras must occur naturally, resulting from the correct development of mindfulness. One must not try to shift or move sensations to any bodily parts. If there is any deliberation to move the sensations to any chakra point, one-pointedness (of absorption concentration) will not emerge.

Bodily components (*kāyasaṅkhāra*): One of the essential components is the breath.

Mental components (*cittasaṅkhāra*): The essential components are perceptions and feelings (saññā and vedanā)

The placidity of bodily components: The characteristics of the first, second and third jhāna.

The cessation of bodily components: The characteristic of the fourth jhāna.

The placidity of mental components: The characteristics of the first, second, third and fourth arūpajhāna.

The cessation of mental components: The characteristics of the cessation of perception and feeling (*saññāvedayitanirodha*).

Rūpajhāna is the blissful dwelling of body and mind.

Arūpajhāna is the blissful dwelling of mind.

8. "I shall calm the mental components, breathing in... and out."
The four levels of arūpajhāna (the formless realm)

The crown chakra (sahasrāra) is the bodily base of the fourth rūpajhāna. At this position, perception and feelings are important mental components. If one is able to perceive very delicate or refined objects, this will lead to a very refined and subtle state of mind. Therefore, one should refrain from perceiving objects in the realm of form, and try to move further into the realm of formless perception.

The Realm of Boundless Space (Ākāsānañcāyatana saññā): The first arūpajhāna

8.1. Remove one's feeling from the stillness and fixation at sahasrāra. Then extend the feeling out into boundless space and recite: '*ananto, akāso* (boundless space), *ananto, akāso*' continuously. The mind will become very light, leave the realm of form, and move into boundless space.

Absorption concentration at the level of arūpajhāna extends itself out infinitely with no definite limits or bounds. Once the mind extends out thoroughly and fully, it will automatically discard the recitation. This signifies that the mind has successfully entered the first arūpajhāna.

The Realm of Boundless Consciousness (Viññāṇañcāyatana saññā): The second arūpajhāna

8.2. Within the infinite and unbounded space, the consciousness also extends itself. Since the element of consciousness is subtler and more refined than the spatial element, the mind tends to absorb the conscious element as its object while chanting '*anantang viññānang* (boundless consciousness)' continuously. As the chanting gradually comes to an end (one cannot chant any further), it signifies that the mind has entered the second arūpajhāna completely.

The Realm of Nothingness (Ākiñcaññāyatana saññā): The third arūpajhāna

8.3. The task of consciousness is to be aware of internal and external objects. It also arises and falls apart continuously and endlessly in the cycle of rebirths, until the state of enlightenment is reached. Since the rising and falling of consciousness continues infinitely, let us then concentrate on the state of nothingness which is void even of the knower and the known; let us delve into the state that is void of every object of consciousness by reciting '*nattikinci* (nothingness or emptiness)' repeatedly.

The state of nothingness, or emptiness, extends infinitely and boundlessly. When the state of nothingness appears fully and completely, the chanting ceases automatically. This signifies that the mind has entered the third arūpajhāna.

The Realm of Neither Perception Nor Non-perception (Nevasaññānāsaññāyatana saññā): The fourth arūpajhāna

8.4. Perception records and recalls the objects of consciousness and represents them back to the mind continuously. The rising and falling of mental components is like an endless stream that flows eternally. As long as the aggregates rise and fall continuously, suffering is not to be terminated. Realizing this truth, the mind inclines to the more peaceful and placid state which can terminate the flow of perceptions and feelings. Let us chant '*santo santo santo* (extinction).'

Then, the chanting ends. There remain only three last rhythms of the rising and the falling of perception…three...two...one… these last rhythms are almost extinguished, but not quite. They appear in an ambiguous state that may be described as neither present nor non-present, neither extinguished nor non-extinguished.

To summarize, at this level the perception expresses itself in an indeterminate manner, neither existing nor non-existing because the lifespan of the perception is extremely short; it arises and passes away very rapidly. Once it is extinguished, there is complete stillness for quite a long time before the perception reappears again and is immediately extinguished. This signifies that one has reached the fourth arūpajhāna.

The description of the characteristics of rūpajhāna and arūpajhāna have been given in detail in topics 4 through 8.4. One should maintain this state of mind as Ven. Sāriputta did.

"And those states of Dhamma…were defined by him one by one as they occurred, known to him they arose, known to him they were present, known they disappeared. He understood thus, 'So indeed, these states not having been, come into being; having been, they vanish.' Regarding those states, he abided unattracted, unrcpelled, independent, detached, free, dissociated, with a mind rid of barriers. He understood, 'There is an escape beyond,' and with the cultivation of that, he comfirmed that there is."[159]

Finally, one has arrived at the highest stage of Dhamma within the cycle of rebirths! However, as long as vipassanā insight has not been perfected, it is impossible to experience the complete termination and extinction of aggregates, because the fuel, i.e. craving, clinging and ignorance, still generates the continuous waves of rising and falling away.

Section Three: Contemplation of the Mind

9. "I shall be aware of the mind, breathing in…and out"

At this level, one keeps observing the characteristics of mind in both the four levels of rūpajhāna and the four levels of arūpajhāna.

---

159 A.N., op.cit., Hare.

10. "I shall experience joy, breathing in ...and out."

Amid the flow of continuous rising and falling phenomena, what has never happened has now appeared, what has happened has now dissolved. Continuous changes occur. Without craving for the pleasant or aversion towards the unpleasant feelings, one is free, and has disentangled from defilements. This is how to train the mind to experience joy.

11. "I shall secure the mind firmly, breathing in...and out."

The mind in the first to the fourth rūpajhāna and in the first to the third arūpajhāna is supported by the seven noble attributes (right understanding, right thought, right speech, right action, right livelihood, right effort and right mindfulness). As a result, the mind is firm and unshaken. Once the mind is firm and unshaken, the Four Noble Truths (the truth of the nature of suffering (five aggregates), the truth of the origin of suffering, the truth of the cessation of suffering, and the truth of the path leading to the cessation of suffering) are then clearly realized.

12. "I shall disentangle the mind, breathing in...and out".

"Disentangling the mind" means to liberate, removing the mind from the imprisonment of desire, or craving, which is the cause of suffering.

Section Four: Contemplation of the Mental-Qualities

13. "I shall contemplate impermanence, breathing in...and out."

A false view takes the five aggregates as permanent, as a source of happiness, and as a source of self. Such misperception is a cause of suffering - samudaya. When the right view of reality becomes strong and clear, the mind will be freed from the **misperception of permanence, happiness and self.** Then, dispassion (*nibbidā ñāṇa*) from attachment to the five aggregates will emerge.

14. "I shall contemplate dissolving desire, breathing in....and out."

As dispassion becomes stronger, all kinds of passion, desire, and attachment in the aggregates will be repeatedly released and dissolved as one intensely experiences the impermanence of the rising-falling aggregates. Equanimity regarding all formations (saṅkhārupekkhā ñāṇa) then arises.

15. "I shall contemplate cessation, breathing in...and out."

The mind moves from the state of equanimity and enters the realm of supreme knowledge. This threshold, which transforms a meditator into an enlightened being, happens in the sequence of appanājavanamaggavithi, the important changing process of the whole mental structure in which the knowledge forwarding one into the threshold of change (anuloma ñāṇa), knowledge of the threshold moment (gotrabhū ñāṇa), knowledge of the path (maggañāṇa), and knowledge of the fruition (phalañāṇa) occur successively (see detailed diagram on page 124 in Chapter Five).

16. "I shall contemplate renunciation, breathing in...and out".

Next, the retrospective knowledge (paccavekkhana ñāṇa) occurs. It reconsiders the process of change in the threshold moment beginning from anuloma ñāṇa, gotrabhū ñāṇa, maggañāṇa and phalañāṇa respectively. Special attention is given to the knowledge of the path whose function is to destroy all fetters and bondage. It considers which fetters have already been destroyed, which have been renounced or removed and which fetters still remain.

Remark: For the detailed description of the entire process of attaining liberation, please see Chapter Five.

Techniques of Entering into Absorption Concentration

1. *Kasiṇa* - focusing on various meditative objects
2. Focusing on perception or memory
3. Focusing on breathing
4. Developing mindfulness, observing the rising and falling state of all aggregated components

Figure 19: Fire Contemplation (Tejokasiṇa)

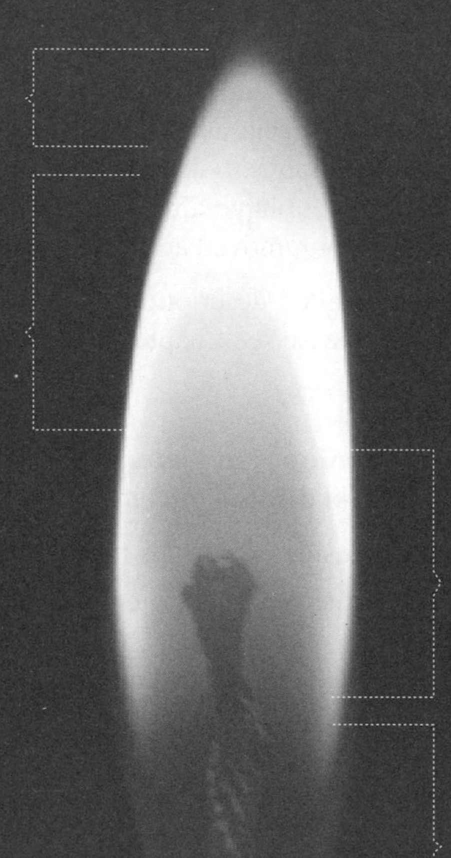

1. Kasiṇa (Focusing on a meditative object): Only the fire kasiṇa will be mentioned here, as an example.

Light a finger-sized candle and place it one meter (three feet) in front of the body. The practitioner should then concentrate on the candle flame, which can be divided into four parts.

The first part is the area at the base of the candle wick and is green in color. The second part covers the top of the candle wick, the third part is the brightest part of the flame and the fourth is the top part of the flame.

The first and the fourth parts are not appropriate as focus points, since the eyes will most likely become dim and not stable enough for concentration. The third part will cause a blurry effect after a long gaze. **The second part of the flame then, is the best part for focus and concentration.**

Gaze continuously at the candle. When all conditions are met, the mind will move into the path of absorption concentration. The feeling of one-pointedness will move up to the pineal.

When one-pointedness establishes itself firmly at the pineal, the eyes are firmly fixed on the candle flame and remain open. Then, as the mind moves further into arūpajhāna, it removes itself from the fire kasiṇa and the eyelids will shut automatically. There is no need to make a wish or any determination to remove the mind from the focused object. When the perception of form ceases (as the mind moves into the formless realm), the knowing elements at the eyes will also cease.

2. Perception or memory: The practitioner recites any religious stanza or prayer and uses this as the object of concentration. Particularly effective is the homage to the Triple Gem, for example, *na ma pa ta na*…. or *sammā ārahang*... or *kīnang pūrānang navang*…. or *suvatthi hotu*… etc. While reciting these stanzas, feeling will be concentrated at the conscious element in the heart. Those who make use of this technique must learn not to pay attention to all other kinds of physical sensation including the in and out breath. Just maintain a light and gentle feeling without any attempt to force or control the mind.

Then, the power of one-pointedness will lead and draw the mind to the pineal and fix itself firmly there. The mind will cease from reciting the words.

3. **Breath**: Those who use this technique, if successfully applied, will receive great benefit. Upon gaining proficiency in observing one's breathing, the practitioner will develop wisdom in realizing the rising and falling away of all phenomena. At the beginning, the characteristics of concentration are distinct. Then, the wisdom of insight will become clear. This ānāpānasāti technique has invaluable benefits, as described in the chapter on the Ānāpānasati Sutta.

A practitioner of this technique will realize the interrelatedness between **breath and mental state, namely, between inhalation, exhalation and the perception of past and future.** These four categories are interrelated from the coarse to the subtler levels. Once realizing this truth, the practitioner will find the technique highly supportive to spiritual development.

Experience in this technique will enable the practitioner to perceive the breath from coarse to subtler levels, until it ceases completely in the fourth jhāna. "Rāhula, … when mindfulness of breathing is developed and cultivated in this way, even the final in-breaths and out-breaths are known as they cease, not unknown."[160]

For those who have not practiced this technique, it may be inconceivable that life can be sustained after the termination of breathing. **The breathing ceases completely when the mind dwells in the fourth jhāna**. Even wearing thin clothes in freezing temperatures, the body will remain warm, and the warm sensation will spread throughout the entire body.

4. Developing mindfulness of the rising and falling of the aggregates in the present moment: The mind maintains equanimity, not accepting or rejecting any objects of consciousness. Just remain fully aware of the passing phenomena in the present moment.

The continuous rising-falling flow occurs within the dimension of time (the mind roaming in the past or future) and is manifested through the changing conditions of the aggregates. The rising-falling phenomenon will appear from the coarse to the more refined levels, from the sensual realm to the realm of form and formlessness, and then will cycle back from subtle to the coarse levels again.

Those who practice this technique will develop deep understanding. If the mind is not attached to the blissful peace, one will able to attain the noble path into nibbāna, which is the final goal.

The first and second methods have to depend more on deliberation and intention. Therefore, mind in jhāna based on these methods, especially the kasiṇa, will face great difficulty in developing vipassanā, or insight wisdom.

---

160 M.N., Majjhimapaṇṇāsapāḷi, Mahārāhulovāda Sutta, p. 532, Bhikkhu Ñāṇamoli and Bhikkhu Bodhi.

Figure 20: Mental Process While Attaining Absorption Concentration*
(Appanājavanavāravithi)

		3 adaptation moments for the Mandhapuggala				3 thought-moments of jhānacitta			
O	O	O	O	O	O	O	O	O	O
Bhavaṅga	*Mano*	*Parikamma*	*Upacāra*	*Anuloma*	*Gotrabhū*	*Jhāna*	*Jhāna*	*Jhāna*	*Bhavaṅga*
		7 moments of javanacitta							

		2 adaptation moments for the Tikkhapuggala			4 thought-moments of jhānacitta				
O	O	O	O	O	O	O	O	O	O
Bhavaṅga	*Mano*	*Upacāra*	*Anuloma*	*Gotrabhū*	*Jhāna*	*Jhāna*	*Jhāna*	*Jhāna*	*Bhavaṅga*
		7 moments of javanacitta							

* Adapted from Sujin Borihanwanakhet, *The Concise Paramatthadhamma* (in Thai), p. 510-511.

A Memoir on the Meditation Experiences of an Anonymous Bhikkhu
Wisdom of a Stream Enterer (Sotāpattimaggañāṇa)

During a night of the waning moon, a group of truth-seeking practitioners and celestial beings gathered in a cave where peace reigned. It was a special night. They had come to listen to a sermon given by a Pure Lord (*visuddhi deva*, here signifying an arahant).

Streams of Truth flowed from his voice like the splendid rays of dawn. The sacred rays of Dhamma overarched and lightened up the sea of saṃsāra. Lotus flowers blooming above the water surface all tried to stretch themselves to touch that glowing light.

A painful sensation occurred at the right knee. Insight understanding of the present phenomenon also arose. The mind moved to the abdomen and fixed itself there firmly and peacefully. The power of one-pointedness had never been so clear and strong. Insight consciousness of the painful sensation at the right knee was also very clear, enabling the mind to perceive the rhythm of sensation, plop... plop... plop. It was like the movement of a hand of a clock.. rising-falling, rising-falling, rising-falling. Chuppp! **The stream of rising and falling came to an end!**

Continuity *(santati*) of the state of things was extinguished! The condition of the knower (nāma) and the known (rūpa) was extinguished. There arose the state where both rising and falling of the aggregates were absent, namely, the nibbānic experience.

After the mind achieved the knowledge of fruition (phalañāṇa), the rising-falling states of nāma and rūpa came back to their normal state. But now some changes to the rising-falling of perception (saññā) occurred. Now, the rising-falling of perception would occur only three times instead of six or seven time as they previously occurred.

The rising-falling of perception was now like drops of water on lotus leaves, unable to penetrate into the deeper layers of the mind. The mind remained aloof, transcending all objects of perception, all thoughts and all conventional truths. Thorough mindfulness was very clear and powerful. All through the night, the mind was fully awake.

The next morning, there occurred a violent physical ejection of coarse bodily waste. The digestion system, stomach and intestine were all cleared out. Everything was squeezed out, even the food intake of that day. Three days later, the body gradually returned to its normal condition.

The Eye of Dhamma opened up on the eighth day of the waning night, which was a week after *Āsāḷha-Pūjā* day.[161] Shortly before that, there happened an amazing and miraculous dream which was an omen of the coming event. In the dream, a group of very fierce dogs was chasing me. After running for a while, a miracle occurred. Both my legs were lifted away from the ground... up, up, and away. Flying in the sky!

Compiler's remark: For sotāpattimaggañāṇa (wisdom of a stream-enterer) to occur, the first level of absorption concentration (the first jhāna) is needed at the turning point of the stream attaining moment on an indispensable basis. This is right concentration in the noble eightfold path.

161 A Buddhist sacred day commemorating the First Sermon and the foundation of the Buddhist Order. This was the full moon day of Āsālha month (the eighth lunar month).

The Eye of Dhamma

Paññācakkhu (the eye of wisdom) is the state of mind that experiences nibbāna for the first time. It is the turning point of one's transformation from a worldly being to an enlightened being. This change is permanent. The person will not be able to be worldly again. He or she will permanently close the door of misery to the four lower worlds.[162] The noble goal is firmly ensured; one will reach full attainment at the latest within the span of seven lifetimes.

That which arises will wither and fall apart as the natural process of all things. This is the translation (from Pāli) and the general interpretation of this sentence is still incomplete. Generally, the statement is understood as **describing the natural state of aggregated things. Such interpretation belongs only to the level of *nāmarūpapariccheda ñāṇa* (the knowledge and ability to discern materiality and mental factors). This is only the beginning level of insight, which still pertains to worldliness.**

The complete translation, which includes the meaning of the nibbānic element, should signify *lokuttaradhamma* (the four transcendent states[163]) which leads to the momentous alteration of the mind. The interpretation should describe the purity of paccavekkhaṇa ñāṇa (knowledge of nibbānic liberation) which emerges at the threshold state: "*virachān vitamalan Dhammacakkun utapādhi yanginji samutayadhamman sappantan nirodhadhammanti.*" This can be translated as: 'The pure eye of Dhamma (paccavekkhaṇa ñāṇa) grasps that

162 The four lower worlds are the world of animals, of ghosts, of demons, and hell.
163 The transcendent states are the states of the stream-enterer, the once-returner, the non-returner and the fully enlightened.

"**The state of things (*nāma-rūpa*) which arise has already ceased**." The continuity of the rising-falling cycle has been broken: no arising, hence no cessation. The nibbānic element emerges precisely in this state, which is devoid of arising and cessation.

Wisdom leading to the Path of Once-Returning (Sakadāgāmimaggañāṇa)

After fifteen days of retreat, special wisdom pertaining to the noble persons led the mind to contemplate and decide that ānāpānasati would be the method and object of meditation which would lead to a higher level of enlightenment. The practice proceeded firmly. The power of ānāpānasati became very intense. The consciousness of breath did not depend on any particular spot or position on the body.

On the fifteenth day, when the mind was fully conscious of the rising-falling stream of thoughts, feeling suddenly became light, like falling into an air pocket. The breath became very refined and a radiant light shone around the body. The mind moved to maṇīpūra position at the abdomen and stayed fixed there very firmly. In a short while, the mind moved up to anāhata position in the middle of the chest. The rising-falling appeared only three times. Both the knower and the known suddenly vanished. The mind moved to the dimension beyond time, the dimension which is devoid of the rising and falling of nāma and rūpa.

Compiler's remark: The second jhāna is needed as the foundation for sakadāgāmīmaggañāṇa to occur. This is the function of right concentration in the eightfold path.

Mind Training of the Higher Level:
(Adhicittasikkha)

The Completion of Right Concentration

At the moment when the mind attained the first absorption for the first time, the first jhāna became the foundation for attaining sotāpattimagga. When the mind attained the second absorption for the first time, the second jhāna became the foundation for sakadāgāmimagga. During the period **from the first attainment to the second attainment, which lasted around one year, the mind could not attain absorption concentration at all**.

However, many special states occurred after the second attainment. The knowledge of breathing meditation became much more advanced. After less than ten minutes of breathing concentration, the coarse breath became subtler. Around the head, the ray of light became much brighter. The mind moved to the point at the abdomen and stayed fixed and firm there (the first absorption). "Don't move from the breath and just keep observing the subtler breath," the intuition suggested.

The breath became much more refined and much deeper. The mind moved up to the middle point of the chest (the second absorption or second jhāna). One-pointedness of mind extended more and more, becoming wider and wider. Peace and tranquility also became deeper and deeper. The subtler the breath was, the brighter the light became. The mind moved up to the middle point of the throat (the position of the third absorption: *tatiyajhāna*) and remained fixed there. Here, the pure white light became very distinct. A cool feeling spread out from the heart and covered the whole body. A very light, agreeable feeling accompanied a very refined and subtle happiness as never experienced before. This was the state of the third jhāna.

As the mind moved to each successive level of jhāna, it was always accompanied by an energy flow moving from the base of the spine up to the bodily base of each jhāna. The breath gradually changed into more and more refined states until it reached the level where there was no longer any movement of breath. Then, the mind moved up to the top of the head (position of the fourth absorption: *catutthajhāna*).

At this point, the movement of the breath no longer appeared. The body was so light it seemed weightless. One-pointedness of mind became one and the same with the feeling of equanimity, and this state was very distinct. Thoughts became very distant and very light. It was as if there was nobody else in this whole world.

Efficiency in jhāna. Skill and proficiency in jhāna had been gradually accumulated. The experiences of getting into and out of jhāna again and again increased. The knowledge of the components of each jhāna from rūpajhāna to arūpajhāna became clearer and more detailed as time went on.

Figure 21: Progressive Abidings; Mental States of Gradual Attainment Cessation of Perception and Feeling

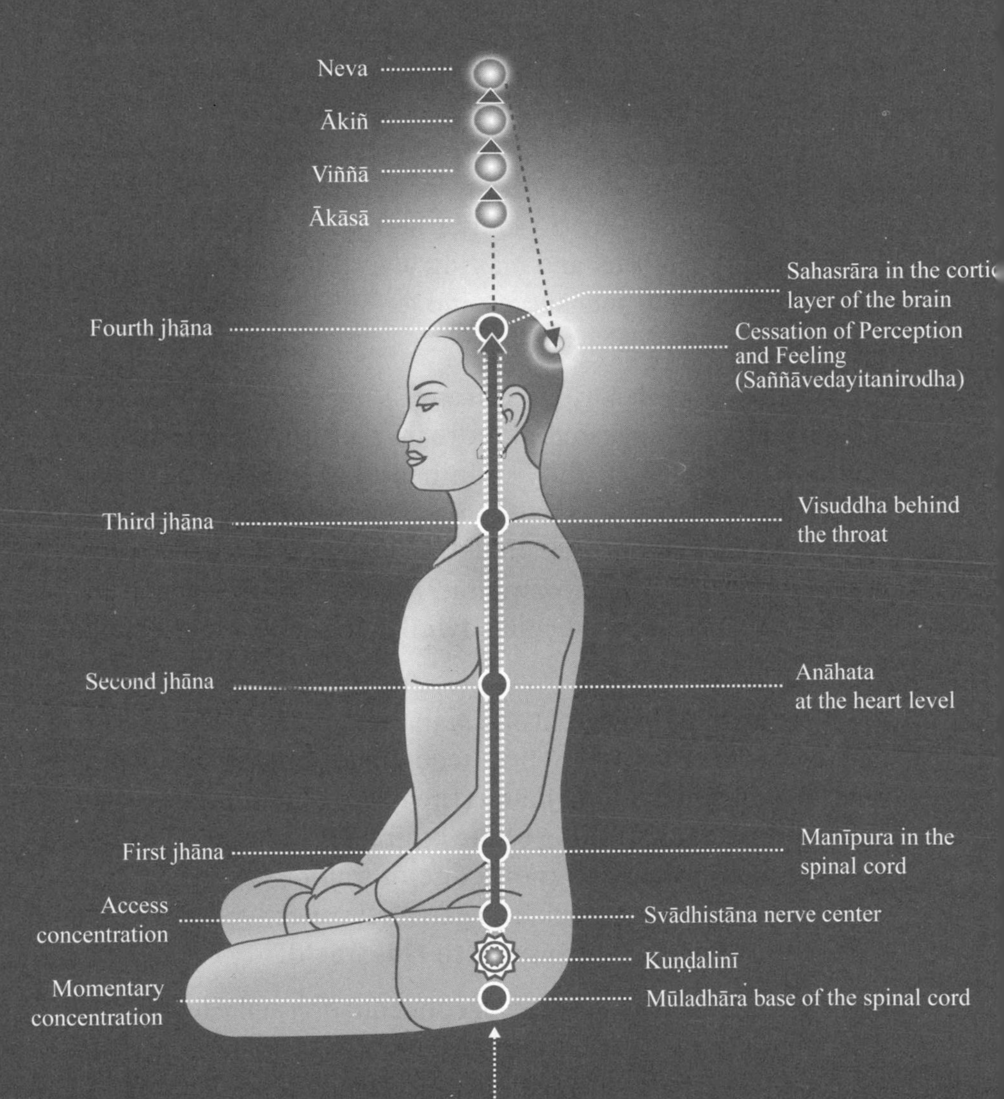

Wisdom leading to the Path of Non-Returning (Anāgāmimaggañāṇa)

The mind dwelled within the world of rūpa and arūpajhānas until it mastered the skill of getting into and out of jhānas, and also gained mastery of making a strong determination (*adhiṭṭhāna*) to remain in each jhāna. After just ten minutes, the mind could enter into rūpa and arūpa levels. As for the four levels of arūpajhāna, the labeling words were no longer necessary. After getting out of the fourth rūpajhāna and making a wish to enter arūpajhāna, the mind could shift into successive formless levels without any accompanying words.

On the seventh day of retreat, a night before the third attainment, there appeared in a dream a visit from a *bhikkhuni arahant* (enlightened, fully-ordained nun). On the next day, before noon, the mind entered into rūpa and arūpajhānas three times. In the afternoon, breathing meditation was used again to enter into absorption concentration, namely the first, second and third rūpajhāna. Then, the mind dwelled for quite a long time in the fourth jhāna.

Next, the mind moved out of rūpajhāna and, after making a wish, entered into the arūpa levels, first, second and third arūpa.... **At the level of ākiñcaññāyatana jhāna (the realm of nothingness), the continuity of rising-falling of the aggregates ceased.** The mind moved out of phalañāṇa (knowledge of fruition). A special type of wisdom called paccavekkhaṇa ñāṇa (retrospective knowledge) appeared. **No more return back to this world!**

Compiler's remark: Absorption concentration at the level of the third arūpajhāna is needed as the foundation for anāgāmimaggañāṇa to occur. This is the function of right concentration in the eightfold path.

Figure 22: Progressive Abidings; Mental States of Gradual Attainment The Backward Order

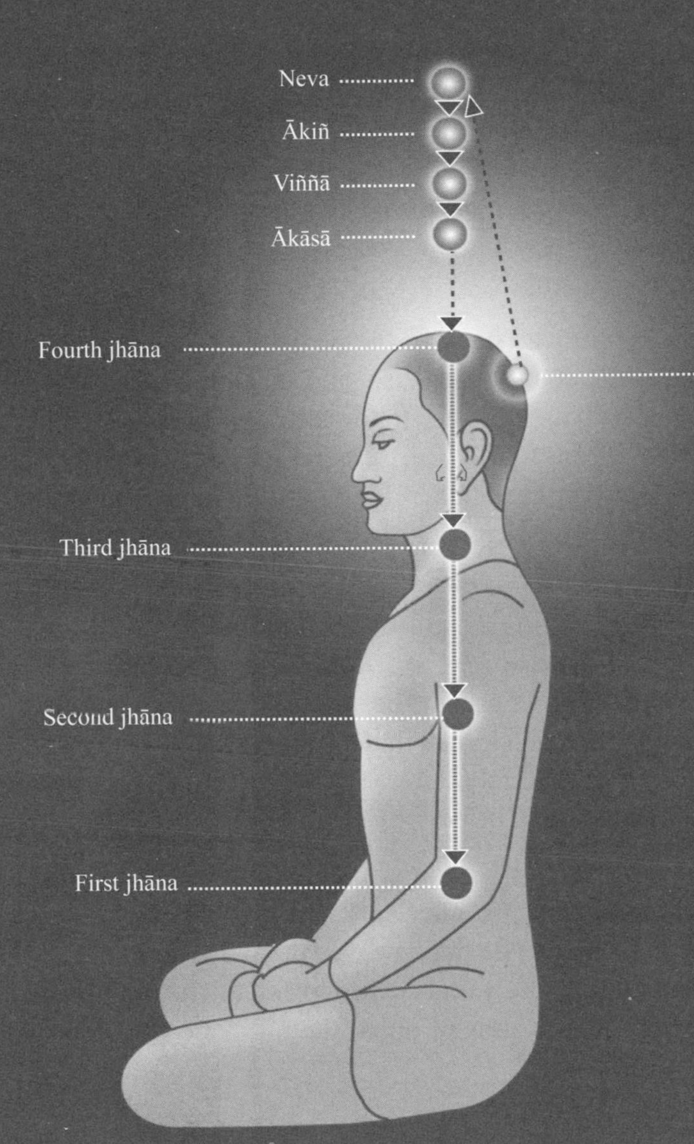

The Cessation of Perception and Feelings *(Saññāvedayitanirodha)*

Here was the experience of cessation of perception and feelings. The mind moved out of the third arūpajhāna with the determination to experience the cessation of perception. Once the mind was released from the cessation position at the back of the head (see Figure 22 on previous page), it made a wish 'reversing, reversing, reversing' ('*patiloma, patiloma, patiloma'* or proceeding backwards).

The mind then moved back to the cessation point, and then moved down to the fourth, third, second and first arūpajhāna. Then it moved backwards further to the four bodily bases which are the positions of the fourth, third, second and first rūpajhāna respectively. Once it moved out of the first rūpajhāna, it made a wish 'conversing, conversing, conversing' ('*anuloma, anuloma, anuloma'* or proceeding forwards).

However, after waiting a long time, the mind did not move into jhāna again! **Lacking advice from others who had more experience, this first experiment and its result were not complete.** Intuition then suggested that the mind make an intention while it remained in the first jhāna. If it moved out from jhāna, the intention would not be effective.

Thus, the experiment began again. This time when the mind entered into the first jhāna, it made the determination 'conversing, conversing, conversing.' The mind moved up to the second, third and fourth jhāna respectively and stayed fixed at the fourth jhāna for a long time. Then, it moved up to the nibbānic position of anāgāmī.

Figure 23: Progressive Abidings: Mental States of Gradual Attainment The Forward Order

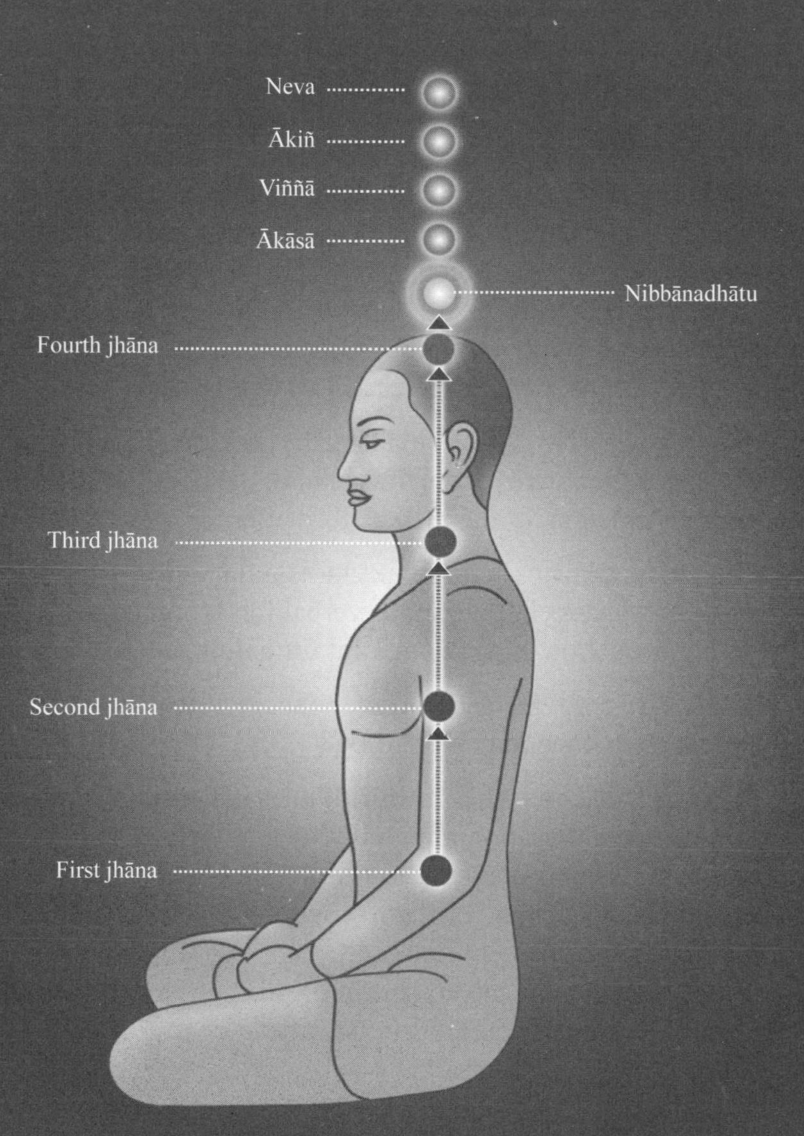

Saññāvedayitanirodha

"On one occasion, Visākhā, a lay follower, went to Dhammadinna, the enlightened bhikkhuni, and asked her the following question:

"Lady, how does the attainment of the cessation of perception and feeling come to be?"

"Friend Visākha, when a bhikkhu is attaining the cessation of perception and feeling, it does not occur to him: 'I shall attain the cessation of perception and feeling,' or 'I am attaining the cessation of perception and feeling,' or 'I have attained the cessation of perception and feeling,' but rather his mind has previously been developed in such a way that it leads him to that state.

"Lady, when a bhikkhu is attaining the cessation of perception and feeling, which states cease first in him: the bodily formation, the verbal formation, or the mental formation?

"Friend Visākha, when a bhikkhu is attaining the cessation of perception and feeling, first the verbal formation ceases, then the bodily formation, then the mental formation.

"Lady, how does emergence from the attainment of the cessation of perception and feeling come to be?

"Friend Visākha, when a bhikkhu is emerging from the attainment of the cessation of perception and feeling, it does not occur to him: 'I shall emerge from the attainment of the cessation of perception and feeling,' or 'I am emerging from the attainment of the cessation of perception and feeling,' or 'I have emerged from the attainment of the cessation of perception and feeling,' but rather his mind has previously been developed in such a way that it leads him to that state.

"Lady, when a bhikkhu is emerging from the attainment of the cessation of perception and feeling, which states arise first in him: the bodily formation, the verbal formation, or the mental formation?

"Friend Visākha, when a bhikkhu is emerging from the attainment of the cessation of perception and feeling, first the mental formation arises, then the bodily formation, then the verbal formation.

"Lady, when a bhikkhu has emerged from the attainment of the cessation of perception and feeling, how many kinds of contact touch him?

"Friend Visākha, when a bhikkhu has emerged from the attainment of the cessation of perception and feeling, three kinds of contact touch him: voidness contact, signless contact, desireless contact.

"Lady, when a bhikkhu has emerged from the attainment of the cessation of perception and feeling, to what does his mind incline, to what does it lean, to what does it tend?

"Friend Visākha, when a bhikkhu has emerged from the attainment of the cessation of perception and feeling, his mind inclines to seclusion, leans to seclusion, tends to seclusion."[164]

---

164 M.N., Mūlapaṇṇāsapāḷi, Cūḷavedalla Sutta, p. 399-401, Bhikkhu Ñāṇamoli and Bhikkhu Bodhi.

Wisdom of the Path of the Fully Enlightened (Arahattamaggañāṇa)

Time lapsed into the fifth year since the day the mind attained the third enlightened state. During that period, the mind had enjoyed traveling innumerable times within the realm of rūpa and arūpa. In this fifth year, the fifteen day retreat took place from the first to the fifteenth day of the waxing moon of the seventh month according to the lunar calendar.

A night before the most important day in my life, the Pure Lord who had given the sermon which led to the first enlightenment appeared in a dream paying a visit to my *kuti*. Then, on the sixth day of the retreat, in the evening after a long day of effort, it was time for bathing. The robe was changed into a towel. The most important moment was about to come!

Before bathing, the mind just wanted to rest. I sat down on a rattan chair with feet touching the floor and both hands resting on the knees, with eyes closed in a relaxing manner. The mind, without any intention, moved into the four rūpajhānas: the first, second, third and fourth jhāna respectively. At the fourth jhāna, the rising and falling flows of aggregates were cut off, finished, a complete extinction!

Compiler's remark: Absorption concentration at the level of the fourth jhāna is required as the foundation for arahattamaggañāṇa to occur. This is the function of right concentration in the completion of the noble eightfold path.

Near the garden in the quiet temple nook,
plumbs are dropping into the nearby brook.

Carried in the wind,
washed in the sounds of the sea,
the song of the cicadas.

Figure 24: Dhammachakra - The Wheel of Dhamma

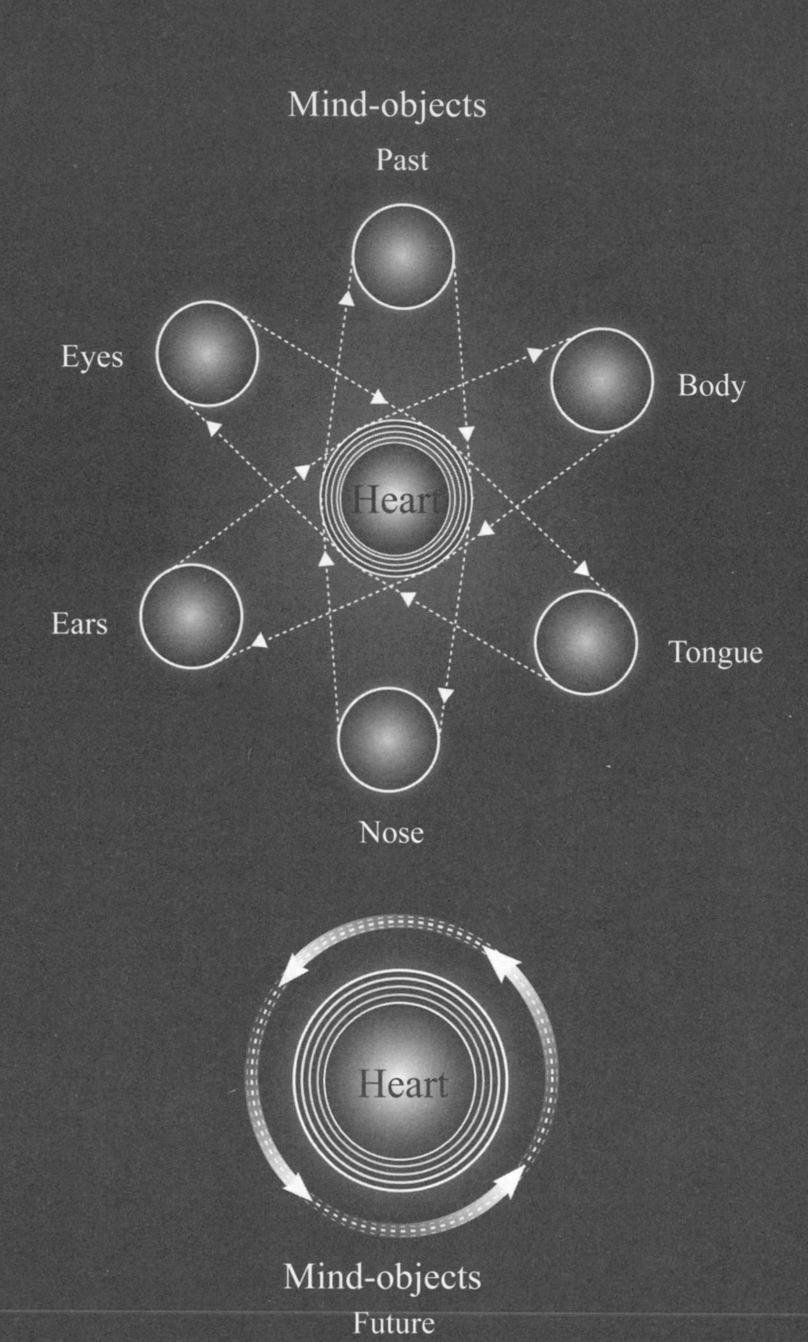

The Wheel of Dhamma (Dhammachakra)

Eight days later, late in the morning before doing walking meditation, a mosquito was trapped by using a glass and was let out of the room. But because the mosquito net at the window was left open, a baby bird flew into the room. It was so naive and fearless that even after being caught in the hand, it was very still. Two eyes met, human and bird.

In the afternoon, during walking meditation in the corridor, there was an encounter with another animal. This time, however, it symbolized death. A large wasp dared to catch a big spider which was waiting for its prey. In the middle of the spider web, a struggle for survival occurred. It was a fierce fight. The wasp used its poisoned sting. The spider used its powerful web. Finally, both fell from the spider's web into a bush below. A short time later, the wasp flew away with its prey.

Some time between three and four o'clock in the afternoon, in the middle of meditation in the standing position, the mind moved into rūpajhāna and arūpajhāna respectively. When it was in the third arūpajhāna, ***Dhammachakra*, or the wheel of Dhamma, began its cycling**. The cycle began first in the head where all cognizable objects of the mind were kept. Then the cycle moved to the heart and back to the head, then back to the heart again. The rotating cycle repeated itself again and again.

Many moments later, the consciousness at the five senses all cycled to the knowing element at the heart (*manodhātu*) and then cycled back to each sensory base. Such rotation, or Dhammachakra, repeated itself from moment to moment. It went on for hours and then for days. Such a state is the pure mechanism of aggregates (eyes met forms, ears met sound, tongue met taste, etc). The mind did not intervene at all. While Dhammachakra moved, the mind dwelled beyond all thoughts, all conventions and all constructions through language.

Wisdom of Liberation (Vimuttiñāṇadhasana)

Silence ruled the atmosphere after midnight. One could feel the power of peace and tranquility. Everything seemed to come to a complete stop, all beings fell into a deep sleep. Midnight songs from all kinds of insects came to an end. It was such a beautiful night. Such a night was like a blooming flower that blessed the heart of the meditator making every effort in the practice of sleep avoidance (*jāgariyānuyoga*).

During walking meditation, the feeling at the feet wheeled back to the heart and then cycled back down to the feet. Such cycling resembled the rotation of a wheel. **Suddenly, Dhammachakra stopped its cycling! The feet stopped moving, the body stood still.** There was a tremendous flow of energy forcing the eyelids to close. Suddenly, that powerful energy flow exploded into a very bright light and an image (nimitta) of a young man in white appeared. Then he changed himself into an old man with white hair and then changed again into a skeleton. Finally, all the bones exploded into dust and vanished.

The body slowly sat down automatically. The wisdom of liberation (vimuttiñāṇadhasana) had emerged. The cycle of rebirths had finished. The Holy Faring had been completed. There were no other duties to be done. One had attained vimuttidhamma, which is beyond all defilements, beyond birth and death. The rumble of thunder from the sky in the north could be heard.

Compiler's remark: The image of the man signifies the mass of energy which had roamed within the cycle of rebirths in various realms of saṃsāra. Its explosion, thus, implies the extinction of such roaming. No more rebirths!

Two Levels of Transcendental Jhāna (Lokuttarajhāna)

The first level is the jhāna of the sekha, one who has already attained the first three experiences of enlightenment. These jhānas are different from jhānas of the worldly people in that when the mind moves from the first to the fourth jhāna, it does not need to stop at the heart position.

The second level is the transcendental jhāna of the arahant. At every level of rūpajhāna and every chakra position relating to rūpajhāna, the mind has to move towards and converge with the heart consciousness. All the rising-falling processes focus at the heart except in the case of the fourth jhāna. Only in this jhāna does the rising-falling phenomenon remains fixed at sahasrāra, at the top of the head.

Figure 25: Vibration of the Refined Physical Elements (Dhammadhātu)

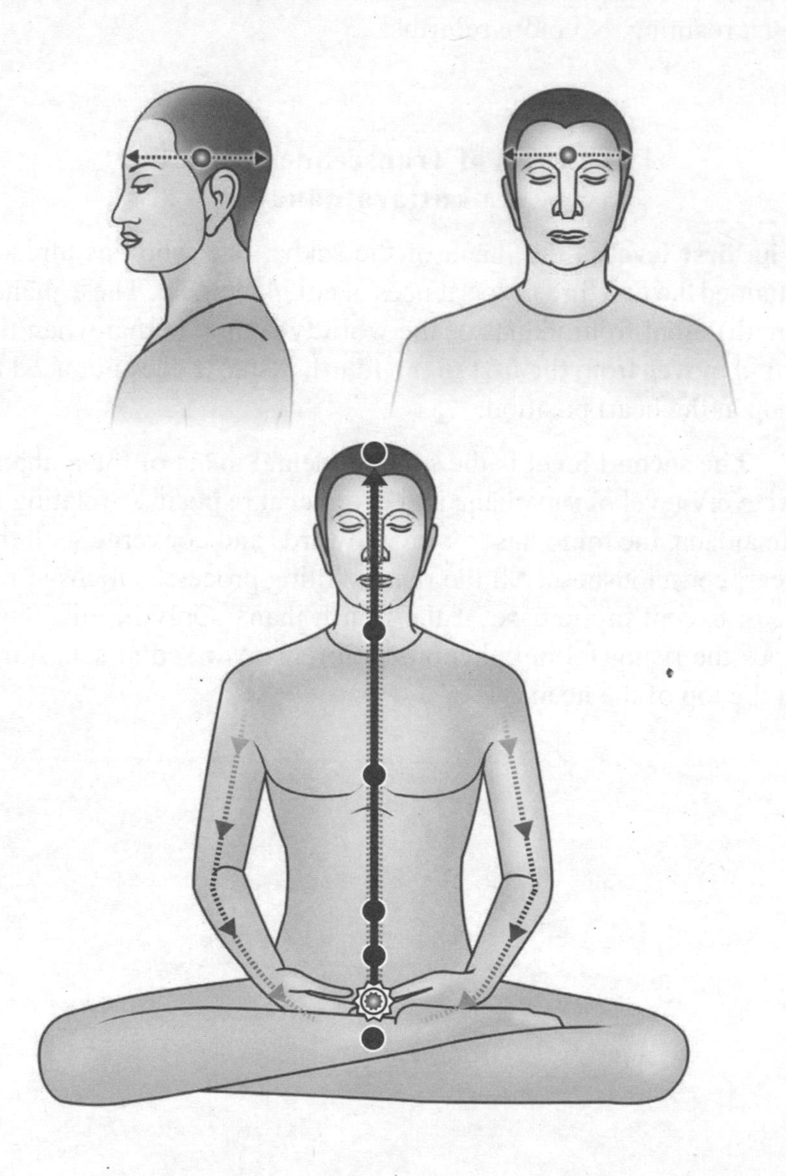

The Vibration of the Refined Physical

The vibration of the refined physical elements *(dhammadhātu)* is the process of cleansing all the remaining negative energies from the body. The coarse, heavy and dark elements will be driven out of the body by this type of vibration wave.

Three levels of Dhammadhātu vibration

First level

1. The vibration begins at the pineal. The direction of energy moves from the pineal to the front and then to the back of the head, alternating in a to and fro swing. Each rhythm of vibration lasts one second.

1.1. The vibration starts from the pineal. The direction of energy goes to the left and then to the right alternately. Each rhythm of vibration lasts one second.

1.2. Each cycle of vibration will finish when it comes to the end of the nerves of the fingers. The heavy elements move from the pineal down along the right shoulder, then down along the arm, the hand until the ends of the fingers.

1.3. Each cycle of vibration will finish when it comes to the end of the nerves of the fingers. The heavy elements move from the pineal down along the left shoulder, then down along the arm, the hand until the end of the fingers.

1.4. The vibration drives impure elements from the pineal down to both shoulders simultaneously until it reaches the ends of the fingers of both hands at the same time.

1.5. Then, the vibration proceeds from the afore-mentioned process, moving down to the heart and then to the lower parts of the body until it reaches the ends of both feet at the same time.

1.6. Then, the mind moves into jhāna and chakra cycles respectively, beginning from the pineal onward.

Second level. The vibration starts at the pineal and moves down to both shoulders, both arms until it reaches the end of the nerves of the fingers of both hands. Once the vibration of each cycle finishes, the kuṇḍalinī energy moves up through various chakras until it reaches sahasrāra.

Third level. All vibration from all bodily parts comes to focus at the right arm and finishes when reaching the tips of the fingers. The vibration starts from the deepest level of the bone tissues (*atthamanchan*).

Dhammachakra and its Cycling

After the entire process of elements cleansing has been thoroughly completed, one can feel that the energy field which normally surrounds the heart consciousness in various layers has completely gone. There is no residue of pulling-pushing energy left. The mind is now free from and remains beyond all contact at the eyes, ears, nose, tongue, body and sense doors. The rising-falling of the knower and the known is now the sole process of mere gestures and contacts. **Every contact is the first and the last happening; nothing remains thereafter.**

The rising-falling of aggregates now is in the state of mere contact between the knower and the known. The conscious contacts at the eyes, ear, nose, tongue, body, thought and feeling - all sensory contacts - go back to the heart consciousness and cycle there. This cycling that surrounds the heart is the wheeling of Dhammachakra.

Tathatā - The state beyond conventional truth

When the wheel of Dhammachakra increases in speed and number of rotations, up to a point, the mind will be able to uplift itself into the state of tathatā, which is the truth beyond all suffering and the maintenance of complete freedom.

Dried, brown leaves have fallen

onto the temple stones;

no hurry to sweep them away;

just sit and observe nature's way.

The excellent Dhammachakra

already declared by the Lord Buddha

is impossible to wheel back

by the effort of the ordained ones,

Brahmin, Angels, Māra,

or god Brahma.

CHAPTER IX

Threefold Attainments

Meditative Attainment
(Jhānasamāpatti)

Having gained the five proficiencies in jhāna practices, the meditator can experience both rūpajhāna and arūpajhāna at will. One can enter a desired level of jhāna and let the mind be firmly established there for a while. As the mind is about to move from that jhāna, one can continue to practice by resolving to remain in that jhāna for a determined period of time. One's mind will then be firmly fixed in such a state and will not move out until the predetermined time is over.

As for entering the fourth arūpajhāna, one should make a determination while the mind is still established in the third arūpajhāna (ākiñcaññayatana).

Fruition Enjoyment
(Phalasamāpatti)

To successfully attain fruition enjoyment, the stream-enterer must be proficient in at least the first jhāna. It has already been mentioned that for a noble individual who is wisdom-oriented (*vipassanāyānika*), namely one who reaches enlightenment by means of the insight force, his or her jhāna attainment will appear only once, in the very moment he or she attains sotāpattimagga, or the first level of enlightenment. Later, after attaining the noble truth of sakadāgāmī, or the second level of enlightenment, such a person can develop systematically the proficiency in jhāna attainment. Therefore, only three types of noble individuals, namely sakadāgāmī, anāgāmī, and arahant, are able to attain fruition enjoyment at will. As for the sotāpanna, only ones who are already proficient in jhāna are able to attain fruition enjoyment.

The four types of noble individuals who wish to enter the state of fruition enjoyment can do so by entering into the level of jhāna which was used as the foundation of their former moment of enlightenment. They should determine to experience fruition enjoyment for an exact period of time. Then, the mind will leave that jhāna and enter into the state of fruition enjoyment. Having entered such a state, the mind has nibbāna as its sole object, with no interference from the passive (or subliminal) states of consciousness (bhavaṅga-citta).

Paramatthadīpanī nāma udānavannanā describes phalasamāpatti as follows: "this...fruition attainment is...to be regarded...as absorption which, having nibbāna as its sole object, consitutes the ripening of that which is both supermundane and skilled."[165]

165 Dhammapala, *The Udāna Commentary* vol.I, trans. by Peter Masefield, p. 60.

Extinction Attainment
(Nirodhasamāpatti)[166]

Wishing to enter extinction attainment, the anāgāmī or arahant who is proficient in progressive abidings (*anupubbavihāra*)[167] in both the forward and the backward order must enter rūpajhāna and arūpajhāna respectively. With wisdom they continue to observe the rising and falling phenomena of the jhāna aggregates until the attainment of the third arūpajhāna, i.e. ākiñcaññāyatana. After the mind comes out of the third arūpajhāna, one should make a wish regarding the three preliminary conditions for entering extinction attainment as follows:

1. During my abiding in extinction attainment, all my personal belongings, requisites and residential properties located near or far will not be destroyed or damaged by any perils of flood, fire or theft.
2. I must release myself from the state of attainment if there is a sangha community meeting which requires my presence.

---

166 Nirodhasamāpatti is the temporary suspension of all consciousness and mental activity. If it happens immediately and automatically following the semi-conscious state of the realm of neither-perception-nor-non-perception, it is called saññavedayitanirodha (cessation of perception and feeling). But if it comes about by way of making a determination for an exact period of time, it is called nirodhasamāpatti. The necessary preconditions for the attainment of these states are perfect mastery of all the eight absorptions (jhānas), as well as the previous attainment of non-returnership or arahantship.

167 Progressive abidings or mental states of gradual attainment indicate the entire chain of jhāna attainment from the four rūpajhānas to the four arūpajhānas plus one higher stage where all perceptions and feelings cease totally. This ninth stage is called saññavedayitanirodha (cessation of perceptions and feelings).

3. I must use the perfect knowledge (*ñāṇadassana*) to foresee the constituents of my life for the next seven days whether or not it will come to an end so that I can be ensured to have enough time to realize and abide in extinction attainment.[168]

While the noble individuals dwell in extinction attainment, no dangers can affect them due to the power of the noble concentration. Having made the determination, the mind moves to the fourth arūpajhāna, i.e. nevasaññānāsaññāyatana. Then the rising-falling rhythm happens two times before ceasing. The mind then moves up to the cessation point of perception (see figure 21). At this point, all perceptions cease completely. The mind, its mental concomitants, and the breath also cease completely (the physical body remains warm, yet there is no in and out breath).

When seven days have passed according to the time-set determination, the mind returns to its normal state. The process of removal from extinction attainment is the same as that from cessation of perception and feeling.

168 *Majjhimabhidhamma: Questions and Answers, Chapter4-5* (in Thai), Abhidhamma Chotika College, p. 56.

Progressive Abiding
(Anupubbavihāra)

The nine states of successive meditative attainment are called progressive abiding (anupubbavihāra). To enter extinction attainment, the noble individual must be proficient in progressive abiding both in the forward and the backward order.

The cessation of perception. One has to begin from the preliminary stage and ascend successively to the highest stage, i.e., from the first jhāna to the cessation of perception and feeling.

Then, if one wants to practice **the backward order**, one should begin from the highest stage and descend towards the most preliminary stage, i.e. from cessation of perception and feeling down to the fourth, third, second and first arūpajhāna, then to the fourth, third, second, and first rūpajhāna.

The forward order. In the process of backward order, when the mind descends to the first jhāna, one should then lead the mind back up to the second, third and fourth rūpajhāna respectively. When the mind dwells between rūpajhāna and arūpajhāna, it then moves into the nibbānic stage which transcends the rising-falling of aggregates, transcending all spheres of being and rebirth.

"There is that dimension where there is no appearance, no ending, and is accessible from all directions.

"There is that dimension where earth, water, fire, and wind cannot be used to intend appearance.

"There is that dimension where the concepts of length, shortness, smallness, largeness, beauty, foulness do not apply.

"There is that dimension where nāma and rūpa are completely extinguished due to a complete cessation of consciousness."[169]

"There is that dimension where there is neither earth, nor water, nor fire, nor wind; neither dimension of the infinitude of space, nor dimension of the infinitude of consciousness, nor dimension of nothingness, nor dimension of neither perception nor non-perception; neither this world, nor the next world, nor sun, nor moon. And there, I say, there is neither coming, nor going, nor staying; neither passing away nor arising: unestablished, unevolving, without support [mental objects]. This, just this, is the end of [suffering]."[170]

"Ānanda, so at a later time, having seen the drawback of the nevasaññānāsaññāyatana, I pursued that theme; having understood the reward of saññavedayitanirodha, I familiarized myself with it. My heart leapt at saññavedayitanirodha, and I grew confident, steadfast, and firm, seeing it as peace. With the complete transcending of nevasaññānāsaññāyatana, I entered and remained in saññavedayitanirodha. And as I saw with discernment, cankers within me went to their total end.

"Ānanda, as long as I had not attained and emerged from these nine steps of anupubbavihāra, both in forward and backward order in this way, I did not claim to have directly awakened to the right self: that is, an awakening unexcelled in the cosmos with its gods, Māra, and brahmas, with its contemplatives and priests, its royalty and common people. But as soon as I had attained and emerged from these nine steps of anupubbavihāra in this way, then I did claim to have directly awakened to the

169 D.N., Kevaddha Sutta (D.N.11), Bhikkhu Thanissaro, ATI.
170 Kh.N., Udāna (8.1), Nibbāna Sutta, Bhikkhu Thanissaro, ATI.

right self, an awakening unexcelled in the cosmos with its gods, Māra, and brahmas, with its contemplatives and priests, its royalty and common people. Knowledge and vision arose in me: 'My deliverance of mind is unshakable. This is the last rebirth. There is now no further becoming.'"[171]

Pairs of Adverse Conditions

"Well said! Well said, monks! Those who should assert what those great disciples have asserted would rightly do so. Indeed, monks, I have said that noise is a thorn to [jhāna]. There are these ten thorns. What ten?

"To one who delights in seclusion, delight in society is a thorn.

"To one devoted to concentration on the mark of the foul, concentration on the mark of the fair is a thorn.

"To one guarding the doors of the sense-faculties, the sight of shows is a thorn.

"To the Brahmā-life, consorting with [the opposite sex] is a thorn.

"To the first [jhāna], sound is a thorn;

"To the second [jhāna], thought directed and sustained;

"To the third, zest;

171 A.N., The Book of the Nines (9.41), Tapussa Sutta, Bhikkhu Thanissaro, ATI.

"To the fourth [jhāna], in-breathing and out-breathing is a thorn.

"To the attainment of the ending of awareness-and-feeling, awareness-and-feeling are a thorn.

"Lust, malice and delusion are thorns.

"So, monks, do ye abide thornless, do ye abide thorn-removers, do ye abide thornless thorn-removers. Monks, the thornless are arahants, the thornless thorn-removers are arahants."[172]

Mental Rust, Golden Rust

"Monks, there are these five debasements of gold by reason of which debased gold is neither pliable nor workable, nor bright, but is brittle and of no use for the best work. What five?

"Iron, copper, tin, lead and silver.

"But when gold is free of these five debasements, it is pliable and workable and bright, nor is it brittle, but fit for the best work; and whatever sort of ornament one wants, whether a signet-ring or an ear-ring, a necklace or a gold chain, it can be used for that.

"In just the same way, monks, there are these **five debasements of the mind** by reason of which a debased mind is neither pliable nor workable nor bright, but is brittle and not rightly composed for the destruction of the cankers. What five?

"Sensual desire, ill will, sloth and torpor, [restlessness and anxiety], and doubt.

"But when the mind is free of these five debasements, it is pliable and workable and bright, nor is it brittle, but is rightly

172 A.N., vol.5, The Book of the Tens (10,8,73), p. 92, Woodward.

composed for the destruction of the cankers; and one can bend the mind to the realization by psychic knowledge of whatever condition is realizable by psychic knowledge, and become an eyewitness in every case, whatever the range may be."[173]

Noble Disciples and the Coral Tree Flowers

"Monks, what time the celestial coral tree, the Kovilāra Paricchattaka, of the devas of the thirty is sere in leaf, those devas greatly rejoice: 'The celestial coral tree is sere in leaf! Ere long now **there will be leaf-fall**!'

"What time the leaves are falling, they greatly rejoice: 'Falling are now the leaves! Shortly, now, **will burgeon every bud**.'

"What time the buds appear, they greatly rejoice: 'Now the buds appear! Soon **the shoots will set**!'

"What time the shoots are set, they greatly rejoice: 'Now the shoots are set! Soon **will the blossoms form**.'

"What time the blossoms form, they greatly rejoice: 'Now the blossoms form! Soon like the red lotus **will the flowers be shaped**!'

"What time the flowers are shaped like the red lotus, they greatly rejoice: Shaped like the red lotus are the flowers! Soon the flowers **will be in full bloom!'**

"What time the Kovilāra Pāricehattaka tree of the devas of the thirty is in full bloom, those devas sport for four divine months at the foot of the celestial tree, dallying and indulging in the five pleasures of the senses.

173 A.N., vol. 3, The Book of the Fives (5,3,22), p. 11-12, Hare.

"When the celestial tree is in full bloom, its effulgence pervades full fifty leagues. The perfume is blown before the wind a hundred leagues. This is the power of the Kovilāra Paricchattaka tree.

"In just the same way, monks, what time **the ariyan disciple minds him to go forth from the home into the homeless life, the ariyan disciple is sere in leaf,** like the celestial coral tree of the devas of the thirty.

"What time **the ariyan disciple has his hair and beard shaved off and dons the yellow robe and goes forth from home into the homeless life is his fall of leaf**, like the celestial coral tree…

"What time, aloof from sense desires... **he enters and abides in the first [jhāna]... his buds appear**, like the celestial coral tree. . . .

"What time, suppressing active thought**... he enters and abides in the second [jhāna]... his shoots set,** like the celestial coral tree…

"What time, **dwelling free from the fervor of zest, detached... he enters and abides in the third [jhāna]** .. his blossoms form, like the celestial coral tree. . . .

"What time, **by putting away ill and ease... he enters and abides in the fourth [jhāna]...** his flowers are of the red lotus shape, like the celestial coral tree. . . .

"What time the ariyan disciple, by destroying the cankers... enters and abides in full realization... his flowers are in full bloom, like the celestial coral tree of the devas of the thirty.

"Then the earth devas utter a shout: 'This reverend sir called so and so, living the life of faith of such a reverend one, gone forth from such a village or market-town, has destroyed the cankers ... and dwells in full realization...!'

"Hearing the shout of the earth devas, the company of the four royal devas... the devas of the thirty... the Yama devas... the Tusita devas... the devas who delight in creating... the devas who have power over others' creations... and the devas of brahmā's retinue roll back the cry: 'This reverend sir, living the life of faith, **gone forth from such a village or from such a market-town into the homeless life, has, by the destruction of the cankers, entered and there abides in that state of emancipation of the mind and wisdom which is free of the cankers, having come to know and realize this state fully for himself, even in this present life.'**

"Thus in an instant, thus in a moment, the sound soars up to brahma's heaven. This is the progressive power of a monk who has destroyed the cankers."[174]

---

174 A.N., vol.4, The Book of the Sevens (7,7,65), p. 78-80 Hare.

Figure 26: Dimensions of Mind

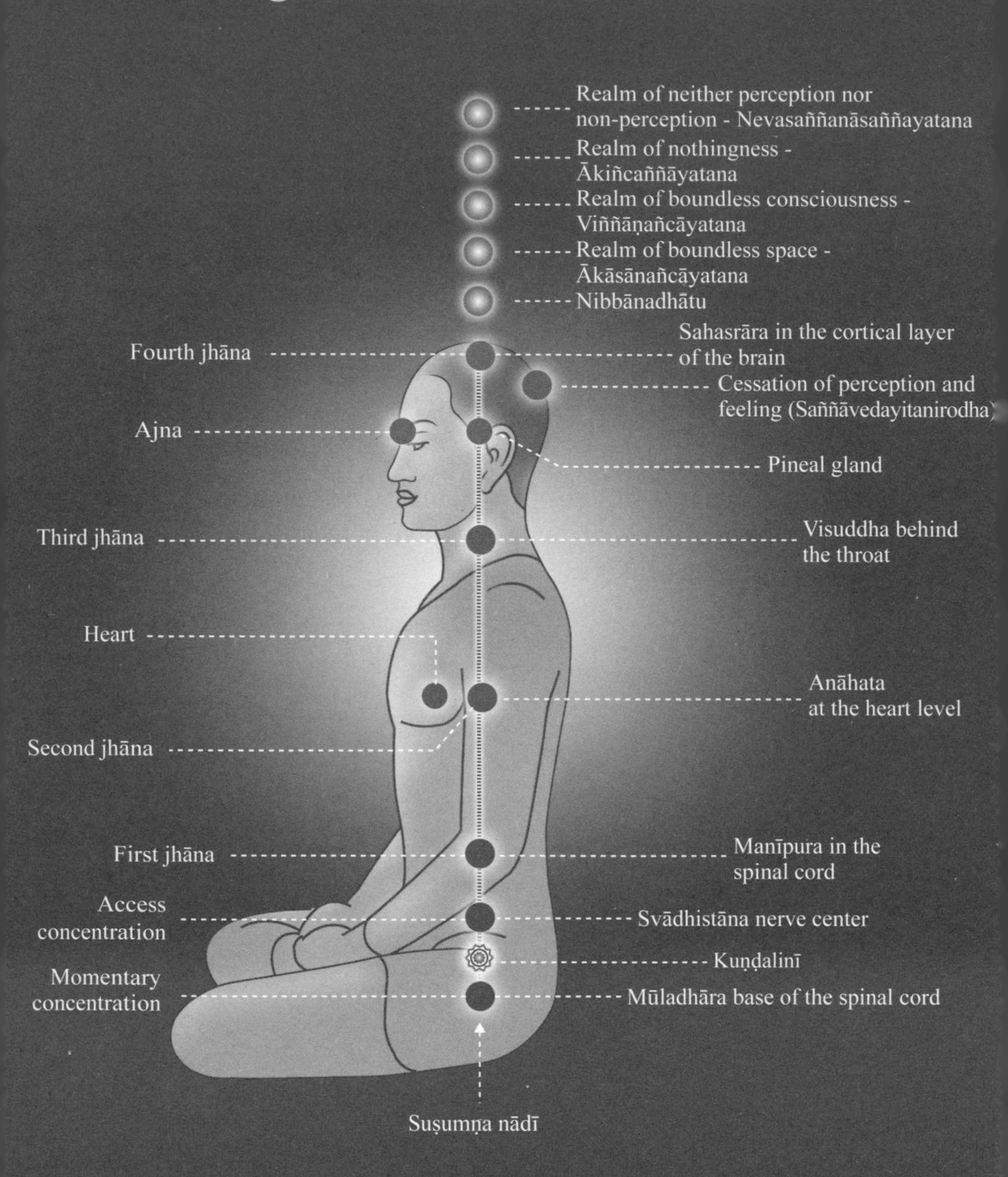

In the realm of the Dhamma,

there is no maker;

all truths of the Dhamma

are inherently true

without any need

to make them true.

REFERENCE WORKS IN THAI

Buddhadasa Bhikkhu. *Ariya Sat Chak Phra Ot (The Noble Truths: From The Buddha's Voice)*. Bangkok: Dhammadana Foundation. 2527 B.E.

Buddhadasa Bhikkhu. *Phutthaprawat Chak Phra Ot (The Buddha's Autobiography)*. Bangkok: Dhammadana Foundation. 2523 B.E.

Burapa Phadungthai. *Kin Yang Rusi, Lang Phit Phichitrok (A Hermit's Way of Eating, Detoxification and Overcoming Illness)*. Bangkok: 2550 B.E.

Chan Suwannaphesaj (trans.) *Huachai Kammathan (The Heart of Buddhist Meditation by Nyanaponika Thera)*. Bangkok: 2538 B.E.

Hatayoga. Bangkok: Sanyo Universal Electric Co., 2521 B.E.

Panha Lae Chaloey : Parichet Ti Si-Ha, Majjhima Abhidhamma Tri (Questions and Answers, Chapter 4-5, Intermediate Abhidhamma, The Third level) . Bangkok: Abhidhamma Chotika College. 2529 B.E.

Phra Dhammapidok. *Photchananukrom Phutthasat Chabap Pramuantham (Dictionary of Buddhism: (Compilation of Dhamma Concepts)*. Bangkok: Maha Chulalongkorn Royal College. 2538 B.E.

Phra Ratchaworamuni. *Buddhadhamma (Dhamma of the Buddha)*. Bangkok: The Third Edition, 2529 B.E.

S. Bunarak. *Photchananukrom Chet Khamphi (Dictionary of Seven Sacred Books*. Bangkok. (no printing year)

Sucheep Punyanupab. *Phra Traipidok Chabap Prachachon (Tipiṭaka : A Popular Version)*. Bangkok: 2525 B.E.

Sujin Borihanwanakhet, *Paramatthadham Sangkhep, Chittasangkhep Lae Phakphanuak (The Concise Paramatthadhamma, Explanation on Mind and Appendix)*. Bangkok: Dhamma Study and Support Foundation. 2530 B.E.

Thanit Yupho. *Vipassananiyom (In Praise of Insight Meditation)*. Bangkok: 2526 B.E.

Tipiṭaka, 45 vols., Bangkok: Department of Religious Affair 2530 B.E.

Tipiṭaka and Commentaries, 91 vols., Bangkok: Maha Makut Royal College, 2525 B.E.

Vipassana Kammathan (Insight Meditation). Bangkok: Abhidhamma Chotika College. 2528 B.E.

Visuddhimagga. Bangkok: Naeb Mahawiranon Foundation. Bangkok: 2528 B.E.

WORKS IN ENGLISH

Accesstoinsight edition 2005, *Aṅguttara Nikāya, Digha Nikāya, Khuddaka Nikāya, Majjhima Nikāya, Saṃyutta Nikāya.* www.accesstoinsight. org

Bhikkhu Bodhi, Ven. (trans.) *The Connected Discourses of the Buddha: A New Translation of the Saṃyutta Nikāya.* Vol. I, II, Boston: Wisdom Publication, 2000.

Bhikkhu Bodhi and Bhikkhu Ñāṇamoli. *The Middle Length Discourses of the Buddha: A New Translation of the Majjhima Nikāya.* Boston: Wisdom Publications, 1995.

Hare, E.M. (trans.) *The Book of the Gradual Sayings (Anguttara-Nikāya).* Vol. III, IV. Lancaster: The Pali Text Society, 2006.

Holmes, David. *Buddhist Perception and Paradox*. Bangkok: Chulalongkorn University Press, 2006.

Horner, I.B. (trans.) *The Book of the Discipline (Vinaya Piṭaka)*. Vol. IV, Lancaster: The Pāli Text Society, 2007.

Masefield, Peter (trans.) *The Udāna Commentary by Dhammapala*. Vol.I. Oxford: The Pāli Text Society, 1994.

Nārada Mahā Thera (ed.). *A Manual of Abhidhamma: Abhidhammattha Sangaha of Bhadanta Anuruddhācariya*. Kuala Lumpur: The Buddhist Missionary Society, 1979.

Nyanatiloka, Ven. *Buddhist Dictionary: A Manual of Buddhist Terms and Doctrines*. Chiang Mai: Silkworm Books, 2004.

Nyanaponika Thera and Bhikkhu Bodhi (trans.) *Anguttara Nikāya: Numerical Discourses of the Buddha.* Walnat Creek: Altamira Press, 1999.

Sathienpong Wannapok, *The Buddha's Verses in Dhammapada,* published in commemoration of the crematory rite of Mrs. Premsri Khemasingkhi, 4 April 1999, Phra Sri Mahadhathu Royal Temple, Bangkok.

Sri Acharya Buddharakkhita, Ven. (trans.) *Dhammapada: A Practical Guide to Right Living.* Singapore: Kong Meng San Phor Kark See Monastery, 2006.

Walshe, Maurice. (trans.) *Thus Have I Heard: The Long Discourses of the Buddha: A New Translation of Digha Nikāya.* London: Wisdom Publications, 1987.

Woodward, F.L. (trans.) *The Book of the Gradual Sayings (Anguttara-Nikāya)*, Vol. I, II, V. London: The Pāli Text Society, 1986.

Woodward, F.L. (trans.) *The Minor Anthologies of the Pali Canon, Part II, Udāna and Itivuttaka*. London: The Pāli Text Society, 1985.

INDEX

A

B

C

❊ D

E

F

G

H

I

J

K

L

M

❊ N

O

P

R

❊ S

T

U

V

W

Y

All existing things are transitory and subject to decay;

objects of the senses are arising and ceasing

every mini-second of the day.

DHAMMACHAKRA

The Buddha encouraged us to push forward the wheel of dhammachakra. That is to say, we have to reach the point where we can see the cycling of dhammachakra within ourselves. The goal of Dhamma teaching is to enable one to see this cycling. So long as dhammachakra exists, human beings will reap the benefit of having a chance to be liberated.

At the time when dhammachakra stands still, our practice will not progress. We will stop short, trapped within our own thoughts, feelings, light, purity and peace.

Ratayano Bhikkhu

ABOUT THE AUTHOR

Phra Ajahn Nawee Piyadhassi is now 51 years old (2011). He was ordained in 1982, and stayed at Ram Poeng temple in Chiang Mai city during his first lent season. He studied and practiced Dhamma with Phra Dhammamangalachan (Ven. Ajahn Thong Sirimangalo), and later with Phra Kru Anusonprachathorn (Ven. Ajahn Rat Ratayano) of Doi Koeng temple in Mae Hong Son province. At present, he is the abbot of Tam Doi Tone Cave Monastery and organizes regular meditation course on monthly basis.